Contents

Part One A Soldier's Tale

Part Two A Nurse's Tale

The Making of Miranda

The Making of Miranda

From gentleman to gentlewoman in one lifetime

Miranda Ponsonby

Acknowledgements

First, to my dearest friend Lisa, whose encouragement and interest were instrumental in producing this book. Also, to Sylvi, whose insight and wisdom lifted so many of the shutters in Miranda's awareness. In the first faltering steps along the path Sarah Allen and Doctor Who gave me unstinting assistance, without which my computer skills would never have developed sufficiently to complete the journey. Dotti Irving and Ruth Cairns of Colman Getty were always at hand to proffer good advice and support, never losing faith.

In bringing the project to final fruition Julia Thorley's editing and Neil Barnes' putting of it all together were invaluable.

Last, to the many soldiers and nurses with whom, through many an adventure, it was my good fortune and privilege to serve. This is their story as well as my own. With respect to their privacy, I have changed some of their names in my story.

Published by Noble Books Ltd 2009

Noble Books Ltd
South Lodge, Corby Road,
Gretton, Northamptonshire NN17 3BN
Reg. No. 06866243

First published in Great Britain in 2009
Reprinted in this format in 2011
Reprinted in this format in 2014
Reprinted in this format 9/2014

ISBN 978-0-9562890-0-1

www.themakingofmiranda.com

Printed in the UK by Impress 01536 462888
Design: Beehive www.thebeehive.co.uk

Part One

A Soldier's Tale

Chapter 1

Summer Lightning

I was born into what now seems to have been the endless high summer afternoon of the years between the two world wars. The Australian, Don Bradman, was filling those idyllic afternoons with runs across the beautiful county cricket grounds of England. The two most talked about Englishmen were also cricketers. They were the majestic Wally Hammond and the ferocious Harold Larwood. The sun was in the heavens and all was well with the world. That is certainly how P G Wodehouse and Dornford Yates pictured it in their books at the time. Perhaps it was indeed a golden Indian summer for the old Empire and the old order. It was so soon to vanish forever, like summer lightning, on the outbreak of war.

This view of things might well have been peculiar to families like mine. They were what, I daresay, social historians would have called upper middle class, for want of a more precise definition. Woolgar, the gardener, shared his sandwiches with us in the potting shed. By us, I mean my elder half-sister, Nada (named after Rider Haggard's *Nada The Lily*), my younger brother John and myself. The potting shed itself had the most delicious aroma, combining Woolgar's pipe, sandwiches and various plants.

Martin, the chauffeur, on the other hand, did not welcome us, fearing that we would leave fingermarks on his gleaming motors. Cook was our great ally, ever ready with secret titbits or a shoulder to cry on in times of need. There were other servants, too, although we did not sport the ultimate, a butler.

I have jumped ahead of myself in order to give a flavour of the sort of background to our life. In the foreground, and very much in the foreground, was the nursery world. There presided the abiding influence in my life, until I was grown up, and beyond, Nanny.

A A Milne's Christopher Robin personified our life. We even embarked on many a minor adventure with our own Poohs and Piglets. We gave them names and characters of their own. Nanny's dressing gown did indeed hang on the back of the door and it was also a 'beautiful blue'. It was a secure and happy little world.

We saw very little of our parents, as was the custom in those days. We would be taken down to the drawing room, very much on our best behaviour, for half an hour after nursery tea. In my recollection, they always seemed to be dressed in evening clothes and just off somewhere. They were gracious and kindly, but the love came from Nanny.

My mother, Prudence, was let loose on us one afternoon a week on Nanny's day off. The nursery maid was in charge of us, or vice versa, until that exciting time. These afternoon outings were usually a bit chaotic and minor disasters tended to occur. Like the experience of another A A Milne character, James James Morrison Morrison, his mother was equally spare. He advised her firmly to 'never go down to the end of the town if you don't go down with me'. She was last seen 'wandering vaguely' and 'seems to have been mislaid'. Other than this, Mother never seemed to have to do anything but enjoy herself. Cook used to come for instructions whilst she was enjoying a late breakfast and dinner parties would be planned. That little interlude would see the catering side of the house sorted as far as she was concerned. We occasionally come across her picking flowers in the garden before visitors arrived. She carried one of those long, elegant wicker baskets under her arm for that purpose. Rich ladies of that era used to be pampered by smooth society doctors. I am sure Mother was no exception to this practice. We children were wheeled in to see her taking her bath; I think it was some current fad, which supposed that children would learn about 'the birds and the bees' that way. I remember her big brown nipples and how dark her skin seemed, as she was a sun worshipper. I think we were subjected to the same treatment with Father.

Mother had been something of a society beauty in the 1920s, with that strong streak of individuality common to most members of the Ponsonby family. Asserting her independence, like Lady Diana Manners, the most renowned of this breed, she also headed for Hollywood. She appeared in a few films. There is a rather faded studio publicity photograph of her with the matinée idol, Clive Brooke. They are in an open motorcar, which, for some obscure reason, had invariably to be driven backwards to appear to be going forwards on film. Having had a glorious time, she returned home and, under pressure from my grandmother, who strongly disapproved of these transatlantic goings on, married a handsome and extremely rich young American who had inherited the Wells Fargo fortune, said to be worth $16 million. Hugh Tevis had just come down from Oxford where he had been a Rhodes scholar and won a tennis blue. He was tall and fair and it seemed a match made in heaven. Needless to say, they did not live happily ever afterwards or I would not be here. During their honeymoon in Egypt, Mother happened to wander into a tent where they were encamped. She found Hugh engaged in some distinctly extramural activity with a Mr Harcourt Smith, who had been a fellow undergraduate at Oxford.

Hugh, however, obviously did also tackle the honeymoon in the more conventional manner as my half-sister, Nada, was born nine months later. Notwithstanding this happy event, when the Harcourt Smith affair proved to be more than a passing whim of Hugh's, they split up and were divorced in due course.

My Ponsonby grandfather, Tony, was a typically rakish figure. He ran away to sea from his public school. He went gold prospecting in Canada and Australia before ending up in South Africa. At the time of the outbreak of the Boer War, he was breeding horses on a stud farm. He was commissioned into a locally raised mounted infantry regiment, called Thornycroft's Horse, after its founder. At long last he had found his vocation in his all too brief life. That was as a fighting soldier. He soon distinguished himself in the battle of Spion Kop. He was recommended for a Victoria Cross but ended up with a DSO. This was awarded for gallantry and when given to a subaltern was a near equivalent to the VC.

At the close of the Boer War, he was granted a commission in a British Cavalry Regiment, The Third Dragoon Guards. The England Tony returned to was basking in the high noon of the Edwardian era. The world map was dotted with the pink denoting the British Empire on which it was said 'the sun never set'. The aristocracy, and even those well below that, led a sumptuous life such as has never been known in this country before or since.

Tony, with his dashing good looks and immense charm, was fêted as a hero. He rode hard to hounds, which, as a cavalry officer of that era, was open to him even on his small income. This small income was to trouble him for the rest of his life. He never really threw off the habits of his earlier adventurous life. He gambled and caroused with his far richer brother officers, often finding himself in debt.

As a scion of the aristocracy and member of a family that held positions at the heart of the royal household during the reigns of Queen Victoria and Edward VII, he was welcomed into the close-knit ranks of Society with a capital S. It was in this rarefied atmosphere that he met, swept off her feet, and duly married my grandmother. Lily Nickalls was the daughter of Sir Patterson Nickalls. He had amassed a fortune in the City and was knighted whilst still a young man.

The Nickalls were probably the most famous Edwardian sporting family. Sir Patterson had owned and completed the Grand National course on the ante-post favourite, Miss Muffin. His three sons Pat, Cecil and Matt, comprised three out of the four members of the England polo team in 1906. The fourth member was W S Buckmaster of Buck's club and Buck's fizz fame. The Nickalls brothers played international polo for a few years in the early 1900s. They represented England against America in the Westchester Cup in 1902 and 1909. This competition was the polo equivalent of yachting's America's Cup. It took place every couple of years or so from 1886 up to the Second World War. It was a great occasion, attracting large crowds. Pat was still in the Hurlingham Handicap list as late as 1936. He still rated four goals then, although he must have been nearing 60. At their peak, all three brothers rated 10 goals, which only a handful of other Englishmen have ever achieved. Pat was secretary of the Warwickshire Hunt for many years and his nephew, John Lakin, the Joint-Master, was also an international polo player. John's mother, my great-aunt, Sybil Lakin, was crippled for life in a hunting accident. As a child, I remember seeing her in a wheelchair.

The most famous Nickalls of all was Sir Patterson's nephew, Guy Nickalls, the legendary oarsman. He won the Diamond (single) Sculls at Henley five times and the Silver Goblets (pairs) six times. Three of these latter were with his brother Vivian, who also won the Diamond sculls. Vivian also won the Goblets twice with another partner. Tom Nickalls, their father, presented a Challenge Cup for this event in 1895. It is still being competed for under the title The Silver Goblets and Nickalls Challenge Cup. Guy's son, Gully, also won this cup twice, with R C S Lucas, in 1920 and 1922.

Gully was a great figure in the rowing world and used to take we children in his umpire's launch at Henley. The launch followed the racing crews up the course. It was a great treat and when we were older we sometimes dined with him at the Leander club during the regatta. Guy, Vivian and Gully rowed in more winning Eton and Oxford University crews than any other family before or since.

In 1914, my grandfather, Tony Ponsonby, was off to war again. My mother was his only child. In a letter to her dated 16th December 1914 he wrote:

My dearest Prue,

I was so glad to get your letter today & so sorry to hear about poor little Zipey being killed. I had bad luck too yesterday as I had my best horse shot in the stomach. We are kept pretty busy between the shells & the aeroplanes & are on the move all the time. It never stops raining & we get no chance to dry our clothes. All the roads are about 6 inches deep in mud. There are an enormous amount of aeroplanes about, scouting & reporting to the big guns the position of the enemy. I saw 13 this afternoon, all in sight at the same time & the Germans bursting shells all round some of them but they never seem to hit them- at least I haven't seen one hit yet, though they fire at them all day long.

At present I am sitting in a glass house, used in peace for growing tomatoes & grapes & am looking forward to a comfortable night but the Germans are rude people & don't mind waking one up a bit, so one never can tell. Goodbye Prue darling- write & tell me all the news you can think of.

Tony

In the Great War, gallantry was usually rewarded by instant death. In his case, it was not so instant as he was badly gassed in 1915 and never really recovered. He died a lingering death, which finally ended on 18th January 1919.

His Colonel completed his letter of condolence with: 'You know how we all admired his wonderful gallantry. He was a great fighting soldier – the greatest thing of all.' The note on the regimental wreath read: 'In affectionate memory of a gallant brother Officer and a great gentleman.' So he died doing what, up to that time, he had proved best at. It was such a shame. His letters show him to have been a sensitive, loving, charming and amusing man.

My father David's family was of an entirely different pedigree. Timothy Davies, my grandfather, was a highly successful self-made Welshman. His father had been an impoverished minor Welsh squire, the demon drink contributing to his financial plight. Young Timothy, showing the enterprise that was to characterise his life, set out for Liverpool, the nearest centre of commerce. He served his apprenticeship in the drapery trade and went south to London. He shrewdly anticipated the growth of shopping centres in the suburbs. He opened a draper's shop in Fulham on borrowed capital. In a short space of time, he paid off this debt and opened a second shop. He continued this movement with ever-increasing success until he owned a string of shops in southwest London.

Timothy was one of the first really progressive employers in this trade. H G Wells in *Kipps* exposed the appalling conditions prevailing for employees in this line of business. They were generally housed in large dormitories above the shops, subject to draconian regulations imposed by their employers. Timothy paid good wages and assisted his staff in finding comfortable houses of their own. They repaid this concern for their welfare by devotion to his. He invariably visited all his shops on a regular basis. He continued this practice even at the height of his later political success in the Liberal Party. Employees were encouraged to talk to him on these visits and voice their concerns and ideas, as friends.

Timothy prospered and became Mayor of Fulham. He was later elected their Member of Parliament. On election night, the ecstatic crowd removed the horses from the shafts of his carriage and bore him and my grandmother through the streets of Fulham in triumph. Throughout Lloyd George's years in power Timothy remained his boyhood friend's right-hand man, adviser and close friend. He refused high office for himself and the baronetcy that was offered to him. He staunchly maintained that his liberal principles forbade him from accepting this latter honour.

It has long been suggested that my uncle, Goronwy, was Lloyd George's son. He certainly had an uncanny resemblance to the great man. There was a scene in a television series, a few years ago, depicting Lloyd George visiting my grandparents' house in Collingham Gardens. He is seen seducing my grandmother on the chaiselongue. My father always strongly refuted these improper suggestions. I must say that it does seem unlikely that a man of my grandfather's strong and independent disposition would tolerate such 'goings on'. He remained close to Lloyd George until he split the Liberal Party at the close of the First World War. Timothy correctly warned him that the party would never hold power again if he went ahead with his coalition initiative. Allied to this, Tadgu, as we called him, it being the Welsh for Grandpa, was a pillar of the Methodist church with strong puritan ideals. He had a reputation for probity, was teetotal and prided himself on a lot of other rather boring things along those lines.

Of course, as is so often the case, it came to light after his death, in his mid-nineties, that he did have a bit of fun like the rest of us. In his later years, on summer afternoons, he would set off with a jaunty stride, Malacca-cane in hand, ostensibly to watch cricket. This caused mild bewilderment to those who knew him, as he had never hitherto shown the remotest interest in the game. John and I applauded this new interest but found him remarkably reticent about the joyous batting of Edrich and Compton or whomever he had supposedly watched. It transpired that he was in fact spending cosy, refreshing afternoons with his gorgeous redheaded mistress. Our admiration for the splendid old boy went up in the same proportion as the rest of the family's went down. It was just a pity about Edrich and Compton.

Tadgu did not forsake his Welsh roots. As soon as he could afford it, he bought back the family place in Wales, Alterverran, where he had been brought up. It had long since gone under the hammer. My father, uncle and aunt had many happy memories of times spent there. Tadgu had one claim to sporting fame. He rode a penny-farthing cycle from Fulham to Wales amidst great national publicity. It was a splendidly eccentric achievement worthy of a Ponsonby: but what a different character. Like them, he was a fearless rider to hounds. His courage was legendary and it was said that even the wildest horse would quieten under him.

There was a famous family story of a journey from Alterverran to the House of Commons to attend a debate. He stopped the car on a Welsh mountainside so that he and my grandmother, Mangu, could relieve themselves. It was a wild stormy night and on returning to the car he drove off leaving Mangu stranded on the mountain. It was never certain whether this was by design or accident. What was certain was that he arrived in London without her. Mangu seemed to have taken the incident in good spirits, as she enjoyed recounting the story. As the years went by the night got blacker and the storm wilder, but his intention was never cleared up.

My Ponsonby Grandmother, Lily, married again after the Great War. Her new husband was a retired cavalry major. He had lost a leg in some long forgotten Imperial skirmish serving alongside Winston Churchill in the 4th Hussars. He was a fine-looking military figure. He must have been a good cricketer in his youth. I remember watching him bat in a local village match. His wooden leg necessitated a runner. This unfortunate boy ran him out on 99. Uncle Trevor was so incensed that he chased the poor boy round the boundary with his bat aloft. We were quite helpless with laughter.

They lived in a house near Haslemere in Surrey. We spent our school holidays there on a couple of occasions. I remember seeing lorries full of soldiers returning from Dunkirk. They were lying all jumbled up, fast asleep and too tired to care. Uncle Trevor used to play a gramophone record every evening. It was the Intermezzo from *Cavalleria Rusticana*. A tear used to run down his fine face and I have wondered to this day what long-gone romantic experience touched this gruff old soldier's heart so.

My father, David, was at Sandhurst in 1914. On being commissioned, instead of joining his regiment, he volunteered for the Royal Flying Corps, which was just being formed then, together with many other daring young officers. They found the prospect of the high adventure of aerial combat irresistible. He duly became a fighter pilot and flew as such throughout the war. They did not have the benefit of parachutes. It was said that the reason for this omission was a deliberate decision by the ruling powers to prevent pilots abandoning their aircraft in a tight situation. Those early fighter planes were difficult enough in themselves, even without the extra hazard of combat. The most dangerous was apparently the Vickers Bullet, which had to be pulled out of a steep dive to land.

In fact, the early formation years were similar to the SAS in the Second World War. They were very much an irregular force of maverick characters who invented their own tie. It was predominately light blue with thin red and dark blue stripes. My father told me that the light blue stood for Eton, the red for the Royal Engineers and the dark blue for Oxford University. The colours represented the proportion of the backgrounds of the officers who joined up.

David, like everyone who survived, had many adventures. He was shot down and crash landed on more than one occasion. In spite of this, he was never seriously injured. If he had joined his regiment instead, his chances of survival would have been minimal. The story that I liked best was of his forced landing on a Scottish laird's estate. On clambering shakily out of the machine, he was charged by an Aberdeen Angus bull. He had to remount in haste. He repeated this manoeuvre several times before the laird himself and a couple of gillies rescued him. He then spent his best week of the war as the laird's honoured guest whilst awaiting the recovery of the plane. Those first fighter pilots were regarded as celebrities.

My father recalled the element of chivalry shown by both sides in those early aerial battles. They felt themselves like knights jousting in single combat. They were close to the elements and had to make use of those same elements. The most dangerous attacks came out of the sun. Clouds were their camouflage. It was a war fought between officers and gentlemen. Cecil Lewis's wonderful book, *Sagittarius Rising*, portrays the sheer exhilaration experienced when flying those planes. Cavalrymen were supposed to make the best pilots, as balance and touch were at a premium. Nothing sums up the spirit of those gallant young officers better than the haunting song sung in all Royal Flying Corps messes during the Great War:

A young aviator lay dying

At the start of a bright summer's day.

To the mechanics assembled around him

These few parting words did he say.

> *'Take the cylinder out of my kidneys,*
>
> *The connecting rod out of my brain,*
>
> *From the small of my back take the crankshaft,*
>
> *And assemble the engine again.'*

At the end of the war, David went up to Balliol College, Oxford with so many of the 'Lost Generation', as they were called. It was therapeutic in that they could unwind amongst their friends who understood what they had been through. Death had stalked them almost daily. Only now did they have a future. A car backfiring in the High would send ex-officers crashing to the ground. The flapping of a marquee in dawn's early light, after a May Ball, would bring a sick feeling in the pit of David's stomach. It brought back memories of the dawn takeoff. Tents had that effect on him for the rest of his life. These men were fortunate that counselling had not yet been invented. They did not beat their breasts and agonise. They kept their own counsel and let the sheer joy of being alive and young do the rest. My father said that he regarded every day from then on as a bonus to be enjoyed to the full. They somehow seemed to feel that they owed this to their fallen comrades.

Life for a rich undergraduate was indeed pleasant. He went out hunting with the Bicester and other packs on winter days. He came back to convivial teas in front of the fire in his college rooms. Evenings were enjoyed with Bullingdon club members. Summer afternoons were spent in a punt on the Cherwell, before setting off to balls in London with a car full of other undergraduates. Study was kept to a minimum. When it came to the finals examination, David paid an impecunious undergraduate to write a synopsis of the required data and ended up with a creditable second class honours degree. On their last night at Oxford, that first post-war generation of undergraduates threw the party to end all parties. David ended by climbing a lamppost. He looked across to see T E Lawrence (of Arabia) at the top of the adjoining one. So by that time those battle-hardened officers had relaxed into more traditional undergraduates.

On coming down from Oxford his charmed life somewhat ended. He was too much of a 'young blood' for the drapery trade. He fell out with his father by marrying a nightclub owner, against his wishes. This marriage produced Dawn and Michael, my half-sister and brother. The marriage failed and he soon married my mother. Both were determined to do better with their second effort. We practically never saw Dawn and Michael. I remember meeting Michael at a dance years later. We eyed each other for most of the evening wondering where we had met. Eventually I approached him and we discussed mutual friends before the penny dropped. The question 'Are you my brother?' caused some amazement to his party.

David and Prudence were an attractive and popular couple. They both had comfortable incomes and lived accordingly. My father by now owned a property company, which took advantage of the increase in the population, with its consequent demand for houses. They purchased the Mill House, next to the mill, in the middle of Wimbledon Common. My brother and I were born there. I chiefly remember the luxuriant, heavily scented garden with its myriad butterflies and bees in the summer.

My sex was in doubt at birth. I was too young, perhaps three or four then, to remember quite how I knew this. I just have a vague recollection of a small, bald man in a long, white coat examining me. I feel sure that I overheard him discussing my predicament. Whether due to this or not, I was never in doubt that I was a girl, despite my being brought up as a boy named Rhodri. This necessitated regular visits to the London Clinic in Harley Street. I was sat in endless canvas baths filled with pink liquid, no doubt following adjustment to my genitalia. Matters were regularised to everyone's satisfaction but my own. This little local difficulty was never mentioned again. There was no such doubt about John, who was born two years later. Hugh Tevis never appeared over the horizon again, but Nada shared our nursery, although she had her own nanny to begin with.

Our nanny came on my birth. She was a highly qualified, Norland-trained children's nurse. My problem probably necessitated her employment. She had a smart, striped uniform with starched collar and cuffs, and a loving disposition. We all adored her and continued to do so up to her death in the 1980s. She had married an Irish medical student at 17. He had suffered some sort of mental breakdown and had spent the rest of his long life in an institution. Being a Roman Catholic, she was unable to get a divorce and marry again. She was thus unable to have children of her own. This was a cruel tragedy for so maternal a woman. I can only hope that our lifelong devotion was some consolation to her. She ensured a happy childhood for us when the war shattered our secure cosy Mill House existence.

I vividly remember hearing Mr Chamberlain's fateful speech while we were on a family holiday in Cornwell in September 1939. At that precise moment, someone rushing to listen slammed the green baize covered kitchen door on my toe, breaking it. My vigorous complaints were met with an answer we were to hear many times in the ensuing years: 'Don't you know there is a war on?' The fact that it was never set has plagued me ever since. On the very same night, we saw a spy signalling with a lamp from the cliffs above our hotel, to a U-boat in the bay. The local military chased up the rocks after him but never caught him. It was said that the reason was that they had army boots on and he had plimsolls. My father, who was on the Reserve of Officers, was called up immediately and never came back.

To our great regret we never returned to our beloved Mill House. We ended up in a thatched cottage in a Buckinghamshire village called Prestwood. Petrol rationing was so severe for civilians that our cars were put up on blocks. The war filled our lives. We watched the Battle of Britain going on in the sky above our heads, whilst eating strawberries and cream in the garden. We helped the war effort by sorting books for sailors and picking wool off the fences. All our children's food luxuries disappeared. There were no more sweets, butter, gollywog marmalade, chocolate and so on.

As I grew, my sexual predicament became more and more apparent to me. By this, I mean my conviction that I was really a girl. I really cannot explain why. I can only suppose that the make-up of my genes caused this. I do not think that I have ever been in any way neurotic. In fact, I am sure that I have a most stable character. I must have been about seven or eight years old then. It was the age when the sexes begin to be more separated. I never mentioned this to anyone, not even Nanny. I think that I assumed that it was part of me and had to be coped with as best as possible. Looking back, I think Nanny tried to make it easy for me to seek her help, but she did not broach the subject directly for fear of putting ideas into my head. Instead we had little chats about the difference between boys and girls. Possibly, she was encouraging me to 'spill the beans' and tell her what was worrying me. Also, of course, my main ordeals occurred at school, away from her. I first went to a local mixed school, named St Christopher's. This was all right to begin with as I was used to playing with Nada's friends at home. I gravitated to the girls and found the rough and tumble of the boys not my cup of tea at all. When it came to being separated to spend the night in the boys' dormitory I was unhappy and felt out of place. This fortunately was a rare occurrence, only taking place during air raids. We normally returned home every night. Little did I know what was in store for me in the near future. In fact, the main thing that I remember about St Christopher's is being forced to drink copious quantities of water out of enamel mugs when not thirsty. This was obviously some fad of the time. It is surprising how many other people's nonsensical fads I have been subjected to in my life. There is a rare intensity shown by individuals in pursuit of their particular lunatic fad that brooks no opposition.

After a particularly hard winter, which we had spent tobogganing and skating on the Tyrhitt Drake's lake at Shardloes, Mother found that her daily journeys up to London were too difficult. As I know now, she had become engaged in some hush-hush war work. Much against Nanny's wishes, who was worried about our safety in the bombing, we returned to London. We moved into 29 Montpelier Place. This was situated in Knightsbridge, almost opposite Harrods. The house had belonged to my grandmother since the 1920s, as her town residence.

We missed the country terribly and things like blackberrying to make summer puddings. These were a rare treat to us. We complained that we would no longer be able to search the woods for German airmen hanging from trees by their parachutes. We indignantly mentioned this loss of our services to the nation to a war cabinet friend of Mother's, called A V Alexander. He only laughed and wanted to hear the story of the German pilot we had found, on a frosty morning, in that predicament. We had rescued him with a ladder from the orchard and taken him home for breakfast, whilst awaiting a military escort. I seem to remember that he was charming and thanked us, clicking his heels with old-world courtesy. Later, at the time of the Nuremberg war crimes trial, John said, 'I do hope they won't hang our German.'

By that stage, of the war few Londoners still bothered to trudge down to the Underground during air raids, although the bunks remained on the platforms until the war finished. I always remember dear Nanny telling us that during bad air raids she only used to grab Teddy and Boy Boy, our favourites, leaving behind jewellery, money etc. at Hitler's mercy! During the holidays we slept in our own bunks in the night nursery. By sleeping in the bottom of these it was hoped that we would be protected in the event of the ceiling collapsing. This proved effective when the nearby Cooper's store received a direct hit. We climbed out unscathed, and, being British, I trust unruffled. The only occasion when Hitler's ears must have burnt was when our carefully set up soldiers and farms were knocked over by bomb blasts. It was fortunate for the Führer that he was in his Wolf's Lair in Eastern Prussia at these times.

There was a remarkably friendly spirit prevailing in the war years, from the General who lived opposite us, to the milkman who used to chat to us whilst his horse was enjoying his nosebag for breakfast.

Paradoxically, Nanny told me years later, that I was the easiest of all the children she had ever looked after. When I asked her what she meant, she replied that I was invariably even tempered, cheerful, never moody and with a great sense of humour. She said that John, my younger brother, was far more difficult and as for Nada, my sister, 'the least said the better'! Yet John always seemed to me to be a really straightforward 'rough and tumble' little boy. I do remember getting 'beaten up' by him from time to time, even though I was two years older. I always lost our fights. Although tall, I did have a very slender build. It was humiliating, but I consoled myself with the secret knowledge that I was a girl and that was the reason. Nevertheless, this sense of deep humiliation has made me guard this secret until this day.

Growing up in the war, we were a very unspoilt generation. Death was near to us, whether it was our own parents or those of our friends. In fact, I vividly remember my father telling me, before he left us, that he expected me to 'die like a gentleman' when my time came. Sadly, I will be a disappointment to him about this! Thus my own gender problems at this time were the least of the terrible things that we all felt awaited us. It put them in proper perspective. I have since met people obsessed with this predicament in a way that I never have been. I did, however, constantly inspect my body for signs of female changes taking place. I felt it was rather like a time bomb ticking away that would explode at puberty. On the plus side, I was inwardly proud of my smooth, unmuscular arms and legs and particularly my small round bum. I thought that these were real assets that an attractive girl should have.

Thus, as I approached the next phase in my life, I was not unhappy. I was full of the joy of being alive and young. I looked forward to whatever adventures lay ahead. I had many failings, but lack of courage was not one of them and never has been.

Chapter 2

The Bending of a Twig

The greatest disadvantage of all about returning to London was the fact that I would now have to go to boarding school. It was when I was sent away to prep school that the problem of my sexual identity began in earnest. From this time on the problem was to steadily grow in the years ahead, be ever with me and colour my whole life. In some ways, before the onset of puberty, I was less set apart from the boys around me physically, but mentally and emotionally the gulf was immediate. I still never felt able to confide in anyone, even under intense cross-examination.

The school belonged to a Mr Hornby, from the famous cricketing family, immortalised in Francis Thompson's poem, *At Lord's*. Part of it was on one of the walls and is still ingrained in my memory.

> *'For the field is full of shades as I near the shadowy coast,*
>
> *As a ghostly batsman plays to the bowling of a ghost,*
>
> *And I look through my tears on a soundless clapping host,*
>
> *As the run-stealers flicker to and fro,*
>
> *To and fro,*
>
> *O my Hornby and my Barlow long ago!'*

The headmaster, Mr Hornby, himself a former Oxford Blue and Hampshire county cricketer, was a kindly and understanding man. He was, however, too distant to be able to help a little lamb, lost, and far from home. On my very first night there was some larking about in the dormitory after lights out. The master in charge announced that he would beat the entire dormitory. We were ordered to bend over the end of our beds and drop our pyjama trousers. Along with the others I was hammered on the bare bottom with the hard heel of a slipper. The master said to me that as a new boy I was probably not to blame, but: 'This is to teach you that there is no justice in this world.' In this instance he was only too right. I had been lying quiet as a mouse in my bed. The other boys laughed at the fact that I had been blameless. Eventually, instead of 'blubbing', I joined in their merriment. I have done so, on suffering 'the slings and arrows of outrageous fortune', ever since. I think that this reaction to adversity has helped me, in no small measure, to be the happy individual that I am. It certainly endeared me to my companions. Thus I have seldom met animosity in respect of my sexual predicament. The world has tended to laugh with me rather than at me. Having spent so much of my life in close-knit societies, this has been doubly fortunate for me.

The school was set in the most beautiful grounds. An abiding memory, during the lovely summer weather of the war years, was of boys in Aertex shirts, with floppy grey hats on their heads, chasing butterflies with large green nets. One of my favourite pastimes was raiding the walled kitchen gardens for gooseberries, deliciously warmed by the sun. A rather extraordinary ritual took place at the end of every term. We were made to strip naked in our respective dormitories and parade, in that state, along the passage to the matron's surgery, to be weighed. In the surgery there would be not only Stubbins, the matron, but also her assistant and invariably a group of masters. I used to find this performance increasingly embarrassing as the years went by, as I imagine any girl would. My sister, Nada, had told me that it made her feel physically sick to be seen naked by a man. In fact it did eventually lead to my being examined by the school doctor. I kept quiet during this ordeal and as far as I know nothing more was said on the matter. My other ordeal was suffering severe abdominal pains daily, usually worse around teatime. Stubbins did not believe me; because when they subsided I wanted to play in the seven-aside football tournament, which went on during the last few weeks of the term. I somehow survived until that wonderful day when we boarded the train back to Victoria station and the Christmas 'hols'. To this day I remember those joyful homecomings. On Christmas Day, the pains were worse than ever and I could not eat lunch. Nanny summoned Dr Lorraine. He must have diagnosed severe constipation, as I seem to remember Nanny carrying out a manual evacuation and subsequent enemas, which cured the problem. Mother and Nanny were furious with the school for not believing me and getting medical help. The down side to this was that Stubbins was even crueller to me than ever. I suppose she must have been ticked off. The trouble was lack of time and privacy. There were no doors even in the communal loos. This, I think, was to prevent masturbation. I was to suffer something similar at my public school.

Recently, I came across a poem that I must have written to my mother about this time. It was hidden in a secret drawer in her old desk. It must have lain there unseen for over sixty years. I was about eight or nine years old then. It was a small boy's cry for his mother and his home. Poor Mother, having survived the worst of the blitz and what Hitler could do to her in London, died a violent death in Germany. Her grave is in Frankfurt. She so hated the Germans. I still wear the wristwatch she brought me back from one of her clandestine trips. It was made by Henri Blanc of Geneva and unobtainable in wartime Britain. It still keeps perfect time and has always been my most precious possession.

Homesick

Summer weather

Us together.

Breezes blowing

Old Tom sowing.

Rural charm

With it's calm.

City's grind

Far behind.

Oh God above

That's my love.

Prestige in the school really depended on prowess on the games field. I did find physical contact sports impossible, but I had inherited a fine 'eye for a ball' from my illustrious family. I adapted this to excel at tennis and hitting a cricket ball. Neither of these games depended on sheer physical strength but more on sweet timing. My success was rewarded, in my final term, by my being appointed captain of the cricket team. I afforded myself a private laugh about this honour, particularly when I topped the batting averages at the end of the term. We won all our matches and the headmaster congratulated me on my sympathetic handling of the team and getting the best out of the boys. In fact, I felt that the boys had rallied round me and supported and protected me. I found this reaction again when I moved on to my public school.

By this time the war was at long last coming to an end. There were gangs of German and Italian prisoners of war working in the school grounds. Finally VE day came. This marked the end of the war in Europe. Nanny, Nada, John and I walked down to Buckingham Palace. The King and Queen, with Winston Churchill, came out on the balcony. There was a wonderful sense of solidarity. We really felt that Their Majesties, Winnie, Nanny, John and I had beaten the Hun. We excluded Nada from this great undertaking, as being too vague. We joined in the dancing round the bonfires in Green Park. We went home happy to sleep our first night's sleep for many years in a country at peace. No more listening for the doodlebug engine to cut out or identifying the German bomber's engines by their 'wong, wong' noise. No more quickening of the pulse at the wailing of the air raid sirens. 'After the war' was now.

At the end of that first summer of peace it was time for me to move on to my public school. I had been treated with sympathy and understanding at prep school. I had been given time and space to develop as an individual. It was a small school and I had gradually found acceptance with the boys. One's happiness at these institutions so much depends on this acceptance. The sensitive and aesthetic side of my nature had been encouraged to flourish. I had found a kindred spirit in a boy named Mark Boxer. Mark was later to distinguish himself in the world of journalism, after a glittering career up at Cambridge. Together we started a school magazine. The highlight of this was his cartoons satirising school life. The many touching tributes to Mark on his untimely death showed how lucky I had been to have him as a friend.

I found no such friend at my public school. It was a large and incredibly Spartan place in that first post-war winter. The scarcity of fuel meant virtually no heating. We sat in overcoats, with mittens on our hands, in the classrooms. Sleep was difficult in our freezing dormitories. The food was inadequate and we were only allowed one hot bath a week. Of course, the wartime spirit of cheerfully enduring hardships helped us to put up with these miseries.

Bathing was, perforce, a communal activity. There were only six baths in my boarding house. These were situated side by side in one room, with no partitions of any sort between them. One of my duties as a Fag was to scrub my Fagmaster's back when he returned from performing great deeds for the school Rugger Fifteen. There was hell to pay if I failed to have the bath ready at the correct temperature for him. The steam played havoc with my stiff wing collar. I had to wear this at all times, together with black tailcoat, striped trousers and waistcoat. The Fag was the servant of his Fagmaster. He was a new boy and his lord and master was a very senior boy. I think that the system was instituted to teach each how to treat the other. It was a lesson in leadership.

With the onset of puberty there was the constant threat of secondary female sexual development. This made communal bathing an ordeal for me. I used to try and take my bath on a Sunday afternoon when there were few other people about. I often used to cycle round the countryside and then return, heat up a tin of sardines and eat these sitting in the bath. Nanny provided them, together with other provisions, to help keep body and soul together. They were kept safely locked in my tuck box.

I unwittingly gained kudos from my companions at the choir practice for new boys. The choirmaster played a note on the piano for us each to sing. My response was so erratic that I was deemed unsuitable for the choir. The boys thought that my response was deliberate and were suitably impressed. Generally speaking, however, I was somewhat of an outsider. The school ethos was to mould us into a rigid type of Empire builder. This was a bit outmoded, even then. Any individuality was frowned upon. I am sure that I was a disappointment to my housemaster. He looked to me to follow in the footsteps of my half-brother, Michael. He had been Captain of the House and School Rugger Fifteen.

In my first year an older boy, Alan, was very good to me. His uncle was a famous actor. His parents had been friends of my mother and Alan had been detailed off to keep an eye on me by his father, who was then a leading light in the BBC. Alan was a bit of a rebel and consumed with Polish nationalism from his Polish ancestry. He used to take me on forbidden adventures to the local cinemas, followed by wonderful meals in the various old teashops in the town. These were magical places with roaring log fires on winter evenings.

Alan told me that it was frowned upon to befriend younger boys and to keep our outings secret. His kindness was therefore doubly dangerous for him. Eventually a school monitor spotted us at a teashop. We were punished with a 'school beating'. These events were more serious than a 'house beating', which was a more informal affair, carried out in a House Prefect's study. Our punishment was posted on the school notice board. Poor Alan was to receive six strokes and myself three strokes on an appointed day at an appointed time. It was rather like an execution and attracted the same morbid interest.

When the time came Alan and I paraded outside the school library. Inside were the school monitors. These senior boys were responsible for school discipline. I remember Alan humming the Polish National Anthem. It was a stirring tune. I felt 'God Save The Queen' would not quite fill the bill for me, so I remained silent until I was called in. I was ordered to bend over a library chair by the Captain of the School, who then felt the seat of my trousers for extra padding. Then a monitor ran up half the length of the library and delivered a stinging blow with a cane. He then handed the cane to another monitor who repeated the movement and then to a third. All the monitors finally shook my hand. As I departed Alan marched in past me, head held high, like a Polish patriot facing Gestapo torturers. On returning to my house I was treated as something of a celebrity. My battle scars were inspected by all and sundry. All I wanted to do was to crawl into a corner like a wounded animal.

At last the summer term came and cricket again saw an upturn in my fortunes. There was a mix-up in the names and I was put down for the final Senior Colts practice match. The Senior Colts were for boys up to sixteen. I was an immature fourteen and should have been a Junior Colt, for boys up to fifteen. I was put in to open the batting and made some stylish runs before rain stopped play. The famous Kent and England cricketer, Frank Woolley, ran the first eleven and happened to be watching. He recommended my inclusion in the Senior Colts team to play Tonbridge School the following day. Colin Cowdrey, who had already made a name for himself by scoring a century at Lord's in the annual Clifton v Tonbridge match, as a fourteen-year-old, was in the opposition. I cannot remember how he performed on this occasion, but I scored some runs again. Frank Woolley took me under his wing and spent many hours coaching me in the nets. He was a tall, immensely dignified and rather remote figure. I never saw him play in a match as his eyesight was failing by then.

Later on he was one of the first ex-professionals to be made an honorary member of the MCC. When I became a member I used to see him sitting in the Long Room in the Lord's pavilion on test match days. He was nearly blind by then. I never dared approach the great man, as he was usually surrounded by other heroes of my youth.

It is sad that the only ancient public school fixture still played at Lord's is the Eton v Harrow match, and that has been reduced to a one-innings affair. When I was young there were many of these enjoyable occasions: Rugby v Marlborough, Clifton v Tonbridge, Beaumont v Oratory, to name a few. These matches would surely provide much better entertainment than some of the dreary professional encounters held at Lord's today. The public schools are the nursery for so many of our best cricketers, as they always have been. Something wonderful was lost when the amateur player disappeared. The MCC abdicated responsibility for ruling the game over the South African affair. Things have never been the same since. I suppose that I can count myself lucky to have enjoyed so many happy summer days watching cricket as it should be played. Certainly my happiest times at school were associated with cricket and playing on beautiful school grounds.

Match days were magic days for me. I would leave the rest of the school, apart from the team, incarcerated in their stuffy classrooms on those summer mornings and cycle down to the ground or board the bus for away fixtures. Sumptuous meals were laid on in the pavilion during the luncheon interval, quite unlike the usual school fare. Opposing teams must have wondered about this lithe female figure tearing round the boundary with such obvious joy or stroking the ball away gracefully whilst opening the batting. I was very slender, with brown hair, hazel eyes and a fresh complexion. I somehow felt that, as a girl, I had put one over on the system.

I was always selected for the leading female roles in the school and house plays. I accepted this as a matter of course and enjoyed playing the roles. My tour de force was as Ophelia in *Hamlet*. An old photograph of the cast does show a remarkably pretty girl in her fair locks. The master in charge did get very overexcited about dressing me up and always insisted on assisting with my changes of costume.

One spring, whilst in the school sanatorium recovering from a nasty bout of influenza, I was subjected to advances by an older boy. It started with a rather bristly kiss. I was uncertain how to respond to this. I was part horrified and part fascinated. Eventually it led to him climbing into my bed and removing my pyjamas. The feminine side of me found his hairy muscular body against my smooth one strangely disturbing. At the same time I felt that it was 'not quite cricket'. I remained passive but felt guilty and ashamed at not repelling him. He must have taken my passivity for acquiescence, for he then slowly rolled back the bedclothes. I was gently turned on my front so that I was lying naked beneath him. 'What a nice smooth girl's bum you've got,' was whispered in my ear. Some margarine, that he had somehow got hold of, was put up me with his finger. This seemed to allow penetration to take place without pain. I gradually moved in unison with him to his climax. I had felt utterly feminine during our lovemaking and was happy and deeply satisfied by it. His name was Jones. I have never forgotten that. The odd thing was that following this event the young nurses in the sanatorium seemed to be jealous of me in some funny way. It was as if I was a rival and I was subjected to some unkind treatment. After Jones left me the feeling of guilt returned with a vengeance. I avoided him in future and nothing like this ever happened to me for the rest of my time at school.

Looking back on my school days, I think that I was rather a lone figure, without close friends, but this did not altogether crush my naturally happy nature. I believed the other boys sensed that I was different, but respected the fact that I competed with them on equal terms, without seeking favours or complaining. Indeed when it became increasingly apparent, at least to me, that my physical development was heading in the wrong direction, they tended to close ranks round me and protect me.

I worked away at my studies and passed my Higher Certificate early and into the Upper Sixth, determined to follow in my father's footsteps up to Balliol College, Oxford. It was at this time that fate took a hand in my future. Hugh Tevis, my mother's first husband, suddenly reappeared to see his only child, Nada, my half-sister. I was at home for the Christmas holidays and he invited us all to dine with him at Claridge's hotel. He was apparently very taken with me and offered to escort me out to the family cattle ranch in what was then Southern Rhodesia (now Zimbabwe), with his party. The wretched Attlee Labour Government was still in power and the future looked bleak for enterprising young men. Africa, most of which was still part of the British Empire, looked like a land of opportunity.

Nanny, knowing Hugh's past, was very against this move. She also knew how I had set my heart on going up to Balliol. I saw it as a great adventure and a chance to get off on my own and find myself. My impetuosity carried the day. I went to Rhodesia House in the Strand to see if I could get help with my passage fare. They agreed to pay it if I joined the Rhodesian Civil Service for a minimum of a year. My Higher School Certificate (the equivalent of A-levels today) was the only qualification required. If I left earlier than that, I would have to repay a proportion back. So my school days came to an abrupt end. They had not been 'the happiest days of my life', but I had survived and emerged still my own person. The traditional schooling of that era had taught me that nothing could be achieved without hard work and single-minded application. I was under no illusion that rewards would fall into my lap undeserved. I would have to make things happen.

It was thus that this strange charismatic boy/girl who was me attained adulthood overnight and set out into the world on the great adventures that stretched across the years and are still being embarked upon half a century later.

Chapter 3

Into Africa

On a cold January morning I said my goodbyes and joined Hugh's party on the boat train to Southampton. He had a strange entourage consisting of two distinctly AC/DC men, an elderly lady and a youngish couple who were business partners of Hugh's. Belford, Hugh's chauffeur and general factotum, looked after us and ensured, partly by dispensing large gratuities, that we were treated as VIPs wherever we went. It was the days before air travel was general. Our ship, *The Edinburgh Castle*, outward bound for Cape Town, carried all normal passengers travelling to South Africa, as the Union Castle Line had been doing for generations of passengers before.

There were many young people aboard. I naturally gravitated to them and we split into various groups of friends. My constant companion was a girl of about the same age, named Millie Cullinan. Her family were connected with the Cullinan Diamond in The Crown Jewels. We first came together amongst the only passengers unaffected by the rough weather in the Bay of Biscay.

I began to realise how much I had missed female company. Almost my only connection previously, apart from Nada's friends who were much older, had been with tongue-tied debutantes. My mother's old friends had occasionally implored me to attend these Deb Dances when short of a man. The debs invariably seemed to have thin arms with down standing up on them either through cold or fright. I never did come to a conclusion on which it was. It was difficult to get anything but 'Yes', 'No' or 'Oh Really' from them. When dancing they were apt to try and take the lead, due to being tutored at all-girl schools where they often had to simulate the male role. This habit meant that a running battle took place for control, which could end with both of us on the floor. I used to find this hilarious but no one else seemed to, especially my petrified partner.

Millie was blonde and beautiful. She shared my own high spirits and sense of fun. Our exuberance attracted a group of like-minded young round us. As we entered warm seas the sun filled me with a wonderful sense of wellbeing. I was to experience this again and again in the years ahead. Millie's affection gave me a certain confidence. If she found me appealing why should I worry about my sex? I was me and I was going to remain so. The world could either accept me or not as it pleased. So spoke the innocent optimistic voice of youth. Leaning over the ship's taffrail we talked by the hour, watching the dolphins and flying fish playing around the ship. At night we danced under the stars. Belford approved of this attachment and became a great friend and ally.

I dined at Hugh's table with his party and we always met at noon for drinks and to bet on the ship's run for the following 24 hours. We stopped at Madeira and had a splendid lunch at Reid's Hotel. Millie and I rode on the sledges down the flower-strewn streets and vowed to return there for our respective honeymoons.

All too soon, Table Mountain was on the starboard bow and I set foot in Africa for the first time. A fleet of Buicks, each with a silver knight on the bonnet, flying the Tevis pennant, met us. We were transported, like royalty, up to Monterey. Hugh had built this beautiful house, high above the Cape of Good Hope, at Constantia. It had a large formal garden with lovely little alcoves, ornamental fountains and trellised walks. Beyond the garden was a vineyard and woods. The sun shone from the bluest of skies. Every morning I awoke to new joys. Taking breakfast in the dining room, with the French windows open on to the lawn, England in January seemed to belong to a different life. The food was superb and served by discreet footmen in blue suits with white gloves. Hugh gave a party for my eighteenth birthday. Some of the old Cape families were invited and as a special treat for me, Millie Cullinan. We danced until the early hours when Belford offered to take us down to Hermanus Bay for a swim. The waves were lit up by phosphorescence. We stripped off and swam naked in this magical new world. It was a very happy Rhodri that finally climbed into bed as dawn was breaking.

After that, during the month I spent at Monterey, Millie and I saw a great deal of each other. Hugh had an Ex-Naval Motor Torpedo Boat moored at the Royal Navy base at Grahamstown. We all often went out fishing in the bay in this. When opened up it went at a terrific speed, up to 40 knots, I seem to remember. Hugh was still a very keen tennis player, and Millie and I had our work cut out to compete with him and whomever he chose as his partner, even though we wiped the floor with most of the other opposition.

We visited some of the Old Dutch Colonial houses round the Cape whose owners happened to be friends of Hugh. I remember one particularly magnificent place belonging to the Van der Byls. Mr Van der Byl had been a fellow Rhodes scholar with Hugh up at Oxford. He had an oar above the great fireplace. It had a dark blue blade and commemorated his winning row in a 1920s boat race.

The Duke of Bedford visited, with his son, who I think must then have been Lord Tavistock. I believe Hugh was helping him obtain big game to open the Woburn Safari Park. Another visitor was Tommy Sopwith, whose planes my father had flown in the First World War. I had been brought up with tales of the Sopwith Camel and the Sopwith Pup.

Hugh was impressed by the way that I was able to hold my own in conversation with his guests. I forbore to explain that one of the reasons was due to his daughter. Nada was more than just vague with her social arrangements. Frequently she would agree to go out with more than one young man on the same evening. It was left to me to deal with the second or even third arrivals tactfully. Sometimes more than one would arrive on the doorstep simultaneously. I would sit them down in the drawing room, give them a drink and go up to Nada, who always took an age to get herself ready. When asked whom she wanted to go out with, she would say, ' Oh I don't know, you choose, Rhodri.' This took considerable tact and communication skills of a high order. At least she never complained about my choice and Montpelier Place was always full of flowers. It was just as well she was such a blonde beauty or she would have ended up without any boyfriends.

Also, Nada was very extravagant. Even in my teens I was despatched to deal with our bank manager in the Brompton Road. Mr McGann of the National Provincial Bank and I held many a conference to try sort matters out. My debating skills were greatly enhanced in this manner. When Mother had met such a tragic death, her friends had rallied round to help us. One of them, knowing Nada of old, had promised to employ her at Elizabeth Arden in Bond Street. They were very long suffering but it still took a considerable 'Gift of the Gab' on my part to smooth matters over when Nada had one of her 'dos.' She would chuck bottles around the shop and lock herself in the staff loo. Following this they would ring me up to come down to Bond Street to sort her out.

Eventually the time came to head north up Africa. We stood on the tarmac of what was then a tiny airfield, in the dawn light. I had enjoyed the happiest month of my life up to then. It had indeed been the Cape of Good Hope for me.

We spent that night in Johannesburg, after a very bumpy flight. Hugh had some business to attend to there. It looked like New York to me and I suffered a headache from the high altitude. I was relieved when we took off for Rhodesia the following day. Salisbury (now Harare) was a beautifully set out little capital in those days. It had wide streets lined with brilliantly coloured jacaranda trees. Cecil Rhodes stood proudly on his plinth in the main street near the government buildings, where I was due to work. We spent that night in Hugh's flat in Salisbury. The manager of the cattle ranch was there to greet us. We set out for Two Tree Hill the following morning and after a long dusty drive, on strip roads most of the way, I saw Two Tree Hill for the first time that evening. It was situated northeast of Salisbury, beyond Sinoia, in the beautiful Umboe Valley. The house stood on a hill flanked by two giant acacia trees, which gave it its name. It was a large old white Dutch Colonial house and had wonderful views out over the bush towards Mozambique.

I so much wished that I did not have to leave it and determined that I would save like mad in order to buy myself out of the Civil Service before my year was up and return. We stayed a few days and rode round some of the ranch on the intelligent little Basuto ponies of which the ranch had a dozen or so. Belford then drove us back to Salisbury. We had tea with Sir Godfrey Huggins, Prime Minister of Rhodesia, who promised Hugh that he would keep an eye on me. He was a kind little man with a sandy moustache. Hugh told me that he had been a vet.

It was then time for Hugh to leave Rhodesia and me to start work. By then I only had £5 left. Hugh very kindly offered to give me some money, but he had already done so much for me that I refused. The first thing that I had to do was to find somewhere to live. The only place that I could afford was a sort of transit camp for new arrivals to the country. This was a tented encampment on the edge of Salisbury. There was an old Bedford army lorry that transported us into the centre of the town in the morning and returned in the evening. There was only a nominal charge for all this. When I received my first pay packet at the end of the month I invested £15 in a bicycle, so that I could travel under my own steam.

My first post was in the Clerk of the Civil Court's department. I issued driving and vehicle licences. The majority of the natives could not read or write so I had to take their thumbprints and put these on their licences. I met an awful lot of Rhodesians in my time there.

I found the transit camp a lonely place, as most of the occupants were ex-service men a good deal older than I was and they didn't stay long. It was certainly a rude awakening after my ritzy life with Hugh. The great advantage was its cheapness and the fact that I was able to save money fast. There was a central ablutions tent with a line of basins and some shower cubicles. What happened to me must have stemmed from this place. I was on nodding terms with one or two of the chaps who used it. Seeing me with little or no clothes on must have inflamed the passions of one of them. He entered my tent in the middle of the night and after a violent fight penetrated me with damaging results. He behaved like a madman. The shock was even greater as I was fast asleep when the assault took place. I was badly split by the penetration and generally knocked about. The sheets were covered in blood. One of my neighbours, hearing the hullabaloo, came and my attacker fled. My rescuer, very kindly, helped me into his car and ran me into the hospital. Whilst the nurses were tending my wounds they tried to find out who had caused them. Fortunately I had the presence of mind to keep quiet and, as far as I know, the matter never got out. I was aware that disclosure would have led to a very public trial. I would have had to relive my torment in court. It would have been headline news in the newspapers and doubtless my family back home would have heard about it.

I learnt later that the rapist had been torpedoed twice during the war and weeks in an open boat had unhinged him. He had fled the camp immediately following the incident. Even though I was sure that I had done nothing to encourage him, I still felt terribly guilty and ashamed. I think that this was a follow on from the Jones incident at school, which I could have stopped and did not. Like then I was convinced that he had seen me as a girl. How was I going to get through the years ahead living in the wrong sex? From now on this quandary never left me and became a secret source worry and yearning. I just had to screw up my courage to continue and take pride in that courage. It seemed to be the only way ahead.

Sitting on my hard stool dispensing licences was almost unbearable after this, as was cycling. I travelled in the lorry, standing up, to avoid the latter. Almost immediately I was transferred to run the criminal court office. This eased the pain, as I was no longer sitting down all day. The previous clerk had got the office in a shambles and been demoted. I gradually made order out of chaos and was congratulated on my work. It was an interesting job and involved working closely with the British South Africa Police. This police force had originated from The British South Africa Company founded by Cecil Rhodes to run the country as a commercial enterprise.

My task was to prepare the criminal cases to be presented in court. Directly I had got the office running smoothly, I increasingly used to accompany the police to the scene of serious crimes. I found that I could ensure that the correct data was collected better this way. It was particularly important to ensure that photographs acceptable to the court were taken. I spent some of the day in court, assisting the judges, when big cases were being tried.

I birched native offenders. Birching was the most usual punishment for non-jail offences, as few natives had money for fines. Natives mostly went barefooted and, if met on the pavement, would get off it to let whites pass. There was no apartheid and, in spite of everything, a pleasant friendly atmosphere prevailed amongst all races.

Quite a few of the people working in the Law Courts were Ex-Indian Army officers. On Independence they had been made redundant. Rather than returning to Britain, some had gone to Rhodesia where the colonial style life was more what they were used to. We even had a former Major General. When I got to know them they were friendly to me and often used to ask me to tennis parties and things like that at the weekends. It was at one of these that I first met Kitty. Her family farmed at Marandellas, which was not too far from Salisbury. She was a tall strong attractive girl. She was a very good tennis player and we won the mixed doubles together at the club tournament. We became friends about the time that I had saved up enough money to buy myself out of the Civil Service and head for Two Tree Hill, at long last.

McDonald, the farm manager, met me at Meikles Hotel in Salisbury and we set off on the long journey to Sinoia and beyond. It was a great day for me, and what I had come to Africa for. The strip roads that we travelled on began a short way out of Salisbury. They consisted of two parallel lines of tarmac each wide enough for a vehicle's wheels. On meeting another vehicle on had to get the nearside wheels off the tarmac to pass each other, causing clouds of dust to rise. We passed a few native women carrying bundles on their heads and the odd lone male. These men would often walk a hundred miles to get home or return to Salisbury.

I was given a large bedroom with several netting covered windows. Light African breezes always seemed to keep it beautifully cool, even in the hottest weather. It was an almost unbelievable luxury to be living in a house again after nine months spent in a tent. There was no electricity and hurricane lamps hissed and popped away after dark, throwing shadows across the white walls.

Two Tree Hill ran over a thousand head of cattle and grew maize and tobacco. The latter crop was very profitable and McDonald was tied up with its 'curing' at the time. The leaves were stored in great kilns and the temperature had to be monitored day and night. I was asked to help with the cattle. This suited me fine as it meant long days in the saddle out in the bush. The cattle were a mixed bunch with Hereford in them, judging by the preponderance of white faces amongst them. The bulls were Afrikanders. These were large brown animals with humps on their backs. One of my main tasks was to take out large posses of mounted native ranch hands, to round up groups of cattle, to be dipped in long tanks filled with a solution to protect them from tick fever.

We spent days at a time out in the bush, camping at nightfall round blazing fires to keep away wild animals. The natives sang the most beautiful tribal songs of their own before turning in. The soft velvet African night cooled one voluptuously in its embrace after the burning heat and dust of the day in the saddle. Lying under the stars, with the cold metal of my rifle at my side, I felt at peace with the world.

I found the Africans good company. We conversed in a bastard language known as 'Kitchen Kaffir'. This was a mixture of English, Afrikaans and their own dialect, Mashona. It was fairly easy to pick up, spending days alone in their cheerful presence, without any other Europeans. They addressed us as 'Boss' and we them as 'Boy'. They lived in their own little villages in round straw huts, called Rondavels. They had lived this way for centuries before we disturbed their pastoral tribal existence. They still had something of the dignity of the warrior in their demeanour but they invariably seemed courteous and charming. They maintained their essential freedom. It was accepted that they turned up for work as they pleased. As long as there were enough of them for the task in hand, which there invariably seemed to be, nobody worried. To be any use one had to be able to handle one's boys. A certain amount of firmness was necessary, but I found a cheerful good-humoured approach best. If you could make them laugh you were made.

Life at Two Tree Hill was not all hard work. The Rhodesian ethos was to work hard and play hard. My cousin John Lakin, the renowned polo international, was staying at a neighbouring ranch, which I think belonged to Lord Cowdray. He encouraged me to start playing polo and organised ponies for me. From then on most weekends I would set off to the various tournaments that abounded in the Rhodesia of those days. My good eye for a ball, coupled with my present life in the saddle, enabled me to make quick progress.

With the polo went a lively social life. Kitty's parents, very kindly, gave a party for my nineteenth birthday, during the Marandellas tournament. I was by then a pretty highly sexed young man. All sorts of puzzling desires filled me, some male, others female. Kitty was a year or two older than I was. She had been schooled in England and had that statuesque carriage peculiar to girls of her generation who had had deportment lessons, supporting books on their heads. I found her bare strong brown arms and long heroic legs most attractive. She was straightforward and friendly. I made her laugh with my chatter. We danced until the African dawn was stirring, clasped in each other's arms. So ended another blissfully happy birthday.

We danced many times through that Rhodesian summer, but nothing quite matched those magical moments for sheer sensuality. Of course I fell for her 'hook, line and sinker'. Kitty, however, had many suitors. There were always too few girls to go round, as was the case in most colonies then. Half the young blades in the BSA Police stationed in our area seemed to be vying for her hand, but Kitty remained her own person and refreshingly unattached.

We saw a great deal of each other at the social events that circulated with the Polo Tournaments. I was beginning to make a name for myself as a dashing Number One. My low handicap got me into the Sinoia team for the premier tournament of the season in Salisbury Show week. I replaced one of Kitty's policeman admirers whom they considered a trifle over handicapped.

The week was the great sporting event of the year. There were cricket matches, show jumping events, racing and of course the polo. I was organising the showing of a Two Tree Afrikander bull. I had brought two or three of our boys up with me. The rains were coming and great clouds were massing with the welcome smell of rain in the air.

Kitty's father was a prominent farmer and politician. He had a large house in Salisbury and invited me to stay. It was rather like the Dublin Horse Show week, with dances every night. Kitty said how much she enjoyed my company and missed me when we were apart. She treated me, however, more like a younger brother than a potential lover. I could not seem to get through that final barrier. Maybe she maintained this barrier of reserve with others, but I doubted it. We seemed destined to be 'just good friends', as they say.

To me the week sped by in a blur of music, dancing, galloping hooves and Kitty, Kitty and always Kitty, by my side. Sinoia did well and we exceeded everyone's expectations by reaching the final. We were due to meet Salisbury, captained by Rodney Morris, Rhodesia's highest handicapped player. The rain came the night before the final with deafening claps of thunder and the vivid sheets of lightning peculiar to Africa. Salisbury was awash that night. When we took the field the following afternoon, in spite of the hot sunshine, the ground was still slippery. Morris' long hitting put us behind. In a desperate attempt score in the final chukka I had a crashing fall on the skiddy turf and was knocked out. I came to in hospital with Kitty sitting by my bed. I spent a day or two recuperating at Kitty's house. This was the high point in our relationship. I had never known her more loving.

Sadly for me, we never came as close again. I think in loving relationships one is either coming together or moving away. One seldom remains just the same distance apart. The loveliest times are often the start of the move towards one another and just before the closest point. Undoubtedly the saddest is the moment of the very first, almost imperceptible, move apart. This was just such a moment.

I returned north to Two Tree with a heavy heart. The summer was over and we were busy clearing new land for the next crops. We ploughed with great teams of oxen. This operation provoked great merriment amongst the boys and, I must admit, we did manage to get ourselves into a rare old tangle at times. Then the rainy season came and we were cut off from the outside world for weeks on end. Kitty and I saw little of each other again. I had come so near to finding a sexual partner for my own peculiar person. I could be both man and woman with her.

There were many other eccentric characters in the Africa of those times, with the freedom to live as they chose. One such was a man who ran the native store in the area. He was called Major Reddy. He had 'Gone Native', as they used to term it. He lived way out in the bush with several native wives. Like them he went about virtually naked, except that he wore an Old Harrovian tie round his bare neck and a monocle over his left eye. He greeted one with an effusive 'Hello, old boy'. His favourite tale was of an Eton versus Harrow match at Lord's around the turn of the century. Apparently in the final over of the match he had got the last Etonian batsman 'plum LBW', as he termed it. The natives in the store used to listen with rapt attention to this story, although they must have heard it many times before. What they made of it goodness only knows. The umpire had disagreed with his verdict and Harrow had lost. He used to ask me, 'Trumper still scoring all those runs?' As Victor Trumper had died in 1915, the outside world had obviously stood still, in his imagination, at the time of his golden youth. He was the best shot in the district and an invaluable man in a lion hunt. He appeared to be a truly contented man.

In the rainy season, the elephant grass used to grow head high. One often used to hear lions grunting round the house at night and never went out unarmed. The most dangerous animal was a rogue elephant. It would devastate everything in its path. Reddy's services were much in demand when one of these was on the loose.

The seasons went by and I began to have increasing trouble with my bottom again. I sometimes used to come back out of the bush with my saddle covered in blood. Hugh came out to Two Tree Hill in the spring of 1953. He persuaded me to go to Sinoia Hospital to have the problem dealt with. After the operation Kitty joined us, to look after me, and we all went up to Hugh's hotel in the hills of Inyanga. It was deliciously cool after the heat of the plains. Kitty was most expert at changing my dressings and forcing me to take it easy. It was a happy time. But I never saw her again.

I had been away two-and-a-half years by then and Hugh thought it was high time that I had a holiday. He offered to take me back to England with him. Belford and I travelled overland to the Cape in a Willis Jeep. We spent a week at Monterey and then set sail for England in *The Capetown Castle*.

So fate was to take a hand, Otherwise I might have settled in Rhodesia. It was then such a happy, well ordered, prosperous land. This contrasts starkly with the murderous, poverty stricken, shambles that is Zimbabwe today. The Africans appeared genuinely happy being left to lead the sort of life they had led since time immemorial, with the added security and access to justice afforded by British rule.

I know that in the years ahead I looked back with almost unbearable nostalgia to those days of freedom in the bush. Setting off at dawn with the mist up to the horse's withers and the midday rest under in the shade of giant acacia trees with the champ of the hobbled horses grazing round us. Of the chance meeting with Reddy's ever growing brood of piccaninnies and their cheery greetings of, 'Hello, old boy.'

I have so often wondered what happened to Kitty in the terrible times that lay ahead for Rhodesia. I have never ceased to miss her, but her memory fades a little as the years go by. She will be an old lady by now but to me still that vibrant, warm-hearted girl that held me in her strong arms and shared a little precious moment of my own youth.

Chapter 4

The Brigade of Guards

We docked at Southampton in early May. I returned to Montpelier Place with many decisions to be made and affairs to be sorted out. Dear Nanny was there to greet me. John had returned to school and Nada was in one of her perpetual crises. Nanny and I decided to sell Montpelier Place and move into my late grandmother's place in Belgrave Square. This move would help to provide comfortable incomes for us all for the time being.

John could continue at school and in due course go up to Oxford. Nada's debts could be paid off and she could continue in her own sweet way. I decided to try and get a place at Oxford myself. I studied hard throughout that summer and was duly offered a place for that autumn term.

Fate again altered my plans and the course of my life. The army stepped in and said that I must do my two years' National Service first. Due to my family connection I decided to try for the Life Guards. A Ponsonby ancestor had even commanded the Household Cavalry charge at Waterloo, which had put Napoleon's army to flight, after his own, much vaunted, cavalry had failed to break the British infantry squares, prompting Wellington's renowned remark, 'Thank you, Life Guards.' John Lakin arranged an interview for me with The Silver Stick-in-Waiting to the Queen.

Colonel Jackie Ward, who interviewed me, was a quiet, much loved, rather sad officer. I never fathomed the cause of this sadness as he had a beautiful fair young wife. I believe that she was the daughter of the agent that ran his Irish estate. He had plucked her out of nowhere, so to speak, and whisked her into London society, which was undergoing a post-war renaissance before disappearing forever in the 1960s. The Colonel was a rich man and Susan Ward became a leading light in that society. She and Mrs Gerald Legge (later stepmother to Princess Diana) looked out, almost daily, from the pages of glossy magazines and newspapers in the '50s. I found Colonel Jackie a kind and sympathetic officer. He had heard of my polo exploits in Rhodesia from John. My regimental colonel, Gerard Leigh, was apparently a very keen player. At any rate I was accepted as a potential officer to join the Brigade Squad at the fearsome Guard's Depot at Caterham.

The Brigade Squad was comprised of all potential officers for the five Foot Guard and the two Household Cavalry Regiments. The Household Cavalry consisted of The Life Guards (the senior regiment in the army) and The Royal Horse Guards (The

Blues). The Foot Guards were, in order of seniority, Grenadier, Coldstream, Scots, Irish and Welsh Guards.

My Oxford college agreed, with some reluctance, to defer my entry for two years. I was called for a medical board examination, in Fulham for some obscure reason. I queued up stark naked with dozens of other young National Servicemen and waited my turn with not a little apprehension and, of course, a great deal of embarrassment. The talk of the nervously giggling bunch was mainly of what ailment they could think up to avoid going into the army. My worries were of the opposite nature. Finally, my turn came and an old 'Saw Bones' of an army doctor, with bushy eyebrows and a hearty manner, barely looked at me to begin with. On noticing The Life Guards on my form and my slender frame he asked me, 'What weight do you ride at?' He obviously assumed that I was an amateur National Hunt Jockey. That seemed to take his mind off medical matters and he passed me A1.

I reported to Combermere Barracks, Windsor, the Household Cavalry Depot, to be kitted out, for onward transmission to the Brigade Squad. What I chiefly remember of that time was breakfast in a vast dining hall full of noisy soldiery. This was before dawn. It always seemed to be pitch black outside. Strangely enough I was never to return there to serve, in my years in the army.

There were seven of us 'donkey wallopers', as the Foot Guards dubbed us. Our arrival at Caterham was a taste of things to come. We were marched flat out 'at the double' to our hut. We were in full kit with packs on our backs and carrying leaden kit bags. We arrived in a state of near collapse to greet our Foot Guard companions.

They were a really elite bunch of predominantly Old Etonians. From the first I liked them and became one of them and fitted in. There was nothing macho or hearty in their demeanour, which was casual. They went to great pains to hide enthusiasm. They welcomed eccentrics and were fairly unbreakable in their own humorous, urbane way. The one quality that they all possessed 'par excellence' was confidence in themselves. They were born to lead and would do so effortlessly without the need to be assertive. They abhorred heroics and displays of keenness. If ever the time came, one knew that they would be prepared to get up under intense fire and lead their men into battle. The greatest accolade for them would be to 'die like gentlemen'. Their manners were impeccable and their charm enormous. If they had a fault it was a thinly veiled contempt for lesser mortals. By this I certainly do not mean their own men, whom they lead with sympathy and kindness, and with whom they were invariably on the best of terms.

The Guardsmen appreciated their officer's qualities and would not have had them any different. The NCOs were a buffer between themselves and boring details that were too dreary to deal with. The NCOs were thus given a completely free rein to do what they did best, loyally supported by their officers, who in turn were given absolute loyalty and respect. The art was that neither should step on each other's toes in the line of duty. This was an art that had taken centuries to perfect.

To me it was all charmingly feudal in concept and, whilst aristocratic officers predominated, it was only a mirror of life outside. The other element was the family nature of the regiments, where son followed father. Most of the officers of the same age had known each other as early as prep school days, if not before, through family connections.

As far as I could gather, the exact opposite applied at West Point, the American Officer Cadet establishment. Supposed meritocracy should have produced equal fighting units to our own, but it had not. For all their bravado, history had shown American units wanting when the going got really tough. In fact, even their Marines could not stand comparison with our crack Household troops in action.

The Household Cavalry possessed all the Guards' qualities, outlined above, to an even greater degree. The eccentric individual was positively encouraged and the outwardly amateur spirit zealously guarded. This had something to do with the cavalryman's traditionally superior social status over the infantryman. Alone in the army we never addressed superior officers as 'Sir'. Officers called each other by their Christian names. The only exception to this was to address the Colonel as such. Officers with a superior rank to colonel were addressed according to their rank. Thus a general was properly called 'General' and never 'Sir'.

Unwittingly I had wandered into the one male adult community where I would be totally accepted for the sort of qualities that I did possess. The Guard's Depot in the old Caterham days was a very tough baptism of fire for recruits and none more so than for the Brigade Squad. The spirit, however, was wonderful within this squad. During our weekly communal shower, which was the only one allowed us, the old wooden hut echoed to the strains of the 'Eton boating song'. 'Swing, swing together, for nothing in life shall sever the chains that surround us now' was very true. I was regarded with amused tolerance.

My companions considered the incident where I had marched slap into the only tree on the parade ground, because the peak of my cap had obscured my vision, as 'absolutely splendid'. They assumed that I had done this on purpose to pull the Drill Sergeant's leg. He did not view this in the same light. Sergeant Huggins was a Grenadier (addressed as 'Saant'). He later became a famous figure at Sandhurst and a maitre domo at Blenheim Palace for the present Duke of Marlborough, himself a former Life Guard officer. At any rate I ended up in the Guard Room. I was the only Brigade Squad member to suffer such a fate. A poor guardsman recruit, finding life too hard to bear, hanged himself in his cell during my incarceration there. I emerged something of a hero. Fortunately, our officers took a benevolent view of my accident thinking it showed 'good form'. 'Typical donkey walloper,' they chortled approvingly. Good Household Cavalrymen were all slightly mad, in their view.

Our period at Caterham was spent in the depth of the winter and I did feel the cold badly. The old Esse stove, with its pipe going up through the ceiling, in the centre of our hut did, however, keep us cosy in the evenings when it was alight. We endlessly practised the arcane art of 'spit and polish' under the watchful eye of our 'trained soldier' who lived with us in the hut. Our best pair of boots had to gleam like glass. The first procedure was to burn all the grease and supple goodness out of the boots so that they became brittle and uncomfortable. They were completely unwearable off the parade ground.

Physically it was a very demanding time. We had to survive many rigours, which were made worse for me by an accident. We had to practise rescuing a 'wounded comrade'. My comrade was just too heavy for me and I damaged my back. This injury was to plague me for months and often only sheer willpower kept me going. Overall, in spite of this, it was a good time. Some of my companions were scions of the 'landed gentry' and I spent some carefree weekends at various stately homes. I returned their hospitality at Belgrave Square, where we now lived, and we had some jolly times.

This training culminated in attendance at The War Office Selection Board on Salisbury Plain. This was a make or break test of two or three days' duration. One was sent to an Officer Cadet School if one passed or the dreaded 'Returned to Unit', to serve in the ranks for the rest of our National Service, if not thought 'Officer Material'. Salisbury Plain was deep in snow and it snowed during most of our tiresome leadership tests. It was like organizing a bunch of snowmen to cross imaginary rivers with the aid of a pole and a loo seat, or something equally silly. It was all a case of showing blind confidence in the face of disaster. When stumped, saying optimistically 'Follow me, men' or 'Beware polar bears' seemed to impress the invigilators. I was not too clever at the 'trick cyclist' tests, which involved putting blocks into different sized holes and things like that. My final ordeal was to give a lecture on any subject. I chose 'Grand Opera'. This went down well, if with a few too many laughs for comfort. At any rate I was marched in front of the board and informed that they were impressed how well I had marshalled the 'snowmen' and deemed 'Officer Material', like most of our Squad. The Foot Guards were sent up to the Infantry Cadre at Eaton Hall in Cheshire and us cavalrymen to Mons Officer Cadet School in Aldershot. The few regulars amongst our numbers went off to Sandhurst for a two-year course. It was sad to be separated from so many good friends. Looking back over nearly fifty years I consider that group to be finest people I have known.

The course at Mons lasted about six months and was first class. In six months it gave us the knowledge to command an armoured troop in the field. The standard expected was high and some fell by the wayside, but most of us rose to the occasion, gave everything we had to succeed, and that is what it took. I remember seeing a squad, senior to ours, coming out of a hut on a May morning. They were bronzed young men in the peak of condition. Their morale was so high that you could imagine them being invincible in battle.

At last that long winter, with all its hardships, neared its end. The sun shone and I bought a motorcar. We began to get out and about in it. We mixed with a small circle of girls in London. I set my cap at a tall blonde girl with a physique similar to Kitty. She was very pretty and had just become engaged to well known rugger playing naval officer. I still wonder about our relationship and quite why it took place in the circumstances. Certainly the naval officer was at sea during the period of our romance. I can only suppose that Lydia was having a last fling. She had mixed with the upper crust at Oxford and it could be that she saw me as a part of that magic circle that was going to be lost to her forever as a navy wife. We danced away the nights at the 21 Room, a club in Chesterfield Place, off Curzon Street, to the haunting music of a quite wonderful pianist called Bobby Harvey. He later became much sought after as an entertainer by London Society. He never quite matched again the incredible sweetness he engendered in the ambience of that dear friendly old club, where the young used to gather in those far off days.

It was a romance with a time limit. The sands of time were running away for us. We both knew it and accepted it. We would soon both be far away. Because of this there was to be no illusion or disillusion, just happiness and young love. There was no need for Lydia to accept or reject me or question what I was, but just accept the love I felt for her. We would never meet again. Recently, by chance, I happened to drive down Tregunter road, and past number 36, where Lydia had lived that summer. That little oasis in time came flooding back to me with such tender memories.

I really did quite well at Mons and became a 'Stick Orderly', which was a parade appointment for the two smartest cadets of a particular troop. We were drilled under the watchful eye of the famous Coldstream Guards Sergeant Major 'Tubby' Brittain. His great commands echoed round Aldershot during parades. He had appeared in several films about the Brigade of Guards and was held in great veneration by us all. In spite of his fierce bark and imposing appearance he was a kindly soul at heart with an engaging twinkle in his eye.

I do not know quite what qualities they saw in me beyond high spirits and enthusiasm. I could not afford to play polo or ride in point–to-points, during my time there, like other better connected and well-heeled cadets. I passed the various blocks of the course without danger of being RTUed. I was happy to be myself and as a Life Guard was expected to be just that and allowed great licence. Eventually the great day of our own Passing Out Parade arrived. We were granted the Queen's Commission during Wimbledon week 1954.

Then came a bombshell. I was called before a Medical Board at Millbank to be told that X-rays had revealed a congenital weakness in my back. I counterattacked spiritedly. I assured them that my back injury was all but cured and that if I could not stand up to active service after all that I had endured in the past nine months no one else could either. The Major General President looked into my defiant eyes long and hard and I could see sympathy dawning in his own gaze. He told me to go and put my uniform back on. When I was called back in before the board he told me, 'We have decided that you are a highly motivated young officer and pass you fit for service.' Relief flooded through me as never before or since. I saluted, turned smartly and marched off to start my career as an officer in Her Majesty's Life Guards. I felt that had overcome the supreme test of my ambivalent sexuality. I drove back down Whitehall, through Admiralty Arch and up the Mall towards Buckingham Palace with a feeling of great exultation.

That afternoon Lydia and I set off to Glyndebourne to hear Mozart's sublime Opera, *Die Entfuhrung aus dem Serail*. The necessary ritual of donning evening clothes on a hot summer afternoon, for the trip down to Sussex, ever afterwards brought back the joy of that unforgettable day. With that beautiful blonde girl on my arm I felt the envy of the world. During the extended interval between acts we dined in the restaurant built round a tree. We drank deep of the nectar in celebration of my victory. It did indeed taste like the cool drink of the Gods that night.

The next day there followed the exciting task of being measured up for my uniforms at the designated tailors, shirt-makers and hatters in London. My embarkation leave, spent with Lydia, passed by in a rosy glow of happiness, only touched by sadness at the very end, on our parting. It was then time to join the rest of the surviving 'donkey wallopers' for the flight out to Egypt to join the regiment. We witnessed dawn breaking over the desert for the first time. The sun was like a great red ball sitting on the horizon of the vast empty ' Land of the Pharaohs'.

Chapter 5

A Life Guard in the Land of the Pharaohs

Joining a regiment as a newly commissioned officer is never an easy affair. It pays to keep one's mouth firmly shut when in the Officers' Mess and oblige protocol in as low profile a manner as possible. As a naturally high-profile character this was particularly hard for me. I was, however, assisted in this by the other officers who totally ignored my presence at first. When I did forget myself enough to venture a remark or two, I was firmly advised to bear in mind the maxim for Second Lieutenants which was to 'keep your mouth shut and your bowels open'. Since a young age I have found the first part of the maxim congenitally impossible and the second part increasingly problematic since the damage to my nether regions in Rhodesia. I am sure that my advisor meant the warning to be helpful. He was the Second-in –Command of the Squadron to which I had been assigned. He was affectionately known as Toad by his brother officers. This was due to his small stature, bombastic manner and love of driving large cars at breakneck speed.

Mess life mainly took place in what was termed the 'Anteroom'. This was so called as it was where we gathered before entering the dining room, which adjoined it. To my mind it could equally have been called the 'Post-room', as we also adjourned there 'post' our meals. Even more accurate, I suppose, would have been the 'Ante-Post' room but perhaps that would have smacked of Lingfield Park or some such racecourse, so beloved by our officers. Fortunately I kept these somewhat mutinous musings to myself. There was a rigid protocol observed at luncheon. We filed in strictly in order of seniority to collect our fare from the sideboard, prior to sitting down to eat. The other main courtesy to be observed was to stand to attention and click one's heels to one's Squadron Leader and the Colonel and his Second-in-Command, on the first greeting of the day in the mess.

I later realised that the mess was home to the officers of the Regiment. Wherever it happened to be in the world the familiar silver, furniture and other artefacts, including paintings, were lovingly assembled to create this home. Thus strangers were only welcomed if they observed the proper courtesies due to their hosts.

The Regiment consisted of three Sabre (fighting) Squadrons and a Headquarter Squadron. I was given command of an armoured car troop in 'A' Sabre Squadron. Each Troop was commanded by a subaltern, like myself, with a Corporal of Horse (Household Cavalry Sergeant) to assist. There were about a dozen troopers to man our four Daimler armoured cars.

We were soon out in the desert on exercises. I quickly, and rather surprisingly, learnt that, in spite of inexperience, it was best to trust my own judgement rather than that of my far more experienced Corporal of Horse. This led to a battle of wills and I was relieved when he was posted to Knightsbridge. He was never replaced and the troop became really mine. My troop was a mixture of regulars and National Servicemen. The latter added another dimension and I would have missed them if regulars had replaced them all. At any rate, the combination made a fine bunch of chaps and we got on well during the following year and a half we spent together. The main fact of living in the North African desert was the cold of the nights. We used to wake shivering until the sun came up and warmed one's bones. That was the best moment. By midday the heat was scorching. One was caked in dust and the great luxury on coming out of the desert was soaking in a bath or, if reaching the sea, plunging in.

The normal working day, when in camp, finished in the heat of midday. The Colonel was soon on to me to start my polo. From then on I played every day that we were not out in the desert. The only exception to this was when I was out on 'Z Patrols' combating terrorism in the built-up areas. My Rhodesian experience was a great help and I soon made the regimental team. We played in many tournaments against the other regiments. These were great occasions, with military bands playing, regimental flags flying and marquees set up for spectators. Half the Canal Zone used to turn up to urge their own team on. We won the Inter-Regimental Cup both of the years that I was there. Our star player was Ronnie Ferguson, who even then, was becoming a high-class player. My own game was coming on in leaps and bounds. I was a natural back, but was made to play up front as very much the junior member of the team and at least managed to score the winning goal in both my finals. It was fortunate that I had my bit of outside income or I would not have been able to afford it all on my army pay.

The Life Guards in those days had predominantly pretty rich officers. The mess bills swallowed up most of our pay. There were nightly poker schools in the mess. It was tempting to join these with nothing better to occupy the long Egyptian nights. Later on we were able to visit Cairo and Alexandria. We even played in polo matches at the Gezira Club against the Egyptian Army team. In the first year that I was there the situation was still tense, and we were restricted to soldiering and the Canal Zone. Only our Colonel, Gerard Leigh, known as 'Colonel G' was able to have his wife, Jean, out there. Jean had written the famous love letter, put in the briefcase of 'The man who never was', with the false invasion plans that fooled Hitler and saved so many lives.

The more time went on, the more I missed female company. The odd girl out from England was soon snapped up by the officers that abounded in such a large British garrison. They mostly worked in the Staff HQ at Port Said. Life was similar to that lived under the British Raj in the old India, without the freedom to roam. It was a claustrophobic atmosphere only enlivened, in our case, by the yacht, *Siesta*, that our Adjutant, Michael Wyndham, had sailed out from Cyprus. This was anchored in the Great Bitter Lake near our camp.

Michael lived on *Siesta* and we all used to spend time out there water skiing off it, sailing and drinking Pimms. Colonel G became a member of the Royal Yacht Squadron. This entitled *Siesta* to fly the White Ensign proudly on her stern. This meant that whenever *Siesta* passed the Royal Navy base or a warship, they had to run up flags to salute us. This was a sport that amused Michael. An odd coincidence occurred one day on Siesta. I met Bridget Hornby, the daughter of my old prep school headmaster. Bridget had been the only girl in the school. She had befriended me when I first arrived, homesick, lost and dreadfully unhappy. We had become bosom pals. I think that she had found me a fellow spirit amongst the rowdy rough boys.

In 1955, an event happened which jerked us out of our rut. There was a rebellion by tribesmen in the Aden British Protectorate in the Gulf. These Shamshi had overrun the upcountry airstrips and cut them off from the outside world. The Political Officers administered the Protectorate from forts that these airstrips serviced. Overland travel and communication was hazardous due to the mountainous terrain and the vast distances involved. The Shamshi laid in wait to ambush travellers in the wadis through which it was necessary to travel. They painted themselves blue to camouflage themselves against the background of the sky. The wadis were dry riverbed passes through the mountains. The British Army had not been in this region since Lawrence of Arabia's days in the First World War.

My Squadron Leader, Kenneth Diacre, was chosen to lead the operation to relieve these forts. He was a charismatic figure and a born leader of men. It was said that he was the son of the Duke of Rutland, born 'on the wrong side of the blanket'. He certainly possessed the distinctive Manners' looks. His superiors no doubt found him headstrong and difficult to control, but his men worshipped him. There was certainly no doubting his ability. Like most great leaders he had a ruthless streak and woe betide anyone who got on the wrong side of him. He and I had a somewhat up and down relationship. This was in the days before combat helicopters and so the force would have to fight its way across country to achieve its objective. Browning machine guns, which we had not used before, were mounted on newly arrived Ferret Scout Cars. Armour-plated sheets were erected round their turrets to protect the commander whist firing the Brownings. I note a laconic comment in my diary: 'Dead busy preparing Ferrets and loading them on to the Hastings'. The latter were great transport aircraft.

I was not included in the advance party and all the old doubts about my sexuality assailed me once more. I felt that I should have been at the 'sharp end' and that it was a slur on me. I need not have worried as shortly afterwards I was on a Hastings gazing down on the barren Ethiopian lands, flying south down the Red Sea. We landed at the Khormaksar, the RAF base in Aden, to be met by Kenneth and join the force.

During the next few months we were constantly on the move, covering great distances across the Arabian desert up to the borders of the Yemen. Most of the time I had what could be called an independent command. My troop supported one company or another of the Seaforth Highlanders. They were a fine regiment and a closely knit band like our own. We provided covering fire, when ambushed in the wadis, for the Seaforth to storm the hills to remove the tribesmen. I soon struck up a happy relationship with the Seaforth officers, one of whom was Robin Douglas Home. Later on he fell in love with Princess Margaretha of Sweden. Her father, the King, forbade the marriage on the grounds of Douglas Home lack of royal blood. As our newspapers pointed out at the time, this was a bit ironic as his Stewart blood was bluer than the King's. I do not think Robin ever recovered from the loss of his loved one. He committed suicide whilst still a young man.

An incident occurred whilst on this Arabian adventure that became part of Life Guard folklore. Robin and I sat up late one night, when in the Sheriff of Beihan's kingdom, firmly anticipating that the Sheriff would send us 'dancing girls' for our comfort. The Arabian night wore on but the feast ended and we retired crestfallen to our lonely beds with only sweet dreams of what might have been. I was reminded of this disappointment recently when a friend pointed out the passage about it in the late Willie Loyd's entertaining book, *Challenges and Chargers*.

Robin and I remained close friends from this night onwards. Back in civilian life, for a time, he used to entertain diners by playing the piano at the old Berkeley in Piccadilly. During breaks in his performance he often used to join my table for a glass of champagne, when I was dining there with friends. He still then seemed to share my own love of life and was invariably great company. I miss him, dear romantic soul, and vowed to knock the King off his silly bicycle if I ever visited Stockholm.

During this time in Arabia I began to experience, like other British officers before me, a deep love affair with the desert. It burned deep into my consciousness. The blinding sun by day and the great panoply of stars to sleep under at night, with the pink distant mountains turning to azure at dusk and then the deepest navy blue at night. As in Rhodesia, I valued the space and sense of freedom it engendered. Almost my entire life I have travelled hopefully, always looking ahead for the next goal and the forthcoming adventure that would entail. Now time stood still. In Arabia I neither looked back nor forward. I just lived for the day. The harsh beautiful environment made survival itself an achievement. The cool drink from the chargoyles slung on the side of my Ferret tasted better than the finest champagne. I was built for the climate. Others were not so lucky. They simply could not take it and collapsed.

Typical of the entries in my diary was: 'Operation in Nisab area. Met Bunny (Political Officer) at fort. Attended Arab war council. Lunch with Sheik at his house and went on operation with Audhli Sultan. Blew up rebel houses.' My troop seems to have been constantly busy and in great demand for operations.

One day, on reaching the fort at Ataq, Colonel G greeted me. He had flown down from Egypt to see how long part of his regiment was going to be lost to him. He took me aside for a chat. He informed me that he had good reports of me from the Seaforth Colonel. He offered me a Regular Commission. If I accepted he planned to send me to the Mounted Squadron at Knightsbridge in the New Year. I mentioned my place at Oxford. He said that obviously it would mean foregoing this if I made the army my career. I begged time to consider. I lay under the stars that night and made my decision. The prospect of Knightsbridge was like a dream come true. There was never any doubt in my mind. I wrote to the Master of my college at Oxford and gave it to Colonel G to post.

Looking back I was taking a bit of a risk. I had yet to pass the Regular Commissions Board before my commission could be confirmed. In the event this did not present any problems. I wheeled out my opera talk again and put in the requisite number of 'Follow me, men'. Finally I had to go before the Canal Zone Force Commander, General Sir Richard Hull. He informed me that his mother was a Ponsonby and I left his office with a Regular Commission.

So the course of my life was altered yet again. I have never regretted my decision. I was about to commence the happiest years of my life. Of course I would have gained enormously from Oxford at that stage of my development, but there are only so many things one can do. I would need several lives to achieve all my ambitions.

So in the autumn of 1955 I returned to Egypt with my troop and desert doings nearly done. There was one more adventure before Knightsbridge. That was an operation into the Sinai. The Egyptian winter was setting in when we crossed the Suez Canal on rafts and travelled inland towards St Catherine's Monastery on Mount Sinai. The going was tough particularly through the Wadi Feran. Scammel recovery vehicles were constantly in action. Their commander, universally known as 'Fucking Harry', more for his language than any other activity, urged these on. I believe that he was Corporal of Horse then. His rank used to zip up and down depending on his latest act of insubordination. It was difficult to keep track of and must have ruffled even the unflappable, bemonocled Guy Long, the Regimental Paymaster. Harry, however, was quite indispensable and whatever his current rank he continued to cajole and lead his team of regimental mechanics with the same verve and skill. Whenever I was in a spot of mechanical bother he was invariably the most welcome and reassuring sight. We were then still operating with venerable Second World War Daimler armoured cars and Dingo scout cars, which were long past their sell-by date. Harry had also had the foresight to bring a plentiful supply of anti-freeze, without which our vehicles would have frozen up at night, as we climbed up near the reputed scene of Moses' encounter with the burning bush on the Mount Of Moses, with St Catherine's Monastery on its lower slopes.

It was an unforgettable trip and once again I was fortunate to be in Kenneth's Squadron. Otherwise I might have been denied so many adventures and spent my 18 months in the Canal Zone, and perhaps never have had the chance to win my spurs and be offered a Regular Commission.

On 13th December I set sail from Port Said on *The Empire Orwell* with my old tin trunk firmly painted 'Hyde Park Barracks, Knightsbridge'. It was quite a wrench leaving my troop. We had been together a long time and one's first command, like one's first love, is something very special. Over fifty years on I can still remember their names and picture their faces, particularly my own driver Wayne, who was killed. We were a happy little family and I wonder where they all are now.

The unique smell of an English winter morning filled me with joy as the Orwell docked at Southampton, with Christmas a few days away. It was good to be home again.

Chapter 6

Strange Birds on a Windy Night

After spending Christmas with Nanny and John in Belgrave Square, I visited Corporal of Horse Peart at Hyde Park Barracks to be fitted with my full dress uniform. This consisted of a gold braided scarlet tunic, buckskin breeches, thigh-length black jack boots, front and back cuirass (silver breast plates), helmet with white plume, state sword and spurs. I did not have to pay for these like pre-war officers. They were merely issued to me whilst I was stationed with the Mounted Squadron on what were termed Public Duties. I was also issued with a long, black frock coat used for inspecting the Guard at Whitehall when the Queen was out of London. I had to purchase a scarlet mess jacket with blue waistcoat. The rest of the uniform, like the navy blue overalls with red split stripes down the side, I had already purchased when first commissioned.

I reported for duty on 14th January to be met by my old soldier servant, Freeman, who had travelled back from Egypt with me. My room in the Officers' House, as the mess was called, was spacious and pleasant, looking over Hyde Park. There was no heating in it, so I provided an ancient electric fire, which had belonged to my grandmother, Lily. This used to periodically fuse all the lights in the house.

I also had a groom of my own, Dampier, whom I chose from the troop that I commanded. The charger (officer's horse) I selected from my troop was a lop-eared black mare called Empress. Dampier and I became devoted to her. He taught her all sorts of 'party pieces'. She was a sweet natured animal with a 'sit-down' as smooth as silk: that is, when trotting, she did not throw one up and down. In full dress uniform it was not possible to rise at the trot.

Empress was quiet in traffic and happy to be separated from her pals and ridden down to Whitehall on her own for the four o'clock inspection, when Her Majesty was out of London. This was quite a feat with the increasingly heavy traffic, particularly crossing Hyde Park Corner into Constitutional Hill. Most of the troop horses hated being separated from their companions and going anywhere on their own. This had its advantages if a trooper happened to be unseated. His horse would then remain in its correct position in the ranks and carry out the required manoeuvres independently, keeping perfect dressing.

I first had to pass out of the riding school. This took three weeks. After that I commenced the full dress ride. Riding in the kit was quite an art in itself, particularly keeping the heavy helmet on and handling the long sword. I completed this on 6th March at a Passing Out Parade. I then began Public Duties by commanding a full guard. There was quite a lot to learn for the handing over ceremony from the Blue's Guard at Whitehall. The Subaltern of the Guard had to give all the commands.

Whilst on guard one lived in the officer's flat. One had to provide one's own meals. The standard procedure was to get Fortnum and Masons to send round a ready-cooked meal. This was expensive and what most officers did was to get their girlfriends to bring in some food and cook it in the little kitchen provided. The alternative was to dine with the Foot Guards in St James' Palace. This was not popular with us.

Ronnie Ferguson, who had preceded me to Knightsbridge, was the only officer that I already knew. The other Life Guard subalterns were Nicky Beaumont, who later ran Ascot racecourse for many years and John Gooch, whose father had commanded the regiment during the war. John was a charming and cultivated person. He organised the mess food to a very high standard. It was said that it was the best in London under his direction. He resembled Dennis Price of *Kind Hearts and Coronets* fame, both in looks and manner. Later on, when I knew him better, I asked him why he did not own a motorcar. He replied, 'Where can one get such a thing?' I had seen one in the window of a little showroom in the Brompton Road and took him down there. He took one look at the car, which was a Humber, I seem to remember, and told the rather startled salesman he would have it: 'But I want a more comfortable seat for myself and all the rear seats removed for Calamity June [his Great Dane dog].' No mention of price was made as he walked straight out again. The car was duly delivered to the barracks with a rather strange old leather armchair for John and just a rug in the back for Calamity June. They both travelled contentedly about in this rather strange conveyance for many years to come.

The second-in-command was the Ninth Viscount Galway, an autocratic, hard-riding, and hard-drinking officer. He was really a throwback to an earlier age. The Squadron Leader was Major Duncan Llewelyn. He was known as 'Black Taffy' on account of his dark moods and uncertain temper. He was a difficult commander to serve under. His favourite entertainment was to sit in the front row of the Crazy Gang show at the Victoria Palace. They used to run special little numbers for his amusement. He invariably wore the same suit and tie when out of uniform. It was said that no one had ever seen him in any other attire.

The Blues Subalterns were also a rich pick of aristocratic young regulars. The four were Lord Patrick Beresford, Sir Nicholas Nuttall, Thomas Dunne and The Hon. Edward Biddulph. The latter was a splendidly eccentric character who always reminded me of P G Wodehouse's Bertie Wooster. Their Squadron Leader was Max Gordon. He was an old-fashioned type of club bachelor. He was intelligent, well educated and a shrewd judge of character. He hid these attributes under a charmingly vague exterior. His officers were very fond of him.

The Colonel who commanded both the Life Guards and the Blues Mounted Squadrons was Sir Rupert Hardy. He was a Colonel Blimp, county squire-type of pre-war officer. He had been recalled after the war to get the Mounted Squadrons going again. We subalterns called him 'Colonel Toast' due to his shouts to the mess waiters at breakfast. He spent most of the winter up in the Shires hunting. He was a rather remote gruff figure with a bristling military moustache.

Max Gordon was in complete contrast to this. He was approachable and friendly. Although a Blue, he took me under his wing in this rather daunting atmosphere for a newcomer. In my first week he took me up to Leicestershire for a day's hunting with the Quorn. In the event it was a frosty morning and the meet was called off and we came straight back again. During the next few years we must have motored many hundreds of miles together to take part in polo matches, day's hunting and other equitation events. Although he never mentioned it I felt that he understood something of my inner turmoil. We never became what I would call friends. He would sit silent on most of our journeys 'miles away' with his own thoughts. I never really fathomed what these were or what 'made him tick'. Of course I was a junior officer and twenty years younger. We did of course discuss our mutual sporting interests and I used to prattle away. I suppose that he must have enjoyed my company or he would not have sought it. Mainly I think he saw me as an enthusiastic promising subaltern who needed guiding in the right direction. This was kind and thoughtful of him and I owed him a lot. His Mayfair establishment was just what I imagined Sherlock Holmes and Dr Watson to have lived in: that is a wealthy bachelor's 'pad'.

I do not quite know what the other Knightsbridge subalterns made of me. When I got to know them we got on well together and I think that they appreciated my zest for life and the fact that I made them laugh. Knightsbridge in those days was an exclusive club and as a fellow member I was one of them. Joining them was not like first joining the regiment. The officers there were a hand-picked bunch from the two Household Cavalry Regiments and the new arrivals were already known to each other, if only by repute. In my case this was as a promising polo player. They launched me into London Society and that first summer I was invited nightly to the grand balls that flourished in the 1950s. One evening I would be dining in the Boltons with the likes of Douglas Fairbanks and the next with a cabinet minister or a duke. It was heady stuff for a youngster like myself without connections. London in 'dawn's early light' was a memory that I carry with me to this day from those carefree happy champagne-filled nights. I thus took part from the inside in the old patrician society's final fling.

Young unattached Household Cavalry officers were always welcome, provided they observed the unwritten code demanded by Society. Once broken, and only once, you were out. My mother had instilled this code into me young, so I survived without really realising what it was. Invitations had to be answered punctually and in the correct form. Acceptance of an invitation meant just that and could not be broken. Impeccable manners were essential, as well as the correct dress for a particular occasion. I remember an officer being seen by the Colonel in a dinner jacket, rather than white tie and tails, at a ball. As a punishment he was given ten extra Orderly Officer duties. That is the officer who is in charge of the barracks at night. He was popular with the rest of us as it meant free nights ahead for us. A letter of thanks had to be sent punctually to the hostess of the dinner party or ensuing dance. The girls in one's party had all to be danced with and generally kept an eye on to make sure that they did not become 'wallflowers'. The hostess must be requested for 'the pleasure of her company' on the dance floor. Most likely she would let one off this duty, but the invitation was still valued. The wealthy and powerful hostesses ran their own Mafia and closed ranks on an offender. The lesser hostesses followed their lead.

Essentially 'The Season', as it was known, was a marriage market, although much less than in earlier times. What it did do was to provide the gilded young with 'suitable' friends and a circle of acquaintances, or that was the idea. At least, it was a bit of expensive fun. Well-connected rich bachelors were its prized possession. The rest of us were there to make up the numbers. In my case it was thought that I could enliven a dull dinner party and there were enough of these to keep the invitations flowing in.

At weekends the jamboree moved out to the country and I found these dances the better occasions. When off duty, I was constantly haring off, after polo, to some noble countryseat and many that were a good deal less than noble. The bind was that I would have to rise early on a Sunday morning to speed off to some polo ground or other.

My polo had begun again in the spring. After a last day or two at Archie David's Henley ground, The Guard's Polo Club opened in Windsor Great Park, instigated by Prince Philip. The early days there were fun before it became too much of a social event. There were comparatively few of us players and we enjoyed ourselves. Prince Philip was very good to the young, such as myself. He would sometimes be driven to 'sound off' at pompous senior officers, but I never received a cross word from him in my years playing with and against him. The Smith's Lawns grounds were a bit bumpy then and one noticed the difference when playing on the immaculately smooth Cowdray Park and Cirencester Park turf. At the best of times, hitting a racing ball whilst galloping flat out is a tricky art to master and requires perfect timing, horsemanship and coordination. The higher the class of polo the faster the pace it is played at. The main essential is a very good natural eye for a ball. My polo pedigree had favoured me in this respect. A good few hour's regular 'stick and ball' practice honed one's natural ability. My own ponies were not in the top bracket, but I was well enough mounted to enjoy myself. They were handy and mercifully stayed sound. My favourite, Hazy Music, used to buck when first mounted when in season, providing our own private rodeo show. Frankashal was an ex-racehorse who had been 'warned off' for running under an assumed name. He was fast but did not understand the game as well as Hazy.

I was provided with a second groom from my troop who looked after my ponies, stabled free in the Royal Mews. I just had to pay for their feed. This arrangement suited Smith, as his father was in royal service at the castle. He moved up to the Remount Depot at Melton Mowbray during the winter to care for my hunter, Guard Royal. He was a fine horse with a lovely mouth: that is, he did not pull and could be controlled easily without pulling my arms out. I had chosen him from my troop. We learnt the skills of riding across the big Leicestershire country together and both enjoyed some great days with the Quorn, Cottesmore and Belvoir hunts. Later on I even had a second troop horse, called Biro. Smith would ride out the second horse, halfway through the day's hunting, so that I had a fresh horse to enjoy the afternoon's sport. Before Christmas these late afternoon hunts were often the best part of the day. There was nothing to compare with a really good day's hunting in those days when the Leicestershire country was nearly all old turf, with no wire guarding the big black hedges. One could still ride a line of one's own then and go like the wind over the fences following hounds.

Most of the Knightsbridge officers lived out in their own houses or flats. Thus if one was Orderly Officer one usually dined in splendid isolation in the long high-ceilinged dining room, waited on by a small army of mess waiters. After dinner I used to sit in the anteroom in front of the blazing log fire, that first winter, watching television. I had never seen television before, so this was quite a novelty for me. When I had left for Egypt there were very few sets around as yet. Apart from this most modern innovation it was quite an Edwardian scene, with the flickering fire lighting the old mess paintings. Above the mantelpiece the great Major Burnaby looked down. It was said that he could lift a polo pony under each arm. He had met a heroic death in the Sudan surrounded by a horde of 'Fuzzy Wuzzies', having despatched a good many before finally falling, mortally wounded. Edward VII, when Prince of Wales, had spent many a winter evening playing poker in that very room with Household Cavalry officers.

The snow would be swirling round the old stable yard on my inspections and the 'Black-uns', as we called our troop horses, would be champing and clinking their chains in their cosy stables. It was a scene that had not changed for a hundred years or more. On returning to the mess I would shake off the snow from my cloak and gratefully settle down in front of the fire again with another glass of kummel and a fresh cigar.

It could be a bit lonely and I missed a close female companion. All the girls that

I mixed with during the season were very much acquaintances and too preoccupied to embark upon closer attachments. Debutantes, I found, tended to become alarmed if sex 'reared its ugly head'. In those innocent days any young man showing 'a bit of form' was classed as 'NSIT' (Not Safe In Taxis) and disapproved of by the Mafia.

Ronnie recommended a visit to 'Ma Feathers', as Mrs Featherstonhaugh was called. He gave me her telephone number, advising me to say, 'I am a friend of Ronald Ferguson. Can I come and see you sometime?' Money would never be mentioned, but I must leave a £5 note on the bedside table before departing. I could stay the night if I so wished. Breakfast would be served in the bedroom and the girl might stay too, depending on her plans.

So on the appointed winter evening I duly arrived on the grand old doorstep of 34, Elvaston Place. I had anxiously awaited the 7 o'clock deadline, downing a glass or two of sherry in the mess. I parked a little way along the street, which was just off the Cromwell Road in Kensington. The bell was one of those old-fashioned sort where pulling down a lever activated a little group of bells in the hall. I could see a light on in the hallway but there was no answer. A policeman was approaching up the street. I pulled up the collar of my British Warm greatcoat and sank into the shadows of the porch. Notwithstanding this subterfuge he wished me a cheery 'Evening, Sir' and proceeded slowly on his beat. When he was safely out of earshot I rang again and then knocked, with the same negative result. By this time I was beginning to think that Ronnie had been pulling my leg over the whole the whole thing, when a taxi drew up. Out of it stepped a smart attractive girl. She joined me on the doorstep. We stood for a minute looking at each other, until she produced a key from her handbag and asked me if it was Jennifer I wanted. I replied that I had no idea who I wanted. She gave a little smile and said, 'Come in, at any rate.' She showed me into a room at the end of the hall and disappeared. I waited becoming more nervous by the minute.

Eventually, Jennifer returned with two or three little hand towels over her arm. I accompanied her up the impressive winding staircase. At the top we entered a beautifully furnished room with a welcoming coal fire burning in the grate. Above it was a photograph of a haughty looking lady in a riding habit, complete with silk top hat and veil. I correctly assumed that this of was Ma Feathers herself. We stood warming ourselves in front of the fire. Jennifer said that I looked very brown and healthy and asked me what I did. I told her and without thinking, in turn, asked her what she did. She was a bit taken aback but quickly recovered, replying that she did a bit of modelling. In fact I learned later that she was married to a naval officer who was often away at sea. I should think that she was then in her late twenties and seemed such a genuinely nice pretty girl.

We chatted away making polite conversation. After a little while I began to wonder what my next move was meant to be. Should I leap on her and get naughty or attempt to remove her clothes? She was so like the elder sisters of pals that I stayed with for various social events. Quite apart from this, the aforementioned moves did not seem to be the act of an officer and a gentleman. Eventually, after what seemed an age to me, she excused herself, went into the adjoining bathroom and reappeared naked. I was still standing rather stiffly in my pinstriped suit. She jumped into the sumptuous bed, turned out the light and, with a laugh, invited me to follow suit. I rather sheepishly took off my clothes and, to her evident amusement, folded them neatly over a chair, by the light of the fire. Even when we were lying naked beside one another I felt a bit embarrassed setting about the exciting business in hand with a complete stranger. She said kindly, 'You have never been to bed with a girl before, have you?' I replied 'Not really.' She laughed again and said that she was honoured to be the first. She then took the initiative with remarks like, 'No, not in there.' She was loving and maternal and though I was unable to perform I was happy to explore her lovely body. We parted the best of friends. I returned to the barracks in a bit of a daze with a dawning conviction that I was perhaps too little male to attempt such activities again.

Life at Knightsbridge went enjoyably on. That summer I commanded my troop on my first Trooping the Colour ceremony on Horse Guard's Parade at Whitehall. It was the most exhausting equitational activity I have ever experienced. I think we got mounted at about half past nine in the barracks and did not return there until past one o'clock. The worst part of it was the long periods sitting stock still, to attention, both at Buckingham Palace, where we picked up Her Majesty, and on Horse Guards, whilst the Foot Guards actually trooped their Colour.

My tight helmet gave me a headache and Empress tried to back into my Division lined up behind me throughout these manoeuvres. As a Troop Leader one was out in front with all eyes upon one. There was the constant fear that one would commit some bloomer or other, like dropping the long heavy state sword. Finally, at the end of the ceremony we were on the move at long last. First, walking past the Queen with the two Life Guard Divisions, our Mounted Band, including Pompey the giant skewbald drum horse and the two Blues Divisions. Then came the moment of great relief when the trot was sounded by the trumpeter and my helmet bobbed up and down with the consequent easing of my headache. It was a swelteringly hot June day, which made the thick full dress tunic and cuirass almost unbearable. I was utterly drained by the time I dismounted from Empress and I am sure that she was mightily relieved to be rid of me. Considering it was her first Trooping she had done really well. Colonel G, who had by this time taken over as Silver Stick on Colonel Jackie's retirement, sent me a message later saying how smart we both were. He had apparently seen a video on that evening and all those watching it had picked us out.

As I had ridden at the head of my troop, with the bands playing and the crowds cheering, some deep pride had stirred me. It was as if I was carrying on a long tradition both of my military family and that of my illustrious regiment and great nation. The very fact that I was there at all in that exalted position somehow seemed to be ordained. It was the crowning moment when I carried out the duty due for my generation. This sense of history was enhanced as I mixed with the scarlet and blue clad officers in the old mess for a late lunch and to quench our thirst with the plentiful supply of deliciously chilled champagne.

Ascot week in June was the height of the Season. As a Household Cavalry Officer, I gained automatic entry to the Royal Enclosure. I went to all four days of the royal meeting and enjoyed the occasion, meeting many of my old Brigade Squad and Mons pals, amongst others. I did, however, lose a bit of money backing the wrong horses. On the Monday, I was on dismounted duty at the Knights of the Garter ceremony at the Royal Chapel in Windsor Castle. After this I dashed off to Smith's Lawns to play in the opening match of the Ascot week polo tournament. I was in The Life Guard team and it was an exciting week with dances every night. There was the daily rush to the polo after the racing and on to various dinner parties, which preceded the dances. These were in the Windsor, Henley and Maidenhead area. I can still remember how heavy scented and delightful the evening air was after London, as I cruised along the leafy lanes in my open Sunbeam Talbot.

A member of the Brigade Squad, Peter Verney, invited me to join his house party for the Dublin Horse Show in August. It was to be a fateful week for me. One of the guests was a girl who was to have a far-reaching effect on my life. I used one of my three free rail passes, which were granted soldiers in those days, to make the long journey over to County Wicklow. During the journey I completed Somerset Maugham's, *Of Human Bondage*. The novel was based on his time as a medical student at St Thomas' Hospital. This was to echo in my mind over the years ahead and curiously influence my eventual life.

Peter had arranged to pick me up at the Kildare Street Club in Dublin. Waiting there was another Brigade Squad member, Peter Nutting. With him was a willowy, dark-haired girl, introduced to me as Lady Annabel Penton-Mewsey. The first thing that struck me about her was her soft hazel eyes and long dark eye lashes. She moved with a grace that I was later to find peculiar to her. We sat beside one another in the back of the car on the journey down to Knockmore. She was shy but there was an effervescent quality about her and possessed what I can only describe as laughing eyes. There were other guests staying in the house, but Annabel and I tended to gravitate towards one another. We spent our days at the horse show and evenings at the nightly hunt balls at the old Shelburne Hotel. It was a splendid place for a party, with a minstrel's gallery where one could sit and watch the dancing whilst eating or drinking. Like all Irish events they were lively occasions, with dear old Willie O'Grady, the popular Irish racehorse trainer, whistling for all he was worth. I felt such a pang when I read of his death years later.

Annabel and I danced more and more together as the week progressed. In fact, so much so that She told me later that her friends had increasingly 'button-holed' her to ask who I was. She was such a friendly amusing companion, full of my own high spirits. In the early hours of one morning we all drove down to the sea for a swim in the nude, still full of music and champagne. I shall always remember it as one of the happiest most carefree weeks of my life.

On returning to London we saw a lot of each other, usually ending up in the old 400 Club in Leicester Square. It was a venerable nightclub. My father had been a member in the heydays of his youth, as a young officer. Membership depended on having an unfinished bottle of whisky 'on the go'. This was produced on one's arrival. Considering that it was so exclusive it was not unduly expensive and a really smashing breakfast was served in the early hours. Ronnie Clayton's band played soft sweet music to sway to and whisper sweet nothings to one's loved one.

At first I saw Annabel as the female companion I had so longed for. She shared my own interests in music, poetry and many other things. We went to Covent Garden, Glyndebourne and the Old Vic on many occasions. We also spent weekends staying with friends. On one of these I played for Peter Nutting's cricket team against a local team. I opened the batting and had the misfortune to run out our star Indian batsman. Annabel thought that this was hilarious. No one else did and, though I had scored some runs myself, I was under somewhat of a cloud.

Eventually it was time to meet Annabel's family. One lovely autumn Saturday, after jumping Guard Royal at the Aldershot Show, I travelled on down to Lornay Castle. Her father was known as 'Gloomy Willie'. From the first, I did not find him an easy person to get on with. Annabel's mother had apparently run away with a dashing Master of Foxhounds when Annabel was still young. He consequently mistrusted hunting people. He was a keen shooting man himself, which I was decidedly not. His main passion was forestry, of which I knew very little. It was said, with amusement, that he used the House of Lords as his private London club.

Annabel's stepmother, who had been her father's secretary, was a real dragon. She took an instant dislike to me. Annabel was not too keen on Aunt Agatha herself, so this antipathy endeared me to her rather than otherwise. It was not an easy weekend, although Annabel's elder sister, Penelope, and I hit it off well. The three of us spent some pleasant hours rowing round the lake in front of the castle in the sunshine.

I slowly but surely began to fall in love and could not bear to be separated from Annabel. She used to bring in meals for the two of us when I was on guard at Whitehall.

We used to talk far into the night until it was time for me to ring for a taxi to take her home. She shared a Queen's Gate flat with her cousin, Simon. He was a serious chap and was in the agonising process of qualifying as an accountant. I am sure that he considered me a frivolous playboy and I think this opinion filtered through to Lornay.

We seemed to enjoy an increasingly happy and loving relationship. Eventually one night in the 400 Club I proposed to her. She, I think wisely, said that she needed time to think it over. She said that her father had told her never to make such a decision before ten o'clock in the morning or after ten at night. I had no such constraining influence and would have been too impetuous to heed it at any rate. I was temperamentally unsuited to such caution and had inherited something of the gambling character from my Ponsonby forebears.

A couple of weeks later I was invited for a day's hunting with the Avon Vale by a fellow officer, John Fuller, whose father, Sir Gerald Fuller, was the Master. As their hunt ball was being held that evening, Annabel was invited to stay too. Feeling in high spirits that evening, after a great day's hunting, I proposed to Annabel again. To my great joy she accepted me. So, against Annabel's better judgement, Bubbles, as we all called John, Annabel and myself arranged to dine at Lornay on our way back to London on the Sunday evening.

Gloomy Willie was not too keen to see us and doubtless wondered what was up. Reckless as ever, after a rather strained dinner, as we were leaving the dining room, I stopped him in his tracks by asking him, 'Can I have a word with you, sir?' We were left alone in the vast dimly lit place. I resumed my seat at the far end of the long table to him. He eyed me in a somewhat hostile manner as I blurted out my request for the hand of his daughter in marriage. He first asked if Annabel had agreed to this. He then questioned me about my background, financial state and future prospects. I could see that my answers did not impress him. He did not consider the army to be a financially viable career. He ended by stating that he was not in a position to leave Annabel very well off. On this rather gloomy note Lord Rosemount stood up to leave and his demeanour softened as he said that he appreciated my courage in coming to see him first. He requested that the engagement should not be announced until he had time to talk to Annabel and got to know me better.

It must be remembered that in those days a girl was unable legally to marry, under the age of twenty-one, without her father's consent. The other fact of life in those pre-contraceptive pill days was that normal 'decent' girls remained virgins until they married. This applied to all strata of society. Certainly my friends would not have respected a girl who broke this code and would have been put off marrying such a girl. The consequences for a girl of a premarital pregnancy were indeed dire. Thus keeping strictly out of bedrooms together averted the temptation. Annabel and I, although engaged, had never seen each other naked except for that fleeting Irish moonlit dip of which all I remembered was a flash of white bottoms as we dived into the waves. Therein perhaps lay an obstacle in her assessment of myself as a suitable husband. We knew each other as loving companions who enjoyed each other's company.

In the climate of the time, dear old Ma Feathers provided such an invaluable service to the young. Young men were thus able to 'sow their wild oats' without risk of disease or damage to their loved ones. She ought to have been decorated for her services instead of being had up, as she eventually was, poor old thing. I believe that she was found guilty of running a 'Disorderly House'. Anything more orderly than her establishment would have been hard to imagine. It was all beautifully organised as a most exclusive club. It was, I imagine, similar to what Rosa Lewis' Cavendish Hotel had been to an earlier generation. Also, like Rosa, she tended to charge her 'young gentlemen' what she thought they could afford. Thus the rich, quite properly, subsidised the less well off. All supported this quite splendid arrangement. She was, also, a true friend to many young officers of my acquaintance, who would bring their troubles to her, knowing that they would get a sympathetic hearing. We were 'her boys'.

I sampled the alternative following Colonel Jackie's leaving party in the mess. We all ended up at a club, known as 'The Bag of Nails' to generations of Guard's officers. It was in Soho and ruinously expensive. It dispensed filthy drink passing itself off as champagne. In a decidedly tipsy state I ended up in bed with one of the club hostesses, somewhere in Bayswater. She kept poking me in the ribs every ten minutes or so, telling me to leave. It was pouring with rain when I finally came to enough to dress and stagger downstairs and out on to the street. There were no taxis about at that hour, so I walked, rather dismally, back across Hyde Park to the barracks. By the time that I reached it my dinner jacket was soaked through and I lost my black tie somewhere on route. She had whipped my wallet with quite a sum of money in it.

The officer meant to be taking the watering order out had not returned yet, so I hastily changed into uniform and went in search of Dampier and Empress. The watering order was the morning exercise for all the horses not on guard or lame. The secret was to find a route, lasting an hour, round the streets of London without retracing one's steps. Also, the routes should preferably vary from day to day. Empress seemed to enjoy leading these clattering cavalcades. Behind us every trooper rode one horse and led another. The only thing Empress did not like was milk floats, of which there were many about at that early hour. She would shy across the road on meeting one and I never could cure her of this undignified behaviour.

On this particular morning I had chosen to go round Belgrave Square, as Nanny was an early riser and liked to see us go by. The square still then had wooden blocks rather than tarmac. These had been laid in the carriage days to quieten the noise of the horse's hooves in this exclusive square. It was still raining hard which made the blocks slippery. As luck would have it we came thundering up behind a dreaded float. Empress did her party piece and slipped up, coming crashing down on top of me. The next thing I knew was coming to in St George's Hospital, which was still at Hyde Park Corner in those days. I remember thinking that Freeman, who usually woke me, was wearing a 'rum' uniform, before realising that it was a nurse shaking me. So ended that disastrous night out. I never attempted such an escapade again.

Annabel dined with her father at his London house on the Tuesday following my conversation with him. She told me afterwards that she had never known him act in such a severe way to her before. She was really shocked by him. I never learnt what he said, but whatever it was, it sowed some doubts in her mind. I went round to Queen's Gate at eleven o'clock that night. A shadow of anxiety now lay across our happiness.

On the Friday I went up to Melton Mowbray with Max for a couple of days hunting. I lay in bed that night, in the old Harborough Hotel, listening to the sound of music floating up from the bar below. Tommy Steele's 'Singing the Blues' was played over and over again. I was too miserable for sleep and needed Annabel with every fibre of my being. That song has brought back those haunting memories ever since.

We spent the evening together at Queen's Gate on the Monday. Gloomy Willy's shadow had somewhat receded. By the time that I set off for a day's hunting with my solicitor and trustee, John Dyson, the following morning, I was in a happier frame of mind. My natural spirit of optimism had reasserted itself. John and I enjoyed a cracking good day with the Old Berkeley and sat contentedly in front of a roaring log fire that evening with a bottle of whisky to consume between us. I now had a weekend in Cambridge with Annabel to look forward to. Surely we could never lose each other. It was up to me to dispel her doubts. As essentially a man of action this was a role that suited me better than just leaving things to develop.

Geoffrey Bowman, an old Wykehamist and Royal Horse Guard, who had been both at Caterham and Mons with me, had invited Annabel and I to join his party for the United Hunt's Ball. He was now in his second year up at Trinity, Cambridge. The previous June I had had a disastrous evening with Geoffrey at his May Ball. I had taken a tall, leggy, stunning looking blonde whom Ronnie had nicknamed 'Miss Plum'. I barely knew her, but imagined that we would have a convivial evening together with Geoffrey's pals. We joined them all in his rooms for a meal, before going on to the ball. In fact when we went on there everybody paired off and Miss Plum and I were left to our own devices. She was shy and still at a sort of Finishing School, known as 'The Monkey Club', in Sloane Street. I had collected her from there early in the afternoon. I could not get any reply much beyond 'Yes' or 'No' from her. Even by the time we reached Cambridge I was fast becoming speechless with the effort.

We danced rather woodenly until exhausted and finally, in desperation, I kissed her behind one of the statues in the quadrangle. Her only response to this rather daring manoeuvre was to say 'What fun', but it was obvious her heart was not in it. So we 'Yes'd', 'No'd' and 'What fun'd' our way through the long night. Nearing dawn 'I drew a bow at adventure' and put her firmly in a punt on the Backs. We joined the many other punts already afloat and occupied by carousing couples. The decidedly esoteric art of punting was not my strong suit and I soon left the pole stuck in the mud. We drifted hopelessly down river. The early morning air was cool and the goose pimples on Miss Plum's slender arms soon stood up like golf balls. She began to shiver uncontrollably. Eventually I managed to grab a weeping willow tree branch and hauled the punt into the bank. She then announced that she had to return to London to attend the Antique Dealers Fair. I vowed never again to attend another 'varsity hop' without a close companion.

So it was with thorough approval that I paired off with Annabel after the gathering in Geoffrey's rooms that November. Holding her soft pliant body in my arms to the strains of such nostalgic melodies as 'Room 604' and 'Moon River' I was indeed 'In heaven dancing cheek to cheek'. There is nothing in life to compare with the touch of a young girl's velvet cheek on one's own. Sweet nothings flowed from our lips in those magical hours. By the time we repaired, weary but in a warm glow of happiness, to our hotel I had won her back.

In the morning, after a late breakfast with Geoffrey, we set off for Lornay again. This time I met Annabel's two brothers. We dined with her elder brother, James, who had a house on the estate, prior to attending a nearby party given by some friends of theirs. I could not fail to notice that he was weighing me up carefully, as was her other brother. I had another long and uncomfortable session with her father. Annabel seemed happy and loving but said that they thought that I was rather feminine and that I must dress in a more casual manner for the country. 'Haven't you got any more suitable old clothes?' she concluded, before dropping the subject and reverting to her old self again.

Lornay seemed to blight our happy relationship. I should have been warned and been aware of the storm signals flying. I was naive enough to imagine that the family had only to get to know me to like me and understand my deep love for Annabel. Since joining the army I was so used to being accepted and everybody looking for the best in me. I felt a loved and valued member of a magic circle, which rejected outsiders. The regiment was like a family. Now I was being treated like an outsider myself and hurtful remarks being made about me. My ingrained 'problem solving' approach led me to counter-attack and attempt to change their minds. I couldn't realise that nothing was going to achieve that and it would be wise to keep away from their malign influence before it wrecked our relationship.

During the next two weeks Annabel and I were almost constantly together. She cooked meals for me when I was on guard at Whitehall. One evening she came into the bedroom as I was changing to inspect the Guard. She sat on the bed and watched me. She then made a remark, which sent a cold shiver of fear down my spine. ' I don't know if you are a man at all, my poor darling.' It was said casually and sympathetically, but in that moment I knew that the Lornay remarks had raised serious doubts in her mind. Perhaps, if we had grown up today and freely made love from the outset things would have been different. In every other respect, we were as close as two human beings can be.

The following Saturday James had offered to lend me one of his horses so that Annabel and I could go out hunting with the Wilton, of which he was Master. We were invited to dine with him on the Friday evening before attending the Wilton Hunt Ball in Salisbury. Annabel took ages getting her kit together and when we were well down the Cromwell Road she realised that she had forgotten something vital. We returned to Queen's Gate and set off again in heavy traffic. James' large party were due to dine at 8.30. We arrived at Lornay at nine o'clock, still needing to change. Annabel told me to nip upstairs and change quickly. She would apologise to her father and ring up her brother to tell him to start without us. James was really very good about it all but James's wife was, quite naturally, a bit 'miffed' about her spoilt food. It was not a happy evening.

The following morning I came down to breakfast in hunting kit to be greeted by a furious Earl. He upbraided me with gross bad manners for not apologising in person to him the previous evening. 'A proper man would not have sent in poor Annabel to face the music.' Following this outburst we sat alone in stony silence, as Annabel and the others had not come down yet. We had a rotten blank day's hunting in cold driving rain. By the time we returned for our hot baths and hunting tea, we were thoroughly dispirited. Gloomy Willy and I were not on speaking terms and remained so for the rest of the weekend.

Late on the Sunday, as the winter afternoon was drawing in, Annabel said: 'Let's get out of here.' We wandered up the long winding drive and took shelter in a wood. The wind soughed through the Earl's precious old trees. Annabel took me in her arms and I felt her warm salty tasting tears running down my own cheek and into my mouth. We clung to each other like lost children. Finally, she said 'You know, my darling, it's no good, don't you?' I had half been expecting something like this, but even so, when the blow fell, it shot like an arrow into my heart. I was stunned with the pain it caused me. The full implication of her loss had still not hit me, in my numbed state of shock. All I thought of was why could I not have been born either male or female? Why must I suffer the loss of everyone I love and make happy, just because of a body that is neither one thing or the other.

This was probably the worst moment in my life, yet I was sustained by the thought that Annabel and I would be part of each other for a few more hours yet. In the happiness of each other's company we never looked forward nor back. Everything we lived for was always there at that very moment. The past was gone. The present was life. The future an unknown island neither of us inhabited yet.

Night had already fallen by the time we returned to the castle hand in hand. Annabel's mind seemed cleared. She was now positive and caring. All her thoughts now concentrated on looking after me. I was in a daze and hardly knew what I was doing. She and the butler packed my things and put them into Sunbeam the Talbot. She put me into the passenger seat and drove me back to London. She had never done this before. We stopped at an inn on the way back for a few stiff drinks. She was loving and maternal in her concern.

I had bought tickets for *The Merchant of Venice* at the Old Vic, for the following Tuesday. This was the 18th November, which was her birthday. She asked me if I still wanted to take her. We agreed that we would have one last evening together and then part. I was Orderly Officer on the Monday. I was still in a daze and missed taking out the watering order. I had never done this before and never did again. I was given several extra Orderly Officer duties as a punishment. Normally I would have thought of this as a terrible bind, as it meant missing precious days' hunting. Now I did not care about anything but the impending loss of Annabel. The wonderful happiness that I had enjoyed over the last few years, particularly since joining the army, had gone. I stood naked in front of the long mirror in my room, which was used normally to see if my full-dress uniform was in order. I looked over my shoulder to see the rear view of a girl reflected there. Then for the first time since I was a child I wept bitter tears.

By the time I picked Annabel up on the Tuesday evening, I was in a world of my own. We ended up at the 400. She clung to me on the dance floor with tears gently rolling down her poor little face. She said that she felt as if her heart was going to break. We sat in the car until near dawn and then she was gone from my life.

I never really got over her loss. She was such a sweet tender loving girl. We shared so much that no one else has ever shared with me. Our relationship had, for me, gone well past the point of no return. I understood why she had acted as she did. I never felt any resentment but only love and sympathy for her. Her final remark to me was, ' You need a lot of love. One day someone will give you this.'

In an old mahogany box, with her letters and photograph as a child, there still lays a little poem I wrote to her then. I do not think that I ever gave it to her.

To A.P-M   1958

IN LOVE

We were as two autumn leaves,
As though chained to their tree forever,
Then spinning free on the wind together.
Oh the joy of that flight through the heavens,
Our boundary the limitless sky.
The moon and the stars
All of a sudden were ours,
But I fell and my lover swept onwards,
I to be chained once more.

For years afterwards I never went to any large dance or social gathering without unconsciously searching for her. In my dreams at night I would sometimes find her sitting in a corner of a distant room. We would dance and be as happy as ever. I used to wake in utter desolation when I realised that she was only in my dreams. I wonder what life held for her and if she found happiness without me. Perhaps some day, before it is too late, someone will bring this book to her notice and she will remember the joy that we shared for that fleeting moment, at the zenith of our youth. At least to me she will always be the young and enchanting Annabel I loved so dearly with all my heart but I must go gently, unless I 'tread on my dreams'.

I remember my mother saying how one's senses were heightened when in love. The grass seemed greener, the sky bluer and the world a beautiful place. I now suffered the reverse, but at least I had obeyed Lord Rosemount's stricture to keep our engagement secret. This was a relief now. Nanny said that I looked awful but life had to go on. I spent as much time as my duties allowed up in Leicestershire hunting. I still had a very full social life and, I think, that helped. The sister of a Brigade Squad chum, Bill Bromley Davenport, befriended me. Minnie knew Annabel and had heard about our parting. Minnie was a saintly character and took it upon herself to help me survive. I spent many weekends at their home up in Cheshire. They were a happy family and were very good to me. Their father, Colonel Sir Walter Bromley Davenport, was the local MP and a most entertaining character. In the spring he opened Capesthorne Hall to the public for the first time. I was detailed off to keep the visitors amused. When a sufficiently large crowd had gathered to watch a family tennis four playing, I would come to the courtside and announce, 'The Prime Minister is on the telephone, Colonel.' He would reply in his booming voice, 'Inform him that we are in the middle of an important game and I will ring him back later.' This never failed to cause a stir amongst the visitors, who would stand opened mouth at his audacity. This amused the Colonel greatly. 'Must give them their money's worth,' he would chortle.

Capesthorne had a charming little theatre, built by a previous theatrical member of the family, Kitty Brownlow. They put on shows, with their friends, over Bank Holidays. That summer Bill, Minnie and I sang 'The Lullaby of Broadway'. For some reason, this number was very popular with the large audiences that attended and invariably received rapturous applause.

The house was generally full of lively guests from the political and theatrical worlds. The impresario, Peter Daubeny, often directed our little shows. He had served under Sir Walter, in the Grenadiers, during the war and lost an arm when the Guard's Chapel received a direct hit. He was a dynamic man, very similar to Kenneth Diacre, and great fun. He had brought 'The Comédie Française' to London with great success.

The Bromley Davenports became almost a second family to me in my distress. Bill and Minnie's mother was an American and the kindest person imaginable. Minnie was contemplating taking Holy Orders and becoming a nun. I think I was considered an antidote to this. Minnie and I did have some heated discussions on the subject. She eventually became a St George's nurse under the renowned, Miss Powell, when the hospital was still at Hyde Park Corner. I remember bumping into her coming off duty one evening, some years later. She looked pale and shattered, but her face light up with her old warm smile on seeing me. That was our last meeting as she died of cancer when still young. This was such a tragedy but I suppose it is said that the gods take those they love early. I know that she will always be Saint Minnie to me. She saw me through those dark post-Annabel days and, during my long and often lonely struggles later on, it was to her that I turned in my prayers.

I tried to keep away from places Annabel and I had frequented. One of these was the Allegro club below Quaglinos. Leslie Hutchinson, the legendary 'Hutch', pre-war darling of society, played the piano there. He gave a magic touch to the old sweet songs. The place was packed with my generation. Through National Service we all tended to know each other. That was one of the great benefits of that duty. It made the London of that Post-war era very friendly and great fun for us all.

That summer I threw myself into my polo, in my loneliness, and climbed the polo ladder fast. In the autumn, Max secured the Household Cavalry officer nomination on the Army Equitation Instructor's Course for me. This took place at the Remount Depot in Melton Mowbray in Leicestershire. I left London with a sigh of relief. London held too many memories of Annabel. I often wondered if Colonel Max, as he was by then, having taken over from Colonel Toast on his retirement, knew of my unhappiness in his perceptive way and realised that I needed a change of scenery to recover. It most certainly changed the course of my life.

There were six of us officers on the course, three from the Household Brigade and three from the Royal Horse Artillery. The latter were destined for the King's Troop at St John's Wood. Also there were two NCOs from the Household Cavalry and two from the Gunners. We were issued with three horses each, one trained, one half-trained and one unbroken. By the end of the six months the latter two had to be fully trained by us. Pre-war, the course had taken place at Weedon and turned out so many renowned service horsemen. The objective was to train us as instructors so that we could become Equitation Officers in our respective regiments, in charge of training mounted troops.

In reality it was something of a hunting course and we enjoyed dozens of days with Quorn, Belvoir and Cottesmore hunts. Together with this went the rather wild social life of Leicestershire in the 1950s. We became superbly fit and by the close we reckoned that we could almost have ridden a bathtub across country, with our experience of hunting horses of all sorts day after day. As there were only a handful of resident young males we were in great demand for the various social events. We led a pre-war sort of existence and had a 'whale of a time'. It was most remedial for me and my old 'joie de vivre' began to return. I still missed Annabel acutely but life was too full to brood.

Patrick Beresford, who had been on the course the previous year, compiled a list of all the hunting characters for me, with succinct comments about them all. This soon became known as 'The List' and I was constantly under siege to reveal its contents. Two of the best girls across country were a Miss Comins, popularly known as Miss Come Come, and June Bevis. June's father had been killed in the war commanding a Coldstream Guard battalion. He had partnered the King in the Wimbledon doubles and was the son of a Suffolk squire. June soon became a member of our 'set' and we saw a lot of her. She worked in a hospital in London in the summer, returning home, to her mother, in the winter for the hunting season.

In those London summers of my youth, the evenings seemed meant for fun. I would invariably be setting off for some event or other with the heady mixture of music and champagne to be enjoyed into the following dawn. Now in the Melton winter, after the excitement of the chase on cold crisp winter afternoons, the feeling of well being enhanced the social delights on offer. Nightly there were hunt balls, dinner parties, poker schools and cosy evenings with the various Leicestershire girls. Another great tradition was the Sunday lunch. These were jolly occasions where port and stilton were dispensed liberally. Many old friends would be up hunting and would gravitate to them. The hunting circle was a comparatively small one and one saw the same people night after night. This led to the forming of close relationships, which were part of the life. It was ever thus in Leicestershire, hence its rakish reputation. Hunting is a very potent aphrodisiac and we began to pair off with the girls on offer.

In spite of many outside invitations, I only left Leicestershire twice whilst on the course. The first of these was enforced. One of the newly arrived Life Guard subalterns at Knightsbridge had not passed out of the riding school in time to command his division on the opening of parliament Sovereign's Escort. I had to return to London to take his place. Empress and I were reunited for the day.

I stayed on to compete in the Army Hunter Trials at Tweeseldown for the Life Guard team. That evening I went on down to Arundel, at the invitation of Anne Fitzalan Howard, to escort her to the local hunt ball at Leaconfield House. The Norfolk family still lived in the castle then. It was cold within the stone battlements but I had a cheering log fire crackling away in my vast stone bedchamber. In the middle of the night I was groping around down the passage on a 'loo finding' expedition when I bumped into the Earl Marshal. He was on an expedition of his own. After recovering from the shock of our collision I politely explained my predicament. He rather sadly replied, 'I am looking for my Duchess' and disappeared into the night.

Up at Melton I increasingly began to pair off with June Bevis. We spent so much of our time together, both in the hunting field and at the many social events we all attended. I think that I felt that the kind of love I had shared with Annabel was not possible for me ever to find again. I suppose that I should have given myself a year or two to fully come to terms with what had happened with Annabel. I was, however, far too impetuous to heed that sensible voice in my subconscious. The Greeks believed that one is born half a person and that somewhere on earth, if one can find her, is one's other half. That ultimate happiness had been denied me but I just had to summon up all my courage and go on alone.

I saw in June a strong girl who would allow me to take a female role in our relationship. I hoped that in this way I could find myself again and not disappoint her or pretend I was something I was not. The idea began to take root in my mind the first time that I saw her in evening dress with her well-knit muscular arms. June seemed to enjoy my exuberant company and find me attractive, or so I thought. I needed a female companion and some sort of sexual life desperately.

So the winter progressed. My little grey unbroken horse, which I named, 'Jerry Pot', after a local hunting character, began to come to hand. My efforts at lunging caused much merriment amongst my companions. They claimed that Jerry used to lunge me rather than me him. I must say that I would, more frequently than not, go flying round him whilst he stood stock still in the middle. Jerry was a great character with a distinct mind of his own. My half-trained horse, Pimms, like Hazy Music, bucked when first mounted. Thus minor rodeos entertained the course every morning, until I cured him of these bad manners. This, at any rate, improved my 'stickability' no end and I never feared bucking horses thereafter. Ibis, my trained horse, was a flighty black mare, difficult to ride in traffic. Later, when she joined my troop in London, I had a hair-raising journey to get to Earls Court to jump her in the Services competition. She did, however, go like a bird across country and carried me splendidly on the Passing Out Parade tests at the end of the course.

Officially we were meant to 'do' our three horses and clean the tack. Patrick Beresford again came to my rescue with his little dossier. This advised me to pay an old cavalry trooper, Alf Sherwood, to carry out these irksome tasks. Alf was very proud of his limp, which had apparently been caused by being knocked down by the then Prince of Wales in pre-war Melton High Street. The Prince had been driving back to Craven Lodge, his hunting box, after a night of carousing. He picked Alf up and gave him a £5 note, which more than satisfied the young Alf in those halcyon days. I shudder to think what the reaction would have been nowadays.

June and I began to come really close at the annual New Year's Eve dance at Burley-on-the-Hill, give by James Hanbury, then Master of the Belvoir. It was a snowy night and Sylvia, June's mother, suggested that I spend the night with them at Langham Cottage. Sylvia was the most charming and kind person, who always saw the best in everyone. I never heard her say an unkind remark to or about anyone. The whole atmosphere was so different from Lornay.

From then on I used to spend odd evenings at Langham with June and her mother. On the night of the Quorn Hunt Ball June and I dined with a Leicestershire hunting character, known as 'Call me Glore'. Before we left Quenby, where the ball was held, I had proposed to her, urging her not to answer then and telling her of my fears about myself and that I had been rejected before on these grounds. I was not going to go through all that grief again. June had been very decent to me and I wanted to be fair to her. Yet again I had ignored my father's sensible advice, garnered from his own salutary experience, not to propose to a girl after seven in the evening and before seven in the morning.

I do not think that June was in love with me, but in a perverse way I think that my admission found a way into her heart. The following Tuesday she accepted my proposal. I had no stern father to beard this time. Sylvia, in her own sweet way, gave her blessing to our proposed union. I vividly remember, shortly after this, returning late one clear frosty night along the Melton road. The hubcap of Sunbeam the Talbot spun off and went rattling down the road. I stopped to recover it. As I stood under the bright starry heavens, in the intense cold, I came to my senses. My heart was still full of Annabel and I began to realise that I might be making a great mistake in supposing that, in my desperation, I could replace her. These events, however, have a momentum all of their own, which brooks no stopping. By the time I left Melton for a second time June and I were an officially engaged couple. We went as such to stay with Fiona and David Myddleton at Chirk for the 1958 Grand National, and the ensuing festivities. We stood at the Canal Turn as Mr What came out of the mist in the lead, soon recognisable by the maroon jersey of Arthur Freeman, with its yellow-hooped sleeves. He was soon to marry the sister of my future squadron leader, Christo Phillipson.

I returned to London when the course ended in April. The whole summer went by in a blur of polo matches, ceremonial duties on Empress, times spent with June at Belgrave Square and the myriad social events we attended. We decided to get married at Langham and hire a bus to bring the Guard of Honour down with all their regalia. Langham had never seen anything like it. There was one hiccup before this happy event. Ibis had a little local difficulty with a London bus and I broke my shoulder. This ended my Polo season and forced me to miss the Inter-Regimental final. I was sent down to RAF rehabilitation centre to speed my recovery. It was in the luxurious surroundings of Headley Court in Surrey. It was mainly full of crashed fighter pilots, with their talk of 'Wizard Prangs' and 'Nothing on the clock but the maker's name'. I was discharged just prior to the wedding.

I met June's brother, John, for the first time then. He had been out in Germany completing his National Service in their father's regiment, The Coldstream Guards. It was not a particularly auspicious occasion. He, I think, took the Lornay opinion of me. In the ensuing argument, in the middle of lunch, he chased June round the dining room table. Not being nimble enough, with his somewhat portly frame, to catch her, he built a barricade of chairs with the object of slowing her flight. They then proceeded to hurdle these on their way round. Eventually he climbed on to the table putting his foot in my soup plate. Sylvia and I were, in the meantime, continuing our polite conversation, pretending not to notice these activities. Sylvia's soup, having by this time landed in her lap, she rose to leave with a slightly wan smile, bumping her head on the low cottage beams, for the umpteenth time, for she was a tall stately lady.

John then refused to give his sister away at the wedding, as planned. Their uncle, Monty, stepped into the breach only too willingly but John tried to disrupt the ceremony and hide our honeymoon luggage. My Household Cavalry brother officers, who had come down in force, foiled this. It turned out to be an enjoyable and convivial occasion, which the rain that fell in an otherwise blazing August, failed to mar. The local newspapers were full of it. I was viewing June, in her 'Going Away' straw hat, rather doubtfully when Sylvia made the splendid remark, 'It's the smile that counts'. This became our motto in the difficult years ahead.

The following dawn we were standing in the quiet of Venice, where cars are prohibited. It gave one an inkling what life in a great city must have been like before the invention of the internal combustion engine. That night was my first proper sexual experience and I was 25 years old. It had been a long and frustrating wait, for someone as highly sexed as I was then. I felt like a bride myself when I climbed, naked, in bed beside her. It was my body that I wanted to give to her and be loved and desired by her. It was her initiative that thrilled me. It was the ultimate test of our relationship. In the throes of passion there is no hiding one's true sexuality. It was truly a make or break occasion and miraculously we satisfied one another. At the time I did not attempt to analyse or explain it. I was just content that June had been made happy by me and not disappointed.

After a few days in Venice we boarded a local steamer chugging down the Adriatic to the appropriately named honeymoon destination of Split. June had distinguished herself in Venice with her 'Hunting eye for country'. The gondolier, who had taken us on an expedition along the canals, got lost. June unerringly navigated us back to base.

Later that week we continued on down the Adriatic to the little Island of Hvar. The sun shone, the sea sparkled and we were in the full bloom of youth. The dark shadow of my gender was but a tiny speck on the golden horizon. Such serenity was never allowed us again but nothing could, in the difficult years ahead, erase the blessing of those honeymoon weeks. Even now, I cannot speak for June, but I had come close to finding myself. It was to be thirty long years ahead before I achieved that serenity again.

My military profession impinged on our life immediately on our return home. The following day I was off to Pirbright with the Life Guard Mounted Squadron for the annual camp at Stoneycastle. This was the country holiday for the 'Black-uns'. Empress certainly enjoyed the break and became quite frisky on our afternoon wanderings along the leafy Surrey lanes. In the morning I took my troop on light-hearted excursions through the woods.

We all lived under canvas and the horses were tethered in traditional cavalry lines. I won the squadron show jumping competition on one of my troop horses. Argosy was quite a famous old boy with many successes to his name in his youth.

After this June and I had but a few months together before I was off to Aden again. Fresh trouble had broken out and the regiment was already out there. The abiding memory of those months was the time we spent up in Leicestershire fox hunting. We had a really good set up. Smith, my groom, boarded with Sylvia's stud groom, Phillips. I had both Guard Royal and Biro stabled at Langham. June had Redskin and her Point to Pointer, Tommy Linden. Sylvia's venerable hunter, Cavalier, occupied the final box. Sylvia rode sidesaddle and looked every inch her stately self in a flowing blue habit with top hat and veil. Thus, every moment that I was not on guard or fulfilling my other ceremonial duties, we would repair to Langham. It was a most enjoyable time. All the more so because, for me, it was so soon to end. That end came after Christmas when I set off to Aden for a second time. Sylvia commented that, Tom, June's father had always put his army service first and that these partings were a necessary part of being an officer's wife.

I had been away from the regiment for over three years, whilst serving at Knightsbridge. Those years were probably the high point of my early life. I have always felt that it was my spiritual home in some strange way. My sadness at leaving was tinged with relief that I had, at least, realised this from the outset and made the very best of my time there, living life to the full. Even Sylvia had commented on my zest for life. She said that I was so different from June and John in that I always seemed to enjoy everything and never complained.

June and I had always known that we faced this early parting, but it was not easy, particularly for June, who was, by now, pregnant with our first child. It was decided that she would return to Langham and we would let Belgrave Square for the summer.

On landing at Aden, the familiar furnace-like blast greeted me, together with a bronzed regimental driver and Land Rover. This arrival, feeling white and undesert-worthy, was part of army life that I had experienced before. This time, however, there were many old friends to greet me on arrival at the mess and later when I joined my squadron. I was back in the old comforting family atmosphere of the regiment. We were based at the BP Oil refinery at Little Aden, which could only be reached along a causeway from Aden proper. The great advantage of the refinery huts was air conditioning, which made life much more bearable. Most of the regiment was scattered around the 'Up Country' forts, which I remembered so well from my time out there before.

I was soon promoted captain and second-in-command of my squadron, which, happily for me, was commanded by an old friend, Christo Phillipson. It was time for me to do some serious soldering again. The key to inspiring confidence and appearing 'dead efficient' was to invariably carry a millboard when walking round the camp. I mastered 'double entry' book-keeping in haste, as one of my many tasks was to manage the canteen supplies to our 'up country' forts. These generated large sums of money running into thousands of pounds or the local equivalent. My predecessor had the misfortune to have to find a substantial sum from his own pocket when the books did not balance. I quickly set up a tight accounting system with the Hong Kong & Shanghai Bank in the Crater district of Aden. In those far off days their calculating was still done by the abacus. I was impressed by the row upon row of beads strung on metal frames in the otherwise smart modern-looking premises.

Although I was based at squadron headquarters in Little Aden, I spent many weeks flying around to visit our troops 'up-country', courtesy of the RAF. I had some hair-raising flights in small aeroplanes, landing on primitive airstrips amongst the mountains. During these visits I would often spend nights in Aden Protectorate Levy

Messes. Their officers lived in a little world of their own with private jokes and conversations. They were eccentric characters who seemed to relish their isolation. Far from welcoming a fresh face they appeared to positively resent any intrusion.

The town of Aden itself was in a highly volatile state with riots and terrorist activities. We had a machine-gun post on the roof of the Crescent Hotel, in the main square, for a time. Later, in the same square, on the Queen's birthday, we held a mini Trooping of the Colour to mark the occasion. We paraded past the Governor, Sir William Luce, in our Ferret armoured cars accompanied by the Aden Protectorate Levy Camel Corps. It was a far cry from the Horse Guards ceremony that Empress and I had taken part in for the previous three years. Empress, I was delighted to hear, had been promoted to carry the Gold Stick In Waiting, Field Marshal Lord Harding, our new Colonel-in-Chief, that same day on Horse Guards.

The then colonial secretary, Lennox Boyd, attended our ceremony. He was in Aden to hold talks with the local rulers to decide the future of the colony. Information had been received that a terrorist attack was planned on Government House during his stay there. I had the task of commanding the guard there one night. I remember the long curtains moving gently in the stifling humid breeze, generated by the great ceiling fans, as I prowled round, revolver in hand. It was an anxious night and I have seldom been gladder to see dawn break.

During our time in Aden we played a bit of rather desultory polo, in the great heat, on shingle grounds. Dust from the galloping ponies hooves enveloped us and it was well nigh impossible to see the ball. The local teams seemed to enjoy it more than we did. Pulling off one's polo boots at the end of the day almost required a surgical procedure they were so hot. Cricket was our main leisure activity. We turned out a strong regimental eleven under the inspirational leadership of Ronnie Ferguson. He soon press-ganged me into opening the batting. The opposition was of a high standard and I constantly found myself bombarded by really quick West Indian bowlers on the fast matting wickets on which we played. I scored some runs but due to my frequent absences 'up country' was seldom in good enough practice for that standard of cricket. Ronnie, as regimental adjutant, was permanently in Aden and played some splendidly flamboyant innings. He, with another officer, Tony Pyman, enabled us to win most of our matches. When they returned home I, rather reluctantly, took over the captaincy from Ronnie, as I had at Knightsbridge, on his departure from there. I regret to say that our weakened team did not fare quite as well in their absence. My main memory of that time is of spending hours at the crease, under the blazing sun, blocking away like a poor man's Geoffrey Boycott, trying to hold the innings together.

It came as a relief, therefore, when all these extramural activities came to an end and the squadron reunited for desert operations. This meant a period of intense activity for me, as I was responsible for the logistics of the campaign. The evening, before we left, with these completed, I was engaged in a croquet game in the mess garden when the mess waiter brought out a telegram on a silver salver. June had given birth to a son, Rollo. In true Francis Drake, mode I delayed announcing the good news until our keenly contested game was completed. Joy was then unconfined and many bottles of champagne were consumed in celebration in the mess that night.

Setting off the following dawn, the desert took over my consciousness, as it had five years before, and the rising sun seemed to enter my very being. As we stretched out towards the distant purple mountains I once again experienced that feeling of great peace. Lying under the stars that night my mind went back to those happy nights in the Rhodesian bush. I was in my true element again. Life was now, not yesterday and not tomorrow. We had some adventures during this trip but not as much action as before and mainly of brief duration. One evening, at last light, we laagered for the night on a rather picturesque beech by the Red Sea. We had had a tiring few days escorting a convoy through difficult and dangerous terrain and turned in early. No sooner had I drifted off to sleep than one of the sentries woke me in alarm. Hundreds of giant turtles were emerging from the sea and invading our laager. We were obviously trespassing on their own sleeping quarters and nothing we did diverted them. We were finally forced to move inland to get some peace.

Travelling as an armoured car squadron, without infantry support, we moved fast and covered great distances during this time. Sometimes it was necessary to divide the squadron and I would lead one half and Christo the other. I found navigation the biggest problem, but like most things in those happy days I took it in my stride. The only really nasty moment was when I tried to take a short cut along a beach. One by one the Ferret armoured cars bogged down. The tide was coming in fast and by the time the invaluable 'Fucking Harry' had winched out the last Ferret with his Scammel, its commander, the present Earl of Onslow, resembled a submariner in his turret. For some period afterwards 'A Life on the Ocean Waves' would be whistled at me as I walked round the camp.

It was with great sadness that I came out of the desert for the last time, when we returned to Little Aden. Another cavalry regiment, The Royals, had already sent their advance party to take over from us. They later amalgamated with the Blues to become part of The Household Cavalry and the union was popularly known as 'The Boyles.' I wondered whether I would ever again live in the wild regions of the world. By the time that we embarked on the troopship Devonshire, to return home, at the end of the year, I was committed to resign my commission and leave the army. I made the decision in the interests of the family. I still regret that I had to make that sacrifice. The regiment had been my home and family for so many years. I was going to miss my friends dreadfully.

This was brought home to me, in the years ahead, when I attended regimental dinners and we were all together again. The new colonel, Muir Turnbull, wrote to me about a year later and asked me if I would consider returning. I was sorely tempted but the same reason for leaving still applied.

As the Devonshire sailed up the Red Sea and into the Suez Canal I savoured my last days as a Life Guard. We were a happy band of brothers. I was nearly 28 years old and still young enough to shoulder the many burdens of a farmer's life that lay ahead. All too soon we were crossing the Bay of Biscay and docking at Southampton, to be greeted once more by the familiar smell of an English late November morning. On going down the gangplank the following dawn, the first person to come up to me was an old friend, Tessa Head. She was the sister of a brother officer and a beautiful girl that I had always been very fond of. We were chatting away happily when I suddenly saw June. She almost seemed a stranger to me. It was the best part of a year since my departure and I had resumed my old bachelor way of life again in her absence. I had somehow felt at home with Tessa, as if I had never been away. Nevertheless, I was overjoyed to be with June again and supposed that we would soon settle down into our old familiar ways. After all, I had been away from her longer than we had been together.

Dear Nanny, with Rollo in her arms, was there to greet us when we reached Belgrave Square. It was quite a moment. Although I would remain on the regimental reserve of officers for the next seven years, my Life Guard days were really over. They had been such happy and exciting years but the future then seemed also brimful with promise. There was a cartoon drawn by some Edwardian officer that hung in the Knightsbridge mess. It depicted two Life Guard Officers out on a stormy night in the stable yard, with their capes billowing out and long thin legs, encased in our tight blue overalls with the split red stripe down the side, protruding from these. It was entitled 'Strange birds on a windy night'. John Gooch and I, when similarly attired, with our equally long thin legs, were known as 'the two strange birds'. So the time had come to say goodbye to ' the strange bird' that was me in the full bloom of my youth.

Chapter 7

Rolling Acres

After a family Christmas in Belgrave Square, on a snowy January morning, we all set off for Rutland. We had purchased what in that part of the country was termed a 'Hunting Box'. It had belonged to one of the joint Masters of the Cottesmore Hunt, Marcus Kimball. It was situated in a tiny village called Barleythorpe, near the county town of Oakham. It was a smart little stone house with a nice garden. It was definitely a 'Gentleman's residence', having been done up in some style by Marcus. It cost £6,000, which in 1960, was considered a fair price, but doubled its value in three years.

I had arranged to enter the local agricultural college, then called a Farm Institute, which now sounds more like a 'happy farm' for the mentally wayward. The National Certificate of Agriculture course commenced in the autumn, so I got a job on a large mixed farm, at nearby Cottesmore, until then. It was the frosty depth of the winter. I chiefly remember being detailed to guard the kale fields from attack by hungry pigeons. Great woods surrounded these fields, where the pigeons lived. I moved silently through the icy mists, on sentry duty, shotgun in hand, wearing my long guardsman's greatcoat. My occasional shots rang out, like the First World War cannon, 'Big Bertha', in the intense stillness. It did not take the canny pigeons long to 'suss out' my tactics. Wherever I went there would be no pigeons and they would be contentedly eating where I had just come from.

In Aden, in the mess one day, we had all said what we would like to have been doing were we at home. I remember opting for riding down a country lane on a frosty morning with the sound of the horse's iron shod hooves ringing out. So my present occupation was near to this ideal. Colonel Tony Meredith Hardy's idea of heaven would have been to lie in bed early on a summer morning and hear the sound of the gravel being raked in front of his house, by the gardener. These daydreams said a lot about us all.

Colonel Tony had been a somewhat unmilitary figure, affectionately known as 'Colonel Cucumber' by his officers. This was, in part, due to his rather startled reaction to emergencies, akin to Corporal Jones in *Dad's Army*'. He was much loved by officers and men, who gave their very best to support him. The regiment was happy and successful under him, in this way. The colonel who succeeded him was the complete antithesis to this. He was very able but without the same charisma and a bit of a martinet. I heard later that he had not been a success. Over the years I have observed that this gift of inspiring affection in subordinates is the most valuable asset for a leader in any field.

The farmer that I was now working for possessed this ability. He had what would now be considered a large labour force of over a dozen men. They were a quite extraordinarily contented lot, full of fun and good humour. They were probably the last of the old type of farm worker. Some of them could not even read or write. I only discovered this fact when a new crop sprayer was delivered and I was asked to read out the settings. They seldom left the farm and were totally incurious about life outside Cottesmore. Their one outing was to the Sun Inn in the village on Saturday night. For the rest of the week they would discuss and laugh about the 'goings on' the previous Saturday. They were full of country folklore. It was considered that no good would come of farm tasks undertaken on a Sunday, barring the essential stock feeding. This was in spite of the fact that they needed overtime earnings to keep body and soul together. They earned about £6 per week and worked very hard indeed for those wages doing, in many ways, what their forefathers had done on the same land. Typical of this was a local character who returned from work on a neighbouring farm every evening on his ancient motorbike, wearing an old leather helmet and goggles. One day a police car was following him and ticked him off for not signalling when he turned right. He indignantly replied, 'Every bugger knows I turn right here for Barrowden,' This was, of course, quite true.

Much of the work was still done in gangs, with the camaraderie of being together all day. They were very good to me and I got on well with them and enjoyed their company. I learnt an enormous amount from them, which proved of great value to me later on. I loved the open-air life and will always remember 'clagging' ewes on a beautiful spring day by a wood carpeted with bluebells. I learnt to drive a tractor by being dropped off 40-odd miles away from Cottesmore and instructed to drive it home. It was a memorable journey through the Leicestershire hunting country I knew so well. I climbed out of the Belvoir Vale past such renowned coverts as Sherbrooks and on to Cottesmore. My steed was an old Ferguson T 20 and by the time I had completed my journey I had got the hang of it. Thereafter I worked all kinds and sizes of tractors without difficulty.

The annual seasons raced by and it was soon time for me to commence my course. The agricultural college was housed in Brooksby Hall, in the Quorn hunt 'Friday country' near Leicester. The Hall had been the home of the first Earl Beattie, illustrious sailor and hero of the Battle of Jutland in the Great War. The Principal, Mr Stearn, was a somewhat battle-scarred ex-gunner officer, who had run it since its inception a few years before. He was extremely helpful to me and the two courses were geared to giving one enough practical knowledge to start farming on one's own account. The first year I passed the National Certificate of Agriculture with a high enough grade to go straight on to the management course the following year. The latter course was mainly concerned with accounting, budgeting, and the financial side of modern farming. My initiation into 'double entry' book-keeping in Aden proved invaluable. Every week we went round a local farm. We then analysed the farmer's own accounts, working out how we thought he could improve his profitability. One week later the farmer would come to Brooksby and we would present our conclusions to him. He then gave us his opinion of our ideas. It was a great way to learn farm management from those actually engaged in it. It soon became apparent what systems paid best.

June was very happy with our new life. She still hunted regularly on her two horses kept at Langham with Sylvia. Nanny looked after Rollo until she had trained a girl to take over. We had inherited Marcus' two staff and, looking back, we lived in some style. I went out hunting on Household Brigade saddle club horses when I found time. These were kept at the Remount Depot in Melton Mowbray. Being on the regimental reserve I still qualified to use them. In the meantime the manor house at Drayton, which was in a pretty derelict state, was being done up for us. It made a fine family home situated centrally to its 320 acres of old pasture land in the fertile Welland Valley about 15 miles south of Barleythorpe.

At the successful conclusion of my courses, in true Brooksby style, I set about converting it into modern arable farm, which would support us. I purchased a Massey Ferguson 65 tractor, and the necessary implements to plough, cultivate and drill the land with winter wheat. Then finally, having bumped around in swirling dust clouds for what seemed an age, the land was ready for drilling. It was a glorious autumn morning on September 14th, 1963. Toby, our second son, had been born in the night. So I went back to Barleythorpe for breakfast, in a somewhat euphoric state, and then on to Drayton to hitch on the drill. The first problem was to set the correct seed and fertiliser rates, and then I found that the 12-stone seed sacks were too heavy to lift on my own. So I unhitched the seed harrows and backed the drill as near to the trailer as possible and managed to drag them on to the lid. The hundredweight fertiliser bags I managed by putting my arms round them and hugging them to me, as in dancing 'cheek to cheek'. Fred Astaire would have been proud of me but I daresay Ginger Rogers would found my embrace a bit 'over the top'. Luckily there was no one about to see my technique, as America field was 'over the hills and far away'. Having filled the drill it was with some trepidation that I set off round the headland. The land was bone dry and after my first circuit it was difficult to see my drill wheel marks. Then, as if on cue, the sun broke through the morning mist and shone on the steel wheeling. It was in the days before rubber tyres on drills. This momentous day was over 40 years ago now and I must have drilled many thousands of acres since but it is still as clear in my mind as if it was yesterday.

The following July we moved into the manor house and I engaged a farm hand,

Maurice Bonney, once we had completed building a farm cottage for him. He was the brother of Sylvia's odd job man. He proved an excellent choice, about my own age, and a first class mechanic. The harvest was nearly upon us by then. I purchased a yellow Claeys combine harvester. It cost £3,000 and was a good reliable machine. I don't think we ever had a better one, although later models cost over ten times as much. Maurice operated it and I carted the corn and ran the grain drier, which I had built during the winter. It was something of a pioneering project using air ducts placed under the corn, as it was unloaded. Ours was one of the first in the country and, I believe, the only one to blow across a 45 feet span. It worked wonderfully well and is still in operation to this day. It was the key to the whole farming system whereby two of us could manage over 300 acres of cereals. Hitherto, the continuous driers, which dried the grain before storage, required a man on them day and night.

This first harvest was a bounteous one with few hitches and fair weather. Success is so important in one's first trading year particularly if money is a bit tight, as it was in my case. It laid the foundation for the prosperous years ahead. Since the previous August, I had been working every hour God gave me. There was a staggering amount to do and organise during that year. I was, however, deeply tanned by my days in the sun, brimming with good health and relishing the challenge.

It was great to be living at Drayton and we were happy to be there. We constructed a tennis court and, later, a swimming pool, to make up for the fact that there would not be time to go away on holidays. There was a quite sensuous pleasure in a quick dip at lunchtime during the harvest. One would be covered in dust and itchy chaff. It was like that bath on coming out of the desert. I also used to have a swim under the harvest moon after the long tiring combining day was done. We gave good old fashioned 'vicarage lawn' type tennis parties on Sunday afternoons, in less busy times, with cucumber and watercress sandwiches. Toby became so good that he won the Eton tournament in his first year there and every subsequent year.

I bought a hunter for June. St Michael was a liver chestnut, like her beloved Redskin. He went like a bird across country but was difficult to box. One evening I took the Rice trailer out to collect her at America cross roads, about ten miles away, in the Cottesmore country. We simply could not get him in the trailer. So June, without a qualm, set out across country and arrived home in the dark. It was a remarkable feat. Only someone with June's 'eye for country', noted in Venice on our honeymoon, would have made it. St Michael obviously learnt his lesson on this tiring trek and ever afterwards went in the trailer like a lamb. Later on I bought Robin for myself. He was being trained as a show jumper and one could turn him at any fence, however big, once he got the hang of going across country with all the other horses round him. On my very first outing with the Fernie hunt everyone was looking at me wondering, no doubt, who the 'swell' in the scarlet swallowtail coat on the smart chestnut horse was. In front of the entire field we cantered at a small fence and Robin was obviously wondering who they all were, instead of paying attention to the task in hand, as he took it by the roots and we both ended up covered in mud on the ground.

Both June and I were used to hunting with the big Leicestershire packs and it was a welcome change to go out with the Fernie on a Wednesday, with only a small band of followers. Colonel Murray Smith, who had been a very grand Master of the Quorn in our day, had also stepped down to the Fernie and like us seemed to enjoy the small friendly atmosphere. As always he gave great sport, which was to be expected of an ex-Household Cavalryman, though he had been a Blue and not a Life Guard!

In those early farming years, before our increase in acreage, we also allowed ourselves a break for tea in the harvest. June would bring up a picnic to the field with the children. We would stop the combine and all sit on rugs, including Maurice. Another little luxury I used to allow myself was to sit in the garden during Wimbledon and watch the tennis on television, with dear old Dan Maskell, whenever I could. We bought strawberries and cream and often lobsters too, in true Wimbledon style. Later on when we had a large hay acreage to make I purchased an extra wide 22 feet Centipede tedder, which still gave me some tennis, as going through the hay was such a quick job. Some of my happiest memories were these sunny relaxing afternoons in an otherwise overstretched life. The swimming pool even gave them an almost Mediterranean touch.

The years slipped by and it was strange how situations seemed to reoccur. We always seemed to be combining Middle field during the Oval test match towards the end of August in sweltering hot weather. I used to park the Land Rover under the same old elm tree for shade and listen to the cricket, in breaks between carting the grain to the drier. America field was the furthest away from the drier and rain almost invariably fell when we were up there. It was a race-against-time field. On Stoke's field, thunder storms always seemed to be coming up the Welland Valley at us, so much so that we referred to it as 'Thunder and lightning field'.

In 1969 we started a new enterprise. I bought 30 Welsh Black heifers and a bull called Charlie. They were the indigenous cattle of Wales. This was an inspired choice as they proved the finest of single suckling cows: that is to say, cows producing one calf per year and rearing them on their mother's milk as nature intended. They were hardy animals with long coats and horns. It was said that they would thrive on 'the smell of an oily rag'. They lived out most of the year and we never lost one. In really severe winter weather they would emerge from the mist at their own stately gait, with icicles hanging from their coats, the calves looking like little snowmen. We gradually built up their numbers to about 200, which enabled us to adopt a three-year ley system of farming, rather than monoculture. This kept the land in good heart without resource to high rates of fertiliser, spray and pesticides. The Welsh Blacks were popular with the local butchers for their lean meat, as the advent of supermarkets began to change the fashion of eating. As ours was a pedigree herd, we also had quite a demand for bulls and heifers to start other herds.

That first year it was a case of learning as we went along. Charlie got all the heifers in calf, although we seldom saw him going into action. He just appeared to woo the lady of his choice in a courtly, not unromantic, ritual. It was a hard winter but positively balmy compared to their ancestral home in the Welsh mountains. At first we were a bit apprehensive of Charlie, with his great size and curly mane, but he had a friendly expression on his face and proved just that. We had many bulls over the years and they were all easy amenable creatures. A few of heifers could be a bit touchy when their calves were first born, but provided one did not confront them at that stage, they soon settled once their babies were mobile, and some of their fears for their well being were allayed. At birth they kept their calves away from the rest of the herd, but joined the others, after a few days, as the calves got stronger. They then ran a system of having a nurse cow that stayed with the calves whilst the rest of mothers went off grazing. From time to time another cow would relieve the nurse cow and so on. How they organised it I shall never know but it worked like sentry duty in the army.

The first calving time was a testing experience. I had never assisted a cow to calve before, as in Rhodesia that task was best left to the natives who were born and bred to it. We fed the heifers sugar beet nuts with added magnesium to guard against the dreaded 'staggers'. This is a form of fatal fit, which cows are particularly susceptible to on calving. The nearby Rockingham Castle herd had been decimated by it. Welsh Blacks were not used to such largess and as a result produced gigantic calves, a high proportion of which needed assistance to enter the world. There was no choice but to strip to the waist and get on with it. Suffice it to say I learnt the hard way, by my own mistakes, but over the years became somewhat of an expert in this demanding skill. My motto became: 'When in doubt, pull it out.' This maxim invariably proved best for mother and baby. I never, however, ceased to derive a wonderful feeling of joy at the birth, even if it had entailed my being up most of the night.

June took an immediate interest in the Welsh Blacks, and without her help and skill the animal adventure would never have prospered and flourished in the way it did. She possessed a quite unique understanding of animals, the like of which I have never struck in anyone else. I am convinced that if she had turned her hand to training racehorses instead, she would be a household name by now. June, however, as the leading lady point-to-point rider in Leicestershire, perhaps knew a little too much about the drawbacks of that calling ever to attempt it. As it was she spent most of her mornings during those years, in the saddle, going round the cattle. No 'off-colour' animal ever escaped her eagle and discerning eye.

In many ways we dedicated our lives for thirty-odd years to the well being of our beloved Welsh Blacks. We knew all the cows by name and their own particular idiosyncrasies. They were our dear old friends and it was a great sadness when one became old and stiff and had to go. I would set off to market with her on her last journey. On arrival she would think that it was a rather interesting social occasion, with all the other cows, in their pens, to talk to. I would install her in her allocated pen and begin to walk away. It was at that moment she suddenly felt deserted and would 'moo' for me to take her home again. It was heartbreaking. I never could bear to watch the actual auction.

After about ten years we lost Maurice. This was a great blow. In the adjoining farm cottage, which we had also built, we had employed a very nice couple. Mrs Rogers worked in the house and helped with the children. Old Mr Rogers did the garden. They had been with us since the beginning. About that time they decided to retire. I engaged another couple to replace them. They proved to be troublemakers and rowed with Maurice's wife, who insisted that Maurice depart. I do not think he wanted this at all. I could not find a suitable replacement for him and with the judicious use of contractors for some of the arable work we soldiered on unaided.

This, of course, increased our workload, particularly when I bought some more land and the cattle numbers kept increasing. Hunting had to go and many of our little pleasures. I became adept at managing two man tasks on my own. It was now a seven day a week job. Nevertheless we were very fit and the years rolled on contentedly enough, or so it seemed. There was always the thought that Rollo would join us one day.

An abiding memory of these years, when the children were small, was my nightly bedtime story. It was really a true story about an event that took place when I was at Two Tree Hill in Rhodesia. I had walked down to the stream at the foot of the hill one morning with our spaniel dog. It was a lovely dawn with the doves 'cooing' in the two great trees. As I looked out across the water I suddenly heard a loud snap behind me. I turned round to see a giant crocodile grinning at me with Jessie, the spaniel, inside it. I shouted at it 'Put Jessie down, you silly ass,' adding involuntarily, 'If you want to eat anything, take a native.' This was the bit the children loved best. So much so that the boys' headmaster asked me why when questioned about what crocodiles lived on, they had both replied, 'Natives.' I, of course, suppressing my laughter, replied, 'I have no idea.' At any rate they would never go to sleep without this tale. With many embellishments, I told it night after night throughout their childhood years. The more gruesome I made it the better they liked it, the little savages.

Towards the end of those farming years an alarming thing happened to me. I became impotent. This may not seem a big deal for someone in their mid fifties. It was for me. I took it as a sign that the feminine side was finally taking over. I needed sexual satisfaction and realised I was not going to get or give it as a male anymore.

It was an awful feeling. One could still enjoy the preliminaries of lovemaking, and then when it came to the point of greatest excitement the wretched thing would go floppy. This obviously meant that penetration and the subsequent wonderful joy of ejaculation were not possible. Quite apart from being denied ultimate fulfilment, there was a dreadful sense of failure and weakness. June in no way contributed to this. She was kind and understanding but I had let her down and denied her satisfaction. I felt this bitterly. I wondered whether it was because I was no longer a male.

In those days, my faith in the medical profession had not been entirely shattered. I therefore sought its help. It was an embarrassing business. One does not like to admit to this failing. I was referred to a so-called specialist in this condition. I had to drop my trousers in front of his nurse, to be examined by him. He, in turn, eventually passed me on to a rather notorious professor from the university in Birmingham. He ran a sort of clinic at his house in Edgbaston. I duly set off one spring morning, full of hope for a speedy resolution to my problem. I had difficulty in finding the clinic and was directed to a long building down a winding drive. I walked in unchallenged, to see a long row of bearded men dressed in black wearing tall 'stove-pipe' hats. They were sitting silently in high-backed chairs. By the look on their faces I quickly arrived at the conclusion that they were probably more likely to be celibate rather than impotent and fled.

The clinic turned out to be situated in a substantial private house, its privacy guarded by some rather moth eaten laurel bushes. The professor was a flamboyant figure, sporting a coloured silk waistcoat, similar to those worn by members of 'Pop' at Eton. The ruby ring on his finger, however, dispelled any thoughts of his having had such a sensible education. I was shown into his drawing room. It was full of expensive looking ornaments. He offered me a gin and tonic, which was more than acceptable at that stage in the proceedings. He asked me about my difficulty. He stated that impotence could be caused by physical or mental problems. He treated the physical one by the use of an injection of Paravane, I think it was named. This was done prior to penetration to give an erection. I said it did not seem very romantic. His reply was, 'Oh, the partner could give it,' which sounded painful. It would be perhaps wise to choose a Registered Nurse as a lover, if forced to adopt this method! Also, there was a danger that the erection would not subside. In this case the antidote had to be administered fairly swiftly to avoid permanent damage to the blood vessels. This brought to mind visions of desperate gentlemen in erectile states running around seeking subsidence.

Following the report from the specialist, the professor decided that my failure could be due to 'lack of confidence', as he put it. He suggested a course of treatment.

This would consist of weekly sessions with a carefully chosen 'sex therapist'. These would cost £40 each. He claimed that this solution had proved most successful, particularly with middle-aged men who had taken young lovers, only to find that they could no longer 'cut the mustard'. Fortified by a second gin and tonic, I agreed to 'give it a whirl'.

About a month later I arrived at the clinic at seven o'clock, on a warm May evening, not really knowing what to expect. The professor introduced me to a nice-looking girl with dark hair, probably in her late twenties. She was apparently a secretary at the university. She showed me upstairs to a room with a sort of mattress laid out on the floor. I had never seen anything like it before. She explained that what she was going to do was to gradually 'up the ante' in the lovemaking department over the course of treatment. The final objective would be a sustained erection. She advised me to strip down to my underwear. As I was doing this, cherished memories of those far off happy Ma Feathers evenings flooded back into my mind.

So there we were, facing each other in our underwear. I, in my underpants, and the secretary in bra and knickers. We chatted awhile and then lay down on the mattress. She seemed to encourage what the Americans would call 'heavy petting.' The trouble with this was our relationship. I rather saw her as a nurse figure. You simply do not go to bed with the nurse who is looking after you. Nobody has with me, at any rate, worse luck, in all my nursing years! Also, her whole demeanour was that of a professional advisor. Thus the lovemaking, if it can be called that, as it developed over the sessions, lacked any romantic flavour. Being as this has always been the essential ingredient for me, things rather petered out. Love, quite properly, is my stimulant. So even when we went into completely naked mode, I remember she had a mole on her bottom, I could not sustain an erection. The secretary was a pleasant enough companion and we got on well, but a similar sense of humour was our main bond. We both spent quite a bit of the time in fits of laughter at our 'goings on'.

Looking back on it, the whole business was highly irregular. I do not know why I subjected myself to this strange treatment, except that my need for a cure was so urgent to me. By its conclusion I was more than ever convinced that I was female. The professor's final suggestion was a spot of testosterone therapy. He warned me that this could have the effect of changing one's character and making one aggressive.

By this time I had had enough. I was ready to bow to the inevitable and find a way to surrender to what was in my heart.

Part Two

A Nurse's Tale

Chapter 8

Metamorphosis

My farming years slipped away, at first month by month then the years advanced into decades ruled by the ever-changing seasons. Looking back it is difficult to separate one from another. Crops grew and were harvested. Generations of Welsh Blacks passed by in an almost dream-like sequence until one day it was over. My marriage ended. For the first time since I set off for Africa at the age of seventeen I was a free man. Rollo, my elder son, was by now thirty years old. This was the same age at which I had started farming myself. From a little boy he had always wanted to farm and was, by now, working on the farm. It was an ideal age to begin farming. He had married and settled down but was still in his prime and ready to meet the challenge with a youthful zest. I had noticed how difficult local farmers' sons had found it if they worked into middle age under their fathers.

I felt an overwhelming sense of a new dawn breaking for me. The burden of the years fell away. I felt an irresistible urge to set out on one last great adventure. It was no time for caution. At long last I was going to be true to myself before it was too late. My whole life had been lived under the great handicap of my gender identity. It seemed to me from my first memories that I was female. The fact that I was born with what I thought was a partially a female body had dictated the life that I had led. I had tried so hard to make a success of that life. I had confided in no one. It was not so easy to share innermost secrets in the era I was brought up in. One was expected to keep emotions to oneself. The English gentleman kept a 'stiff upper lip' and 'soldiered on'. Thus, accepting this, I had not been unhappy and had done my best to make the most of the joys that had come my way.

Now it was different. I would be unhappy if I did not, as I saw it, rectify matters. Years of pent-up emotions were ready to burst out. I visited my doctor who was somewhat taken aback. She passed me on to a psychiatrist who specialised in such matters. He informed me that the standard procedure was to undergo a three-year trial period living as a woman. No surgeon would apparently undertake such an operation without this, bearing in mind the irreversible nature of the procedure. He would be worried about being sued in the event of my changing my mind at some later date. At the conclusion of this time I would have to present myself, cap in hand, to a Dr Montgomery at Charing Cross Hospital in London for his decision. I was prescribed a new form of hormone treatment. This was a patch, attached to one's bottom, which released oestrogen and began the onset of female characteristics. The first of these was the early burgeoning of breast development and softer, less hairy skin. The penis and testicles did not seem affected. There was no weight gain at this stage.

My faith in psychiatrists, like vets, was and still is, zero. I have always thought that anyone who consults a psychiatrist is mad! I had already made my decision after a lifetime waiting. Even Field Marshal Montgomery would not have stood in my way. After quite a search I heard of a plastic surgeon, named Harrod, who carried out sex-change operations. I went to the Cromwell clinic in Huntingdon to meet him. We immediately seemed to warm to one another. He was actually out to help me! I typed out a legal-looking document exonerating him from any blame in case I should ever have second thoughts. Mr Harrod said that he backed his own judgement of character. Bearing in mind my age he thought it was right for me to go ahead now, if I could afford the fee of £6,000. The operation was arranged for a few weeks' time. I was on my way!

I then received some disappointing news The Cromwell clinic refused permission for the operation, worried that it might cause some scandal. This was bad luck as subsequently they have carried out many such operations. So, instead of the cosy friendly Cromwell, we would have to go up to Rotherham of all places! At any rate, the momentous day in my life soon dawned. I set off north in wet miserable weather. On the journey I remembered other great days in my life. They all seemed to have been glorious sunny days when it felt good just to be alive. My first Trooping the Colour on dear old Empress, first match in the school cricket eleven, that drive up the Mall on my way to Glyndebourne, the Inter-Regimental polo final and many, many others over the years came to mind. From now on I would be shunned by my friends and probably ridiculed by strangers. My family, quite understandably, did not want 'to know'. Rollo observed that it was particularly strange as I had hitherto had such particularly male occupations, cattle ranching in Africa, soldiering and farming. How was I going to make a living? I was going to be terribly alone. Then I noticed my bag on the seat next to me containing my new female attire and wig. My spirits lifted a bit.

Rotherham on that day appeared as dreary as I had imagined. The nurses treated me as somewhat of a curiosity as they shaved the hair off my nether regions. Then it was all over. Rhodri had gone forever to be replaced by Miranda. I awoke in great pain with a feeling of desolation. It was a staggering shock to my body. If ever I needed comfort it was then. Nurses came to ameliorate my pain but otherwise left me in isolation. When Mr Harrod visited the following morning I begged him to arrange a private nurse so that I could get home and out of that dreadful place. He did this with great efficiency and in a few days she arrived up to escort me back to Drayton. She was a really sweet kind local girl, so different from her Yorkshire counterparts. My new private parts were subjected to one last inspection by all and sundry. It was observed that once my pubic hair had regrown they would look like any other woman's. With that embarrassing ritual over we headed home. Nursey changed my dressings several times a day and the bleeding soon ceased. I was then able to get about supported by her. She had been instructed to insert a sort of dildo up my newly constructed vagina at regular intervals to stop the passage from closing again. I had to continue this practice for several months ahead and everything healed well.

Nursey taught me the rudiments of cooking before she left and little tricks like using silver foil to keep the cooker clean. I began to feel quite the little woman about the house. Then the time came to venture out into the world again. Locally I attracted quite a lot of ribaldry and comment, which was to be expected I suppose. I was seen as no longer a respected member of the community but more of a candidate for the 'funny farm'.

Tractor work proved painful and continued to be so until I went back to Mr Harrod a few months later. Sitting down on a bouncing tractor seat was so uncomfortable that I spent most of the time standing up. This was very tiring. It was lucky that my tractor, in those days, did not have a cab. It transpired that one testicle had been left in error. It seemed a fairly basic omission. After all it wasn't as if I had had dozens of the things! I do not know why I was not furious with him. The whole object of the operation had been their removal. I had paid him £6,000 for just that. Once this rogue testicle was removed, life became more comfortable. A major problem, when out on the farm, was 'spending a penny'. Every time I dropped my trousers, however remote the spot, someone or other would appear. I never did find an easy solution other than traipsing all the way back to the house. My bare bottom was fast becoming an agricultural curiosity. I had recommenced the hormone treatment a week after the operation. I had had to stop this for a week prior to it. I watched with wonderment the dramatic changes in my body taking place. My breasts grew rapidly and soon looked firm and rather beautiful to my eyes. My skin became softer and smoother. What body hair I possessed just disappeared. even in the anal area. I was left with only a faint down on my forearms. I was a bit miffed, however, that I still found it necessary to shave daily. What with also having to shave my legs and under my arms, female life seemed a constant battle against hair. My bottom grew rounder and more feminine by the day.

I would have to put these feminine charms to good use. It was no use just sitting at home admiring them. I contacted an up-market dating agency. I somehow felt the need to establish a female identity for myself; otherwise I would be in a sort of no man's land, neither Rhodri nor Miranda. At any rate in due course the agency produced someone for me. He telephoned and it was arranged that he would come to the house at around six o'clock on the following Tuesday evening. On the appointed day I arrived back home at about four in my farming overalls, less my wig, as I had been doing corn loads which was a particularly dusty job. Lo and behold, he was sitting in his car on the gravel by the front door. I was stunned but it was too late to flee. So I greeted him with the remark that he must have come to see my sister! I settled him down in the drawing room with a cup of tea and dashed upstairs to change. I reappeared in all my finery, apologising that I had not been there to meet him and saying that my brother was off to London so that we would be dining on our own. He said that my brother had looked after him well and were we twins? I faintly replied, 'Rather'. and hastily changed the conversation to safer waters.

As it turned out we enjoyed quite a convivial evening. He liked his port and rather 'banged on' about this and that. I could not even get a word in which was highly unusual for me. He was rather the club bore type in late middle age with a distinctly fruity voice. When it began to get late he requested to stay the night as he had 'imbibed' too much to drive home safely. I gained the impression that he thought he was going to share my bed. He said how attractive I was. He liked tall girls. I was not ready for this yet and also felt that he would consider me a very loose lady if I jumped into bed on first acquaintance. I was later to learn that this was an old-fashioned maxim. The modern girl was expected to bed complete strangers, if so moved.

Thus when the agency produced Bernard a few weeks later, I was all ready for action. He was a retired headmaster of military bearing, complete with clipped moustache. He brought a bottle of good wine. We got on well although he did remark that it was unusual for females to use words like 'esoteric'. I made a mental note to appear less educated in future if that was what it took to be a true woman. Although I thought it was a bit rich coming from a headmaster. I wondered about his late school. The port flowed again and we duly gravitated to my bedroom. Bernard seemed surprised and rather overjoyed at this development. I discovered later on that he had been having a little local difficulty achieving this exciting state in his previous liaisons. Nothing daunted and remembering my first visit to Ma Feathers I stripped off, secretly inserted some of Mr Harrod's wheat-germ oil and hopped nude into my vast old double bed.

Bernard meanwhile was fiddling about in my dressing room. He eventually returned, moustache bristling, in a silk dressing gown, for all the world as if he was playing in a well-mannered Noel Coward drawing room comedy. I fervently prayed that it wouldn't degenerate into a farce. The frantic efforts that I had to employ to keep my wig in place whilst on the job did teeter on the brink of the ridiculous. My gallant lover was all too busy with his own department to notice these manoeuvres fortunately. Penetration was not achieved without some pain but I experienced an overwhelming arousal and sense of my hard-won femininity. The following day twelve red roses from an ex-headmaster, who couldn't believe his luck, celebrated 'the night of a thousand stars' when Miranda lost her virginity.

The third gentleman that the agency thought suitable was named Harold. He lived in Oxford and was very much part of university life and rowing. He had also had a slim volume on punting published. Our romance, if it can be called that, mainly took place on the river or in places connected to it. We spent lazy summer days on the Cherwell in his punt, fortified by Fortnum and Mason hampers. He would instruct me to look away as *Parson's Pleasure* hove on the starboard beam, in order to spare my female blushes. Oxford Dons exercised their ancient right to be sport themselves naked at this point. In the evening we would repair to the Oxford University Boat Club restaurant by the landing jetty. The dons frequented this. The food was excellent and the champagne flowed. On returning to Summertown, Harold's delightfully named part of Oxford; he would prove an ardent lover. To date my only experience of being on the receiving or female end of things had been with the rather courtly Bernard. Going to bed with Harold was like being set upon by a grizzly bear. It was lucky that I was a strong girl! On the other hand he accused me of being a trifle basic in just stripping off and jumping into bed. He purchased me some rather glamorous nightgowns, which I was made to wear in his bedroom.

This was an important lesson for Miranda. I must obviously acquire some feminine wiles and graces. Harold had been a bachelor all his life but was now hell-bent on marriage and I was getting sucked into this fantasy. Even if it had been possible for me, it was the last thing I desired. We did, however, have some good times together. I particularly remember driving up to Oxford on one glorious May morning in my open car. The sun was warm on my bare arms and shoulders and I was looking forward to a day in Harold's punt watching that almost Edwardian scene of the college May head of the river bumping races and doubtless a night of 'how's your father'. For the first time I felt that my change was nearly complete.

What was not complete, however, was that I still had to shave. It was a problem. I had been a member of the Cavalry Club at Hyde Park corner since I was a subaltern in the regiment. The Ladies' dining room area was a particular favourite of mine. Annabel and I had enjoyed so many happy times there. So I took the distinctly unusual step of making myself a member as my own wife, if you know what I mean. At any rate it proved very useful. I had found that you could not meet people easily as a lady. I had got some very funny looks whilst waiting for Harold or Bernard at various places in London, even at my old stamping ground the Ritz. But it was quite in order to sit on one's own at the Club. The difficulty was to get a wash and shave. I obviously could not use the Gents and I felt it would hardly be cricket to use my battery razor in the Ladies. The only private place I hit upon was the lift. It had a mirror and was rather creaky and noisy. So I used to go up and down until the task was completed. If anyone got in at a floor I hastily hid the razor in my bag.

The only time that I did get myself in a bit of a pickle with Harold was the day

Mother (left) with matinee idol Clive Brooke in Hollywood thriller.

Here I look as though I would give anything to be allowed to dismount!

Sail away: Dressed as HMS Rodney's newest recruit.

Standing in charge of my brother and sister, preparing for my early role in life.

A sunny day in Sussex reveals my prep school out in strength, with me in my role as captain of cricket (extreme left of the seated masters).

Officer at play. Here I am out hunting on "Bubbles" Fuller's grey, Lisa. Later, at the evening's festivities, I proposed to Annabel.

The best man. Rollo and me at a Life Guard pal's wedding, for whom the bell tolls.

My old companion and colonel, Max Gordon (holding cup) and me (far right) in victorious mode having won the Tidworth polo tournament in 1958.

A pause on the dangerous Dhala Road, up-country in The Aden Protectorate in 1960. My driver in correct headgear.

Household Cavalry officer in 'the kit' for Trooping The Colour day, June 1956.

A Life Guard in the Land of the Pharaohs. In my role as Orderly Officer, in the mess garden, on a very hot Canal Zone day.

Ready for battle in the service of the King Charles the Second!.

*Miranda on the road to Rio,
late in 1989, sporting the
Princess Di look.*

*Metamorphosis. First photograph after
'the change', Apil 1989. No longer a
respected member of the human race.*

*On board ship off Montevideo
on the same South American
odyssey, still looking demure like
Princess Diana.*

my godson captained the combined Oxford and Cambridge cricket eleven in The Parks. I had carelessly let this information out. Harold insisted on our going to meet him. He even assured me that we could get access to the pavilion! Nothing I could do was going to stop him. My poor godson would have wondered who the dickens this strange lady was accusing him of being her godson. So I formed the plan of greeting another member of the team out of Harold's earshot. Unfortunately in error I picked one of the Australians, their opponents that day. This caused all sorts of confusion and I had to plead a headache in true female fashion, to get back to Summertown when I really wanted to see godson batting. Before we left, I spent almost the entire morning dodging behind trees to avoid said godson, much to Harold's bewilderment.

The next hurdle was to get Miranda a passport, as Harold was planning a holiday abroad for us. The first move involved getting a JP to sign the relevant document. He had to have known me for a few years. David Brentnall, an old family friend, was the only person that I could think of. The snag was he did not know about my sex change. On seeing me he was taken aback and knowing my army background jumped to the conclusion that I was going underground on some secret mission. The more I refuted this, the more convinced he became. At any rate he duly signed with the words 'Quite proper that you should keep this secret, mum's the word.' Later on I would answer awkward questions, in interviews, about my military service by saying that it was something 'hush hush.' They would exchange conspiratorial glances and drop the subject. I even think I inadvertently gained some extra kudos from this tactic. The passport authorities were remarkably compliant and, on my producing David's form, issued me with a new passport in the name of Miranda Ponsonby with an appropriate photograph.

My Nickalls ancestry impressed Harold. We invariably graced the Steward's Enclosure for the full Henley week. I was introduced everywhere as Guy Nickalls' niece, though great- niece would have been more appropriate, I believe. I did receive some funny looks, particularly when I was inveigled into presenting the Silver Goblets and Nickalls cup to the winners of the coxless pairs. The famous Olympic pair were hard put to keep straight faces during the ceremony. Old Harold was blissfully unaware of their merriment and even asked them to take me up the course in their launch. They politely excused themselves from this pleasure much to my relief.

I feel sure that my illustrious forebears had they been looking down must have also had a chuckle or two at my first efforts in a single scull. I was never a candidate for the Diamond Skulls, being a cricketer who regarded 'wet bobs' as large oafs with a strong streak of masochism. Harold duly press-ganged me into one with the coach of the university eight, known as the 'Blue Boat', looking on. They are devilish things even to get into, and tip over unless the oar blades are on the water feathering. Also, as one is proceeding backwards, one has to be constantly craning one's neck round to avoid cannoning into other boats. Why they do not fit wing mirrors I shall never know. When I suggested this to 'Blue Boat' he gave me pitying look and replied, 'You rowed at a good pace'. I forbore to tell him the reason was that I just wanted to get back and out of the wretched thing. I preferred punting what Harold termed his 'canoe', but, as a lady, I felt that I should be excused this task.

Chapter 9

Tradimus Lampada

Florence Nightingale almost seemed, at critical moments, to be standing by my side with her lantern lighting my way ahead in the great struggle that I now undertook to enter her profession. The time had come to leave the farm. I had to now find another way of earning a living. On the grounds of age alone this was going to be difficult enough. Add the extra conundrum of a sex change and I knew that I was in for a major struggle. I joined battle, however, with a light heart, undaunted by the obstacles in my path. There was only one thing I wanted to do that simplified matters. It was to enter the most female profession of all, if you exclude the oldest! Rhodri had succeeded in the most male professions and Miranda was not going to let the side down for her part.

As I had feared it would happen, even my oldest and dearest friends had deserted me. All those years of comradeship and shared hardships across the desert sands of Arabia and elsewhere had counted for nothing against the apparent shame of being a Miranda. The sad thing was that I was still me and never attempted to be anything else. I wondered whether my years of nursing would be like doing a Profumo and would exonerate my shame in their eyes one day. I did so hope so. It would make me very happy.

I moved away from Drayton that autumn, when the harvest was safely gathered in. When the time came to go it was a terrible wrench. For nearly thirty years I had given myself body and soul to the place. It would always be part of me and my imprint would remain on that little bit of England for generations still to come. I vowed that I would return the day I died, and rest in peace in the little cemetery at Bringhurst overlooking my land.

My new home was about six miles away, just out of the valley. It was isolated, outside a village I had always liked. It had a lovely little garden from which I could see Bringhurst church across the Welland River and hear her bells ringing of a Sunday morning, as I had at Drayton.

I planned to try and get a job as an auxiliary at a nursing home to start with. I scoured every local paper for miles around. I went to interview after interview. Everything seemed to go swimmingly and provisional plans were put in place only to be rescinded later. One evening I was even within an hour of going on duty when without explanation I was cancelled. It was a salutary lesson in what I had let myself in for. Previously I had never failed at an interview. People had invariably warmed to my enthusiasm and go. I felt sure that I had not lost that certain charisma.

Advertised jobs were running out so one day when I was passing through a village called Clipston I noticed a nursing home name board and called in. The proprietor was black. He had been an officer in the Ugandan air force and had been forced to flee some political coup or other. I think he recognised officer qualities in me. At any rate he took me on, subject to reference. I was later to learn that coloured people couldn't rumble Mirandas for some reason. The only person that I could think of for a reference was Mr Harrod. He very kindly produced a very suitable piece predicting that Miranda, in his opinion, would make a good nurse. By this time I was one of his success stories, apparently, for what I had achieved already. So I set off to Leicester to purchase two white uniforms, blue, silver-buckled belt, fob watch and sensible shoes. I looked at myself in the mirror before setting off for my first night's duty. I thought that I looked the part and rather glamorous to boot. It was an exciting moment. My foot at long last was on the bottom rung of the nursing ladder. Miranda was on her way again.

The home specialised in psycho-geriatric, long-stay patients. I settled very quickly into what was a backbreaking job at night. The patients had all to be changed and their beds remade at regular intervals throughout the night. All the linen had to be washed and hung up to dry. Two of us were on duty. We took a floor each and one had to handle the patients on one's own, which took considerable strength and not a little skill. We had to work at speed and if something delayed us it was difficult to finish by seven o'clock when the day staff came on. Dawns have never seemed sweeter as I drove home along the misty country lanes ready to tuck into eggs and bacon.

I immediately discovered that I possessed a gift for getting on well with the patients. They seemed to like me and I could handle their mood swings. I also had a happy relationship with the other members of the staff. Adam, the owner, was pleased with me and said that it was rare to find all the attributes of a good nurse in one individual. He most certainly got his money's worth out of me during the time I was there. I grew fond of our charges and particularly remember one old lady who looked and moved just like the footballer Peter Beardsley. Thus started my use of nicknames, which has enlivened so much of my nursing career.

After six months there I decided that it was time to put my sensibly shod foot on the next step up the ladder. I answered an advertisement for an auxiliary nurse at Kettering General Hospital. I presented myself with a glowing reference from Adam. One of the two nurses who interviewed me had been an army nurse and liked my military background. The other Sister thought I 'looked a good strong lass'. She was right about this necessary qualification for an orthopaedic nurse in those days when the majority of patients where on traction. I was chosen for the post.

This time I was issued with two uniforms free. They were cream with brown stripes. Whilst I was being measured up a newly qualified nurse came in to pick up her staff nurse's uniform. This was an altogether grander dress with a royal blue belt. I looked on in awe and imagined the day I might be doing this. I was starting to dream the impossible dream. I said a fond farewell to Clipston and Adam predicted that when he saw me again I would be a qualified nurse.

I arrived early on my first hospital morning. There were a gaggle of nurses round the desk who shot me quizzical glances. Then Sister appeared and I sat nervously listening to handover of all the patients. A nurse was detailed to look after me or, more accurately, for me to help her with the heavy work. My Clipston experience stood me in good stead. I struck up good relationships with our patients, particularly the old dears. The motorcycle accident boys rather giggled whenever I appeared and ribbed each other when I came to rub their bottoms with some cream, as was the practice then. They settled down a bit as they got more used to me. Visitors tended to laugh and whisper amongst themselves. I found that if I made a point of going up to them and cracked a joke or two they soon became friends. They then laughed with me rather than at me.

Consultant's ward rounds were just starting to be accompanied by the staff nurse in charge of the patients rather than the ward sister. Sue, the nurse that I worked with, used to get very overexcited about this. I mentioned to some staff nurses that Sue was having her usual orgasm now that the consultant had arrived. They thought this was a hoot and when they overheard me instructing some policemen who had arrived to interview a patient to 'Follow me, men,' I was made in their eyes.

All of a sudden I had a bit of really bad luck. Our farming neighbour was admitted with a broken limb. He immediately recognised me and 'spilled the beans' about me. The sisters who had interviewed me were horrified but took no instant action. I went through days and days of agonising suspense, anxiously scanning the off duty book to see if I was still included. They were pleased with my work and I was fast establishing myself as a member of the team. I particularly remember one sparky, amusing old lady. She had suffered a stroke and was the very first patient that I had a close relationship with. She would not let anyone else near her when I was on duty. Then the blow fell. I was summoned to a meeting with the Director of Nursing, Mrs Pharaoh, and my orthopaedic directorate manager, Lynne Gale. I was due on duty but was told to come in civilian clothes. This was ominous enough in itself. I feared that this was the end and that all my hopes were going to be shattered.

As I marched down the long hospital corridor I had that sick feeling in the pit of my stomach like before going into battle. I pulled myself together as I knocked on the door. A lifetime's training came to my aid. The last of the Pharaohs, as I had dubbed her, stood up to greet me, and both she and Lynne Gale were friendly and sympathetic. They said that I was the talk of the hospital but that I had falsified nothing in my application form. Sister Jones was very pleased with me and all they were going to recommend was that I try to be a bit more feminine. I must wear makeup and try not to stride down the corridor as if I was changing the Guard at Buckingham Palace. Relief flooded through my whole being. I had even recovered myself sufficiently to answer the advice that it would be more appropriate to call myself Ms rather than Mrs with the remark that it was too politically correct for me and that my children did not want to be thought of as bastards.

I think that is had been a 'damn close run thing'. Lynne Gale could have given me the advice offered quite informally on the ward. I had a feeling that something had changed their minds in my favour. Perhaps it was my success on the ward and growing popularity. I shall never quite know. Could Florence Nightingale herself indeed been watching over me? At any rate, it was decent of them and the hospital to give me my chance. I was not going to let them down. At least the whole thing was now out in the open and I could relax a bit and enjoy my nursing.

Chapter 10

Storming the Citadel

When I had settled into my work on Barnwell C, I began the search for a place at a School of Nursing to qualify as a Registered Nurse. I made an appointment to see the Recruitment Officer of the Northampton and Kettering school. She was helpful but on learning my age she said that I would be too near the then retirement age for them to train me. The only course of action seemed to be for me to request the School Principal for an exception to this rule in my case. I made an appointment to see him in his Northampton office. He changed this on two occasions, causing no end of bother to my Off Duty. Then on the very morning of the interview he cancelled it altogether without explanation.

The next nearest school was The Charles Frear in Leicester. They assured me that they did not discriminate against age. They invited me to their selection day. I arrived armed with a good reference from Lynne Gale. The day went well. I had been instructed to bring my birth and education certificates with me. I wondered what would happen when they saw my birth certificate. In the event the final interviewer only gave them a cursory glance and accepted me subject to a 'stringent medical'. This was on account of my age as they said that they had experienced problems in the past. I drove home full of happiness ready for the next hurdle.

I arrived at the Leicester Royal Infirmary in a bit of a flap on a raw wet spring day. The traffic had been bad and the car park was full. The examination took place in a sort of dungeon underneath the hospital. I had blundered into a changing room, full of nurses in various stages of undress, trying to find it. So I was a bit hot and bothered when I finally found the doctor. He looked a very senior and dignified figure in his long white coat. As a child I had happened to overhear my mother saying that she always made a point of wearing silk underwear when visiting a doctor. Remembering this random remark I had duly put on a very expensive cream coloured silk bra and pants, given to me by Harold I think, with my best silk stockings. The mistake that I made was to wear my Basler jersey as opposed to a cardigan. This proved tricky to take off in front of him without dislodging my wig. My usual practice was to remove wig, take off jersey, then replace wig again. I deemed that this would be a trifle extramural for the occasion. I somehow completed the task but emerged looking, I am sure, a trifle dishevelled. He prodded and poked me, checked heart, wind and limb and finally stood behind me whilst I touched my toes or as near my toes as I could get. He commented that I had a good strong back and that was vital for a nurse. I was indeed very fit having always led an outdoor life prior to nursing.

To my dying day I shall never be able to explain what happened next. He told me to get dressed and to then come and sit down and answer some questions. As I had always enjoyed perfect health my answers about my previous medical history were pretty routine. Finally he asked me if I had ever had any operations. Without thinking I replied, 'Only one.' 'What was that?' he asked. In a blink of an eye, 'A sex change,' came out of my lips. He sat bolt upright and I could have cut my tongue out on the spot. He was appeared fascinated and said that he had had no idea of this when examining my, what he termed as, 'unclothed body'. I thought rather gloomily that at least that was welcome news but I knew that I had blown it and with it almost certainly my only chance. He passed me fit for nursing but...!

Looking back over the years what I should done was to have got him by the scruff of his Saville Row suited neck and threatened him that I would sue him for everything he possessed if he unethically betrayed my confidence. He had after all only been requested to pass me fit for nursing. This he had done. What he did do I discovered later was to append a note on the bottom of the report stating, 'Ask Mrs Ponsonby about her sex.' This completely flummoxed The Charles Frear. They obviously felt that they could not do this. They made enquiries to Kettering who, as they were to do on several subsequent occasions over my career to their credit, closed ranks and said that they could not discuss the private matters of members of their staff. They then apparently asked the Nursing School Principal if he could explain it. He tried but failed to do any better – and serve him right!

The Charles Frear had offered me the place subject to medical, which I had passed. Pasted all over the Leicester stationery was 'Equal Opportunity NHS Trust'. My reference had stated that I was popular with staff and patients and that they would be glad to have me back when qualified. Also, that they were confident that I would pass with 'flying colours'. The school had already informed me that I had the highest educational qualifications of all the candidates. Also they had seen my birth certificate before offering me the place. The weeks went by, however, without them making a final decision, in spite of my ringing them several times.

Harold, in the meantime was pressing me to apply for a nursing degree course at what is now Oxford Brooks University. It was a four-year course with a high science content. We went up to Headington to see them. They were happy to consider me if I could elaborate on my science qualifications. Brooksby Agricultural College, where I had obtained my two Diplomas, kindly furnished me with these to their satisfaction. The main snag of Oxford was its distance and the fact that Harold was pressing me to marry and live with him. I rather feared being trapped. Legally this was forbidden and still was until very recently. I dithered about this putting off a decision until I had heard from The

Charles Frear. More weeks went by without my hearing from them. I eventually requested an interview to clear the matter up.

I was shown in to a panel of about six or seven dignitaries who looked embarrassed. I argued my case with quiet force. The chairman in a rather shamefaced manner said that they had decided that they could not risk me. I stated that it would have been fairer to me if they had let me know sooner. As a parting shot I assured them that I would let them know when I did finally qualify and that I hoped they did not put other aspiring nurses through the ordeal of anxiety I had suffered. It was a sad Miranda who wended her weary way home.

That afternoon I rang Oxford as being my only hope left. They were sorry but all the places had just been filled, but if I contacted Aston University at once they were running a three-year nursing degree course for the first time. These were the only two degree courses at the time. I duly presented myself at their selection day. It was in a part of Birmingham. It was a depressing red brick and concrete place, even worse looking than the Royal Shakespeare theatre in Stratford upon Avon. It was daubed with slogans against the poll tax. The students wandering round looked unbelievably dirty and scruffy. Birmingham was a dispiriting mixture of motorways and pedestrian underpasses. These latter were patrolled by gangs of dangerous-looking black youths almost certainly intent on no good. They had obviously been driven mad by this hellish environment. A world away from our beloved natives at Two Tree Hill in Rhodesia with their dignity, humour and loyalty. Also so different from happy-go-lucky friendly West Indians that I had mixed with when visiting the Leeward Islands. My heart sank. I was but a country girl I thought.

The other candidates for selection were a totally different 'kettle of fish'. They were all smart, young and keen. Before starting we were informed that there were only a very limited number of places. Most of our great gathering were going to be disappointed. I thought it would have been kinder to tell us this in advance. We looked at each other in dismay. As usual I had a good series of interviews only to be told at the end of the day that they thought it was fairer to award the few places to younger girls. I must admit I was nearly old enough to be their grandmother and one rejected little girl did have a cry on my shoulder, so my long journey had not been entirely in vain. Every mile that I put between that nightmare place and myself increased my contentment, but what was I going to do now?

The Charles Frear's messing me about was doubly frustrating, as by now most of the nursing schools had closed their intakes for the year. I began to go further and further afield. I remember going to Coventry, somewhere in Essex (Colchester, I think) and one day I ended up in Norwich. The Recruitment Officer was a very courteous Indian. As I was going out of the door, looking rather crestfallen no doubt, he said that with my educational qualifications it might be worth trying one of the London teaching hospitals. He had heard on the grapevine that a few of them were down on their current intakes. The following day I set about ringing round the famous ones that I had heard of. St Mary's invited me to their selection day. I drove up to London with some excitement. Miranda was going up in the world. The hospital interior was new looking with bright cheerful murals painted on the walls. The only problem was that the car parking was virtually nonexistent. The girls were a noticeably different type. What my grandmother would have termed 'a better class of girl'. What I would have possibly called better educated with a proportion of graduates. They were only filling up a few places due to last minute refusals. I enjoyed the day but was not selected. Perhaps I was not thought of as a 'better class of girl' myself!

The Guy's Recruitment Officer, Marie Brown, agreed to see me for a chat the following week. I travelled up by train this time taking the northern line from St Pancras to London Bridge for the very first time. I passed through the beautiful, old, wrought-iron gates and passed the statue of Thomas Guy and the little chapel, which had stood since his time in the 18th century, with a feeling of awe. As I passed the porter's lodge I was greeted me with a polite, 'Can I help you, madam?' which was good for morale. I was directed to Shepherd's House, the home of the Guy's school of nursing. Mrs Brown was sitting in her tiny cluttered office. She was a black middle-aged lady, friendly but with an air of authority. I believe that she had been Guy's first black Sister. She read my reference and wanted to know all about me. We took coffee and biscuits and I was invited to the selection day in a couple weeks time.

On the appointed day I set off for London very early by car. I had located the multi-storey car park next to the Guy's theatre on my previous visit. It was a misty late March morning. I knew this was my last chance. If I did not make it now it would be the end. Somehow I wasn't nervous, just keyed up with every fibre of my being set on succeeding this time. It was the sort of feeling that I had experienced in my youth before opening the innings in a big cricket match. I remembered it so well even though it must have been forty odd years ago. The morning was spent in various group activities and a brief visit to a ward or two. Marie pointed out what the various colours of buckled belts denoted and said that 'anybody who was anybody' wore one. Then we went for lunch in the big staff dining room. The ward sisters sat amongst themselves. They had an aura of great dignity about them and looked magnificent in their roughs and capes. I palled up with three or four of our girls who were very much the same as the St Mary's type. My recent life had been spent with girls of their age and we chatted away. I was blissfully unaware that we were being watched. At the close of the meal we repaired to the vast coffee room full of nurses, the younger doctors and medical students. To enter one goes through some elegant glass doors and down a couple of steps. As I paused at the top of these the entire company in the room stopped talking and gazed at me as if spellbound. It was like being on parade in front of my squadron. It only lasted a minute and would have unnerved a lesser mortal, but on that day I was prepared for anything.

On returning to Shepherd's House we sat around talking amongst ourselves awaiting the ordeal of our final interview. One by one the girls were called in and on coming out disappeared down the stairs, some with a thumbs up signal. Eventually I was the only one left and it was my turn. Interviewing me were Marie and the school Principal. Marie said that they were impressed how well I had got on with the others. They had had one or two other older entrants who had not fitted into their set and eventually fallen by the wayside. They liked my reference but were worried that I would be a long way from home and 'would my husband mind?' I assured them on that point. For the second time a black person had not 'sussed me out.' Finally, Marie said that they thought I deserved a chance and subject to a medical offered me a place in the July set. I then had what could have been a decisive slice of good fortune. I had been supposed to show them my birth and educational certificates and had them in my hand, but they got up and said good-bye without requesting them. I suppose that it was late and they were tired by that time.

I descended the stairs almost walking on air and allowed myself a thumbs up although there was no one left to display it to. It was one of those rare lovely March afternoons. I took the roof of my car down and I remember driving down the Marylebone road, past my birth place, the London clinic, singing, rather perversely, 'Oh what a beautiful morning, oh what a beautiful day, everything's going my way,' etc. I had so much to look forward to now. I would never make the same mistake again at the medical.

In due course my certificates were requested. I just sent my educational ones and nothing more was said on the matter. I attended the medical in Tabard House well prepared this time. I wore a blouse that undid down the front, shaved my legs with extra care early that morning (by this time I had no longer need to shave my face) and donned the regulation silk bra and knickers. This time the doctor was a quite delightful old boy. He informed me that he lived in Ponsonby Place and had served in the war with a certain Gaspard Ponsonby who sounded a great character like most of our family. He recounted a few amusing stories about him and that it was so nice to see that at least some of the 'old families' still sent their daughters to Guy's to train. He never even requested me to strip. He just weighed me, for some obscure reason, and finally remarked that I looked 'perfectly fit'. He was dead right and thus Guy's and the nursing profession gained a dedicated nurse where Leicester had lost one.

Kettering was more than a little amazed when they heard my news. I had hitherto kept my trials to myself. The time to July whizzed by. They presented me with a handsome set of Spencer wells clamps. We all got pissed and having wished me luck their parting words were, 'What are we going to do for laughs when you have gone?' I was sad to leave them all. I had made some really good friends and they had been really kind and encouraging to me through a difficult time. Without their tolerance I might never have had the chance to set out on this new great adventure.

Harold and I went for a long walk on Boar's Hill near his home to discuss our future. He felt that now I was committed to Guy's for at least three years we might lose each other. This was how it did in fact turn out. If you dedicate yourself to the nursing profession full time it is almost like entering a religious order. One works all sorts of odd hours to a state of exhaustion. On time off all one wants is rest. In this state, the libido is seriously diminished. For me now it was going to be doubly difficult with the ordeal of having to travel 200 miles daily just to get to work and back, let alone all the studying that would be necessary.

Guy's was deliberately founded in the East End of London to minister to the poor and needy. We were the wonderful Bermondsey people's help and succour in times of illness. We looked after them and they in their own way looked after us. In the entire time that I was to be there I never could persuade a local taxi driver to accept his due fare. There was always a table free at local restaurants and sometimes free wine. They always seemed to recognise us and if one ever got into any bother, particularly when out at night, they would appear as if by magic to protect us. In this environment it seemed perfectly natural to dedicate one's life to them and I never regretted my doing so.

I had laid siege to the citadel of the nursing profession. At last the gates had fallen. I was about to enter with a joyous heart. I was going to make sure that both Kettering and Guy's would be proud of me.

Chapter 11

Sheep on the Line at Flitwick

Rather like before entering my prep and public schools I had been sent a list of the things needed for student nurses, like a black cardigan, black stockings and the required type of shoes. I had nametapes with Miranda Ponsonby sewn on my things as urged. I was sternly instructed to 'always' put my hair up when going on wards, etc. So when I arrived at Kettering station on the first day of the course I felt very much the new girl. I purchased an annual season ticket, which set me back £3,600 as I recall it. It was a scorching hot July day. I was wearing a thin comfortable sleeveless navy coloured dress. As it was rush hour the underground was pretty full. Hanging on to my strap I felt the curious, not unpleasant sensation, of a hand creeping up inside my dress and then my pants. I looked round sharply but, wedged as I was, it was impossible to be sure who the owner of the hand was or move away. At Moorgate a few seats became free. I sat down with relief as hand was becoming ever more intimate. A rather smart looking gentleman in a grey pinstriped suit who had been one of the people standing next to me came and sat down in the adjoining seat. He smiled and said nothing but followed me to Guy's gates. Apart from my trip to meet Marie I had not used the tube for about forty years. I was pleased to see the amenities had improved in my absence. Sadly, in the hundreds of times I was destined to travel that route during the next few years a similar incident never occurred. I can only hope that this was not due to my feminine charms diminishing!

Although we did not know it at the time, our July 1990 set was entering Guy's school of nursing at an historic moment. We were following in a long tradition stretching back more than a hundred years and one of the last groups to do so. The certain mystique of nursing still prevailed. We were aware of our part in that unbroken line. A group of experienced dedicated nurse tutors would above all train us as Guy's nurses. We would be imbued with the Guy's spirit of self-sacrifice and dedication to our patient's needs. It was run as a practical nurse's course. We would almost constantly be working on the wards as an integral and vital part of the nursing team. With the advent of Project 2000, the universities would soon take over with their lazy, inefficient ways and dedication to their own interests. In a decade, this would lead to the present crisis in the nursing profession.

All this was far from my mind as I joined the set that summer morning. There were forty of us to begin with, although the next oldest to myself soon dropped out. I always thought of her as the parachutist because she always went about with some sort of pack on her back. At any rate she suddenly disappeared and perhaps had dropped behind enemy lines. I did not recognise any of the 'thumbs up' girls but they were still predominantly the St Mary's model with a proportion of university graduates. There were even one or two boys at the less educated end of the scale. Amongst the latter's numbers I was to experience for the first time a phenomenon that I have found since almost invariably applies. Boys with homosexual tendencies are not at ease with Miranda's and indeed often openly hostile. I really don't know why this should be so. One would think that the opposite would be the case.

I made a great effort to keep as low a profile as possible and only opened my mouth when spoken to. I would try to keep this up until everyone got used to me. I was paired with a tall slim Irish girl called Maggie for a sort of 'find the lay out of Guy's' project. I came to like and trust her. Under a certain amount of duress, much later, I confided in her and never had cause to regret it. Otherwise I kept my own counsel. Looking back I am sure this was wise. People might surmise but as long as they were not sure I felt I was safer. The set as a whole were kind and friendly to me. We all got on well together and had some quite hilarious times when the opportunity arose. Two of the slightly older girls, Joy and Joan, teamed up with me on various projects that first summer. In what seemed an endless heat wave they introduced me to parts of London I didn't even know existed. I was fit, brown and happy.

The long daily journeys were tiring, but it was lovely to return to my own little country world at the end of the day after the heat, dust and racket of London. It did not hurt so badly during the long summer days. It was when the winter set in and I would find myself sometimes, when doing community nursing, in some unknown district with darkness descended. I used to feel very far from home. It was lonely returning in the pitch black to an empty house. I had never really lived on my own before. It was then that I bought the first of my beloved chows, Ming. She later even used to accompany me to London if I was to have a night out.

Her ticket cost £8 and she liked sitting in the window seat looking out at the passing countryside, much to the annoyance of the ticket collector. There was nowhere else for her as people's feet took up the space between the seats and the central gangway was too hazardous. I used to refuse to move her on the grounds that she had a ticket like everyone else. He would walk up and down complaining but did not dare to take me on. We had some adventures on the underground escalators until she got the knack of it. I used to smuggle her into the nurses' home where I would take a room for the night. If anyone heard the odd bark I would apologise for my bad cough.

The time soon came for us to start on the wards. We commenced on the psychiatric ones in York House. Maggie and I were allocated George Savage, which specialised in therapy for young adults. They were a well-educated bunch some with professional backgrounds. I particularly remember one Old Harrovian who was an accountant, I think. The unforgettable thing about York House was the ringing of the alarm bell, which was a fairly regular occurrence. It signalled a dangerous situation, usually a patient wielding a knife or similar weapon. As many nurses as possible would run to the incident and pile in to overpower the culprit by weight of numbers.

The majority of the nurses were male, whereas in the rest of the hospital, apart from A&E, male nurses were almost non-existent. This was just as well in the circumstances. It meant that Maggie and I were in constant demand as chaperones or to carry out treatment of a delicate nature on female patients. Being in their line of business the staff were intrigued by me. One was, I heard, an unfrocked catholic priest. He was amusing, urbane and particularly kind to me. I thoroughly recommend the unfrocked variety to the frocked. David Shaw, my mentor, I found a highly intelligent sensitive person. He had recently returned from the hippie trail to Kathmandu or some such place. He was much the best mentor I had in my years as a student nurse. Years later he invited me to his leaving party and it was great to see them all again. It was near Christmas and as we walked back across London Bridge on that frosty night they regaled me with tales of their patients who had jumped off the parapet into the river. It was rather like trainers recounting the deeds of the horses they had trained.

I had to deal with one incident myself. I was chatting with a young redheaded man who was feeling a bit low, after lunch one day, when a silly girl made a derogatory remark about his potency. Without any warning he suddenly set upon her and would have undoubtedly strangled her if I had not intervened. I shouted to another patient to ring the alarm bell. It took all my strength just to hold him and I was fast losing the battle when the heavy mob piled in. He was screaming with uncontrollable rage and continued to do so for a good half an hour. David debriefed him as soon as he calmed down a bit. This was the standard practice. I had got a bit knocked about myself and directly he left David he came to apologise in a concerned manner. He was quite his normal self again. I had always had a soft spot for him. He often used to come up and have a chat if he saw me round Guy's later on. Sadly, a little while ago I thought that I saw him on the television news in a police car having been charged with murder.

York House was like a tinderbox with a match nearby ready to light it. The silly girl mentioned above used to creep out at night when no one was looking and wander round the empty streets until picked up by the police. She loved the fuss they made of her. We were not allowed to lock the doors as patients had to be 'sectioned' and on special wards for this to happen. The assault seemed to knock some sense into her. I noted this in my report adding, 'more of the same recommended', but was made to alter it. I carried out a little research project on our patients concluding that three failings common in them were that they smoked too much, neglected to clean their teeth and were anti-foxhunting. On the final day of my placement, which happened to be Christmas day, I escorted several of the more sensible ones round HMS *Belfast* to try and cheer them up. The Petty Officer on the gangplank demanded £5 each. Not having enough money on me I marched them straight past him saying 'Guy's Hospital'. He saluted with a 'Carry on, Madam'. So far so good. All went well until we entered the control room where a dummy officer of the watch was sitting. My patients proceeded to 'go spare'. The sailors and I ended up chasing them round the slippery steel decks. It was a very relieved Miranda who finally returned them to base. Asked how it went I replied, 'Fine,' much to the merriment of my unruly brood.

After this it was time for us to start our first proper wards. Mine was an acute surgical one with a reputedly fierce martinet Sister. We had been measured up for our uniforms some time previously. In York House all the staff wore civilian clothes, which led to some confusion to newcomers. One often had to make snap decisions on who looked sane and who mad. It didn't do to ask the permanent staff 'what the devil they thought they were doing'. The uniforms were very smart with lilac stripes. Each year had a different coloured belt. First years were called student nurse. Second years were junior nurses and the third senior nurses. For the first week we were not allowed to wear our belts at all to denote our 'sprog' status.

Luke was an L-shaped Nightingale ward holding thirty-five patients, with three further side rooms for the most acute patients. These latter on occasions led to unexpected results. One day when I had been frantically busy 'Prof' McColl, our consultant, could not locate the nurse in charge of these. He asked me to go round them with him. On entering the first one he asked me how the patient was doing today. Not having the first idea I looked rather frantically at the bed and replied, 'He doesn't look too well.' The Prof joined me at the bedside and replied, 'I should think not, nurse. He's dead.'

On this first morning Sister Gale totally ignored us, as was the old practice at Guy's. I wandered down the ward and noted a man sitting propped up against the pillows looking very white and stiff. I went to investigate. Sister came striding down the ward at that moment and asked me what was the matter. 'He's kicked the bucket' I replied starting to draw the curtains round the bed. 'Kicked the bucket, kicked the bucket, your expressions, nurse'. She then prodded the poor man hard with her finger and he fell over sideways into my arms. It was not a very auspicious start, but she never held it against me and called me Miranda thereafter. The staff nurses giggled discreetly and thought that they might be in for some fun with me on the ward.

It was a strange coincidence that a second Sister Gale was going to prove to have a decisive influence on my nursing career. She used to carry out a daily teaching session round the nurse's station, which was positioned at the point of the L in the middle of the ward. Originally females were down one side and males down the other. Now they were sometimes mixed depending on demand for beds. The patients seemed perfectly happy with this arrangement and, when asked, usually said that they preferred it. It did put an extra emphasis on ensuring patient privacy, but over all improved the ward atmosphere. On these teaching sessions, questions were fired at us and by a stroke of good fortune I usually managed a correct answer. An aged, retired Guy's Sister who was one of my patients further enhanced my standing in her eyes. I did not realise this but apparently she used to report on her nursing care to Sister. My efforts were classed as 'good proper old fashioned nursing', thanks probably to my Clipston and Kettering experience. Also, whilst in charge of the side rooms, I looked after Lady McColl, the Prof's wife, and got on well with her. Later she was to take an interest in my career. All this goodwill was to prove vital to me.

I enjoyed a happy relationship with the staff nurses and they used to like me to join them on their outings. I thus would find myself singing 'Crazy for you' at a karaoke down the Old Kent road or attempting to pass muster dancing to that catchy tune 'Having a gang-bang up against the wall' at the Hippodrome. One of their favourite watering holes was a sort of steak house with telephones on all the tables. Young executive types in lightweight suits with belts and no turn-ups on the trousers used to frequent the place in small groups. They would all ring each other up and have no end of fun. We also used to go to a club where everybody, rather curiously, seemed to be celebrating just having been granted a divorce.

Our set had elected me their representative on the student council, which had somewhat allayed my insecurity. In that capacity I was requested to organise a small party to sell raffle tickets at the British Heart Foundation ball at the Dorchester. I managed to press gang a rather fizzy group of student nurses known as the Forest Hill Mob who all shared an old rambling place in Forest Hill. We duly turned up in full fig with capes. I sat them down amongst the Arabs and ordered afternoon tea as we were all hungry and thirsty having been on early shifts. No sooner had this been put before us than the organiser hurried up and said that we had not got time 'for that'. We were spirited away to a briefing and, by the time it was completed and we had been handed our buckets and red dots, the guests started arriving. They were very much the 'Beautiful People' thirties to forties in age with an air of my old polo fraternity about them. As we sold the tickets we had to stick on a red dot to designate who had already bought them. We collected buckets and buckets full of money. After an hour or two of this, we began to flag. They would not even allow us a glass of the champagne that was flowing. It was an awful long time since breakfast, and I went to try and organise the meal that we had been promised. Disconcertingly, I was confronted by Ann Chiesman whose husband, Tony, had been my Life Guard squadron leader at Knightsbridge. I knew her very well, but fortunately she did not recognise me. She asked me to sell some more raffle tickets to the guests at her table while she enquired about our meal. I recognised the actor, Nigel Havers, without a dot on. As he entered his name and address in my book he commented, ' I am afraid my signature is rather strange, but no stranger than the nurse selling me the ticket'.

Ann returned with the bad news that no meal had been arranged for us. The Forest Hill Mob had in the meantime palled up with a strange-looking, carrot-headed chap, complete with two minders, they said was Boy George. On hearing our plight he generously arranged a room and a quite splendid repast for us all. We then went back to listen to the cabaret performed by Fascinating Aida. A speech was made thanking all and sundry. We were not even mentioned. My girls had by this time got a bit tipsy, bless their little hearts, and were joining in the dancing. They told me Boy George was going to return them to Forest Hill later, so I left and was charged £25 by the hotel car park. I eventually got home a bit the worse for wear and told Ming a few home truths about the British Heart Foundation.

The big annual sporting event was the Hospitals' Rugger Cup, which I had not attended since my brother, John, had captained the winning team. Guy's had fallen off a bit since those halcyon days and St Mary's seemed, since J P R Williams' time there, to monopolise it. It was still great fun and there were some other events celebrating it. The Forest Hill Mob, who had become firm friends since our outing, inveigled me into taking part in a mixed hockey match. I found an old weapon in the attic, which I had not used since my school days. I donned my old army PT shorts and trotted on to the field in what I imagined was the approved manner. As I passed the referee or umpire or whatever he was called he gave me a searching look and said to the opposition captain 'I have heard of mixed hockey but this is ridiculous,' which rather took the wind out of my sails.

The Guy's Ball was the great social event of the year. It was held at the Grosvenor House Hotel in Park Lane, where we held our regimental dinner in the old days and was a splendid occasion. I went with our set every year and danced away the night as I had done there on so many happy occasions as a young officer forty years before. It was almost like reincarnation and being given a second chance at youth's heady wine. I just wished I had been Miranda at that age and experienced the joy of being young and really beautiful. At least I did not have to struggle with a halter neck dress in those days. It was a Guy's tradition that we showed ourselves on our wards in all our finery before setting off. That first year I simply could not get the blinking thing done up at the back so as it was getting late I slipped my cape over the top and dashed up to the ward. Sister viewed me with awe as I removed my cape. 'What magnificent shoulders' she remarked as she did me up at the back. My female patients were duly appreciative, but the men with remarks like 'Here comes magnificent shoulders' or 'How are the shoulders, nurse?' greeted me for days afterwards.

Luke ward specialised in bowel and arterial surgery. The Prof was one of the leading laser surgeons in the country, if not *the* leading one. Our patients were comforted by the knowledge that that they were in the very best hands. That was one of the features of Guy's. Every department had top people in charge. Yet they were most attentive to their patients and daily ward rounds were the order of the day. One must bear in mind also that Prof was private secretary to the Prime Minister at the same time, hence his peerage, but his patients came first. This was the Guy's ethic and we all abided by it.

I was introduced into the wonders of stoma land and cholecystectomies. Every hour one seemed to be learning some new skill. Everyone was out to help and instruct one. This was the great and wonderful difference of being a student nurse as opposed to an auxiliary one. I nursed my first terminally ill cancer patient through to the end. This may sound a sad and depressing task, but it is not. It is at the very core of one's nursing psyche. One draws incredibly close to them as you both prepare for the end. You are the person they confide in as you are with them so constantly carrying out intimate tasks. Very often words are not necessary. It is just the presence of the person they know so well and have shared so much with they need. How they have lived is important but how they die is too. They decide when it is time to go. You both know this and you can feel them go even if your eyes are not on them at that moment. You also build a very close relationship with the family. This can be most rewarding also. One might shed a tear or two in private, and it must be in private, but it is an inspiring time and why one is a nurse.

The other side of the coin is motivating someone to survive when there is still hope. One can play an enormous part in this and it is a major role for the nurse and one that I do feel I have developed a particular aptitude for, or possibly was born with it. The hope of helping to achieve this is why I look forward to going to work in the morning. I had one such patient before I left Luke. She was a wonderful old cockney lady. She had an extraordinary experience at the end of the war. Her younger son had always been very close to her and lived with her before being called up into the RAF in 1939. His troopship docked in Southampton one morning in 1945. He telephoned her to tell her to get his room ready as he hoped to be home for lunch. He never appeared and she never heard from him again. She made dozens of enquiries over the years but there was never any trace. The RAF were equally baffled. He never was demobbed. She always expected and hoped that he would knock on the door one fine day. She lived down Jamaica Road by the docks and had lost her home and all her possessions three times in the blitz. She and I formed a very close bond and by the time that I left Luke she had improved. She was very upset when I was saying goodbye and the nurses told me later that without me she had given up hope and died. I have always remembered her clearly amongst the hundreds of dear people I have nursed who pass across my mind in an endless stream sometimes when I am lying in bed at night.

It was sad leaving Luke. Sister gave me a very good report saying how good it was to see someone with such enthusiasm for nursing and how my high spirits had a beneficial effect on the whole of her ward. This was just as well, as Maggie and I were next placed on a geriatric ward called Addison. In charge was a young newly promoted Sister who was rather stressed. She did not approve of these very same high spirits and my mentor was a Senior Staff Nurse prone to black moods. She found fault with everything I did and eventually a nurse tutor from the school was sent to monitor my progress. There could even have been a bit more to it than that as I had overheard an old boy on the ward say to Senior Staff Nurse, 'That nurse has a voice like a man.' The tutor spent a day with me and a couple of my dear old cockney ladies came to my rescue. When she thought that I was out of earshot I heard her ask them if they minded having their legs pulled. 'We love it,' they replied. 'We love it. It's so nice to see a nurse with a smile on her face.' Since that time I have often heard patients discussing their nurses. They almost invariably they say either, 'She's lovely, always has a smile on her face,' or, conversely, 'I do wish she would smile sometimes,'

Fate took a hand next in the guise of one of my old York House patients. There is a tunnel that runs for miles under the hospital connecting the various parts. It is dark in places and really spooky, particularly at night. My senior staff nurse was on the way along it to the Guy's swimming pool one evening when by the bottom of the York House lift shaft she was assaulted and raped. She was away for a bit on sick leave but when she returned she was all sweetness and light and I even began to find favour in her eyes. There must be a moral somewhere in this story!

Sister Gale was known to be very demanding of her students. Until shortly before my placement, they were even made to take their breaks in one of the patient's bathrooms rather than in the staff room with the rest of the nurses. She had a reputation for panning students if they did not live up to her high standards. Therefore the fact that I had found such favour with her carried a lot of weight. It is quite possible that this was pointed out to my Addison Sister. At any rate, I never experienced any further difficulty.

Queen was my next ward. This was an orthopaedic ward and with my previous experience at Kettering I got on really well and was credited with possibly saving a twenty-year-old girl by spotting a deep vein thrombosis early. From my first day the staff kept mentioning what I thought was 'baloney amputations'. I assumed that these were so named after a distinguished Italian surgeon. It must have been the best part of a week before I enquired about him in a ward handover meeting. I was more than baffled to be greeted with gales of laughter until I discovered that it was 'below knee amputations'.

Queen also sported a plastic surgery unit. I found this a fascinating speciality. I looked after a young motorway surveyor who had been inadvertently dragged along by a mud-sweeper vehicle. The whole of his side had been scraped away and was being patiently rebuilt. I had to dress his wounds thrice daily. Each time this took over an hour. It was almost miraculous how well he healed and I heard later that he made a complete recovery. Being young and fit obviously assisted this.

It was whilst doing night duty on this ward that I first saw one of the famous Guy's ghosts. I was in the drug cupboard doing a stock check with one of the staff nurses in the early hours of the morning. The cupboard was situated in a passage leading from the outside door to the ward door proper. We both noticed this white figure gliding along the passage past our cupboard. We checked with the nurse on the desk just inside the ward. Nobody had entered the ward. I can only suppose that the memories of over two centuries are not easily disposed of.

Also on Queen we carried out some outpatient treatment. One morning a tall slim glamorous looking girl brought in her mother for me to treat. At the conclusion of this she asked if she could have a private word with me. I took her into one of the side rooms, which happened to be empty at the time, expecting that it was to do with her mother. I was taken a back when she asked me when I had had my sex change operation and were Guy's good about it? I rather stalled a bit until she said that she had also changed at a young age. Mr Harrod had also carried out her operation. Someone later told me that she was a well-known fashion model. She had succeeded in an equally female profession to my own of nursing and been judged in it by her female physical attributes. She was intrigued when I replied that I was not sure whether Guy's knew about me or not. Her transformation had obviously been so dramatic as it had been carried out at such a young age. Mr Harrod had told me about this. I still could not see anything but a beautiful girl standing before me. It was amazing. Her voice and all her mannerisms were so feminine. She invited me to dine with her one evening in Decima Street and gave me a card with her telephone number on it. I regret now that I never accepted the offer fearing something might get about at Guy's. It was another time when I suffered a pang at what might have been if only I had changed at her age. Also at my more advanced time of life I had found it impossible to throw off certain ingrained male habits like standing back to allow a lady to go through a door first, standing up when they entered a room and opening the car door for them. Another quite different habit I couldn't break was grabbing hold of the front seat passenger in my car when breaking sharply or going round a hairpin bend. This of course from the time when my own children were small and before the use of seat belts and infant seats. This latter habit led to some very startled reactions sometimes!

Another male characteristic that would never be suppressed is best illustrated by an incident that happened around this time at St Pancras station one night after a late shift. My train home was scheduled to depart at ten o'clock. I was a bit pushed and hurrying along the winding tunnel that leads up to my platform when confronted by two black youths who demanded my brief case and tried to grab it. In it I always carried my handbag and all my little treasures. Instinctively I lashed out at one of them punching him hard on the nose. He fell with blood pouring out of him and a surprised look on his face. His accomplice ran up the far platform stairs thinking that I was pursuing him. I was, however, intent only on catching my train and ran up the nearer stairs. He was looking back over his shoulder when we ran full tilt into each other at the top. We both bit the dust from the force of the impact. It is the only time that I have witnessed a black face turned ashen white. I picked myself up and sprinted along the platform just jumping on the departing train. As I sat down panting I suddenly saw the funny side of the affair and couldn't stop laughing much to the surprise of the other passengers. I scanned *The Daily Telegraph* on the train journey back the following morning half expecting to see some heading like 'Nurse slays Black' but nothing ever appeared.

In between these ward placements we would spend the odd week in the school. In charge of our set was a Guy's Sister named Isobel Hancock. It was rumoured that she had theatrical connections. She liked us to put on presentations and little shows to improve our communication skills. Maggie, Joan, Joy and myself devised a number entitled 'A rough guide to Guy's'. This was a skit on a current television programme by a certain Miranda Devine, if I remember it correctly. I dressed up in a sort of Hawaiian outfit with a grass skirt and a brightly coloured scarf round my bosom. The others were similarly clad. I was announced as 'Divine Miranda' when I entered to the 'Rough Guide' theme tune and delighted applause and laughter. Isobel was 'tickled pink' by this and our little number. This stood me in good stead later when something potentially hazardous occurred during our first Christmas holidays. We joined the traditional Guy's carol singing round the wards and set off home quite like a bunch of schoolgirls at the end of term. The carol singing in itself I found a profoundly moving experience. We wore our capes turned inside out with the red side showing, over our uniforms, carrying flaming torches. All the lights were turned out in each ward as we approached singing and processed down the entire length of the old Nightingale wards and back out again. It presented the most beautiful scene and one very sick old girl told me later that she thought she had gone to heaven already. We even crossed the snow-covered park to the private block. Our efforts there were not so well received. Most of the rooms seemed to be occupied by groups of Arabs sitting cross-legged on the floor. They shot us frightened looks as if we were the Janissaries come to take them away.

As she bade us goodbye Isobel strictly forbade us to work in the holidays, as this was a school rule. They considered that we needed the rest. It certainly had been a packed six months with so much to assimilate both on the wards and in the school. Adam, however, recommended me to the British Nursing Agency who begged me to go and look after a gentleman living in the dukeries to the north of Nottingham. His awkward daughter had, for the umpteenth time, caused the nurse to depart. Over Christmas it had proved impossible to find a replacement. I was on my own at Christmas and needed the money badly, so I agreed, provided I could take Ming along too.

We set off in a snowstorm, but made it to the foot of the long drive up to the old mansion itself, which proved too slippery to ascend. I knocked on the door of the gate lodge. I was greeted with 'My goodness, Madam, you look like a snowman. They are expecting you up at the house. We will take you up in the land rover, your car will be garaged and the luggage put in your room.' So I grabbed snowman number two, Ming, and we were duly escorted into my new patient's presence in a vast hall with a great log fire burning and crackling in the old fireplace. He was a solidly built old boy suffering from multiple sclerosis. He and Ming immediately hit it off well and I only hoped that I would, too. I was certainly needed. His mobility was seriously restricted and it took our combined efforts about an hour to get down from his bedroom to the dining room in the morning and about the same to return at night. We had to travel along freezing passages, up great staircases and round galleries in the course of our journey. He refused the use of a wheelchair fearing that he would seize up altogether if he didn't keep going.

On Christmas day his daughter and a few family members came for lunch. I could understand why her reputation for being awkward had been gained. It was not a very jolly affair and I could see that my charge was depressed and bored. After the guests had departed I hatched a plot with the butler and chauffeur. I had already found out that my patient loved going to the races but had not been out of the house for a long time. We planned that if the weather relented we would go to Kempton Park on Boxing Day for the King George steeplechase. That Christmas evening the patient and I set about a decanter of his finest port in the glow of the log fire with the wind and snow buffeting the battlements outside. We finally travelled north to his bedroom in great good humour singing songs learnt in the Officer's Messes of our long lost youth such as 'On the banks of the Nile stood the Sergeant in waiting', and 'High ho Jerusalem'. When I had finally tucked him in bed he gave a contented sigh saying 'What a lovely Christmas.'

On the morrow he was thrilled to learn that racing was on down south and that provided he used his wheelchair we would go. Martin, the chauffer, brought the ancient Rolls round to the front door and we piled him in with a brandy flask, field glasses, rug and some smoked salmon sandwiches. James, the butler, sat in the front with Martin and we two sat in some style in the luxurious back. I managed to get us into the member's enclosure and laid bets as requested. Quite a few old chums of his came to talk to him and it was a thoroughly successful outing. From then on we went out every afternoon.

On the day of my departure the old boy thanked me for giving him such a good time and said, 'You are a remarkable woman, Miranda, I only wish that you didn't have to leave me.'

When I returned to Guy's I received an ominous request to see Isobel 'at once'. I went up to her office with a heavy heart, as I knew it must be something serious. Apparently the awkward daughter had rung up in a rage about me. Isobel told me that she had cut her short telling her that she was not prepared to discuss one of her student nurses and had put the telephone down. What was said I shall never know. I received a dressing down for working on my holidays when expressly forbidden not to, but that she would overlook it this time. I was mightily relieved and even more so when I gathered later that the daughter had discovered my real identity on the foxhunting grapevine. It just showed how careful I had still got to be.

At the completion of our first year we had to sit our first exam. I never found these very easy, as education had moved on since my day. It was no good just answering the questions correctly. One had to fathom what they wanted to hear and phrase the answer in the approved formula. Fortunately I passed, but some others did not and our set was further reduced. It was around this time that we went out on the district. This increased my daily journey as having reached London Bridge I then had to catch yet another local train to Ladywell near Lewisham. It was not an inspiring placement. All the District Nurses seemed to do was treat ulcers and take blood tests on diabetics if they had anytime left from trying to work their newly introduced pocket computers. These were meant to record their every move. So we would spend hours sitting in their car whilst they tried to fiddle the answers. Like nearly all time and motion studies the end result was more time and less motion.

The Health Visitors were even more of a waste of time. These worthies really preferred sitting in their offices drinking cups of coffee, and pretty poor coffee at that, bemoaning their work overload. When we did ever venture out few would answer their doorbells. One would just notice some old Arab peering out of the top floor window. The only people who did let us in were the unmarried mothers on state benefits. We were meant to check that they were indeed depending on these to keep body and soul together. In fact, of course, they invariably were living with a fellow and it did not require the skills of a Scotland Yard detective to see evidence of his recent presence. On pointing this out I was informed that no action could be instigated unless we found him on the premises. This was unlikely as they had prior notification of our arrival, so that at least the social worker could report that she had seen a client.

The midwives did seem busy but we always dealt with pre and postnatal cases and I didn't see a baby born in anger during my entire time spent with them. What I did see were some rum old parts of London. It was on these junketings that I would find myself stranded in some outlandish place on winter evenings with never a taxi to be found. It then developed into an initiative test to find one's way back to London Bridge or St Pancras. How I longed at these moments to be already at home with Ming sharing some crumpets in front of my warm cheerful fire. There were times even when I would wonder what the dickens I was doing being there at all!

My constant travelling was terribly draining on my energy levels. If I was on an early shift I had to rise at quarter past four in the morning and if on a late shift I did not get home until after eleven at night. The trains were still under British Rail then, but I found them no better than today. At the slightest hitch or sign of severe weather they seemed to take a delight in providing a wayward service. At that time there were frequent IRA bomb scares and one would be stranded at all sorts of odd places miles from one's destination. I was even involved in one 'bomb scare'. At the end of our stint of seven night shifts, it was a pleasant Guy's custom for the shift to all go out to breakfast together. We would usually choose some quite swanky place. That morning we went to the Waldorf Hotel in the Aldwich. Having enjoyed a smashing and convivial meal we departed on our separate ways home. On getting to the top of the underground stairs, I suddenly realised that I had left my treasured briefcase behind by the table. By the time I got back it had already triggered an emergency and the front door was cordoned off. I ignored this and as I entered the hotel I heard the crowd that had gathered say, 'It's a nurse, it's a nurse, isn't she brave?' I went straight to my case and before anyone could react I grabbed it and departed scattering the crowd who presumably thought I was in imminent danger of exploding. I nipped down the underground and that bomb scare was over and my case had had a lucky escape.

About the only good thing about train travel, apart from the opportunity to study, was the breakfast after night duty. One took this in the first class dining carriage. It was a really good old-fashioned spread and I could just finish it by the time the train drew in to Kettering station. It temporally revived me enough to keep awake during the journey and obviate the tiresome risk of ending up in Crewe or somewhere. Even the quaint little excuses British Rail delighted in to explain delays such as 'sheep on the line at Flitwick' did not faze me on these occasions. I just tucked into a second helping of eggs and bacon.

Chapter 12

Guy's and Dolls

At the end of our first year we swapped our white belts for lilac ones and started in the operating theatres. These formed an enclosed world of their own. On entering the area we had to go to the changing rooms to put on theatre 'blues'. These consisted of rather tight blue cotton dresses. We were allocated lockers to keep our own kit in and there was the minimum of arm room to effect the change in. The room always seemed to be seething with naked girls. I found it a very ticklish business to wriggle into my dress without dislodging my wig and even worse to get out of it again. Fortunately everyone else was too busy hurrying into their own things to take much notice of my struggles. There was just the odd 'Get a move on Miranda or we'll be late'. On our first morning we were allocated theatres. Mine specialised in breast surgery, mainly biopsies, removal of malignant breast lumps and glands under the arms up to full mastectomies. The Sister was supposed to be a bit of a terror and there had been a number of complaints by students about her treatment of them, which had resulted in their transfer to other theatres. She was Chinese and had been at Guy's for many years and was nearing retirement age. I got on quite well with her probably because I wasn't cowed by her. I came to like her and she used to pick me out in the theatre canteen and sit with me.

We donned facemasks and pink caps to denote our student status before entering the theatre 'scrub' room. Sister had suffered a 'shunt' in her car recently causing whiplash injury so we were shoved straight into the 'scrub nurse' role. Lee, my fellow student, and I therefore took alternate patients with Sister at our side until we got the hang of it. Lee very quickly became competent, but I am not sure that I really ever did. The job of the 'scrub nurse' was to directly assist the surgeon by handing him the correct instrument as requested and account for everything used in the operation to avoid a foreign body being left in the patient. We had been coached in the names of the various instruments, but often different surgeons would have their own pet names. Also it was difficult to hear what they said through their facemasks. If one ever made a mistake one got shouted at and called some rather uncomplimentary names. I think this was because the surgeon himself was keyed up. We even had one little Indian who had her own type of small instruments. These had to be specially autoclaved so they could be used again. She ended up pointing out to me the instrument she wanted next.

'Scrubbing up' in itself was a long tedious process and my arms used to get sore after a long day scrubbing them again and again. When scrubbed one put on a sterile gown and gloves and woe betide one if one touched anything unsterile. This entailed starting the procedure all over again. This also applied if an instrument was accidentally dropped in the theatre. The surgeons seemed a very hairy breed and being as hair harbours germs they cannot have been as sterile as their nurses. Our great allies were the ODAs (operation department assistants). They were mostly army men 'moonlighting' and well trained and experienced. They came to our assistance whenever we got in a jam.

We were warned that if at first we felt faint viewing surgery we must look away and take deep breaths. It would be a black mark against us if we passed out. I found that I was always so busy when in the theatre that I never thought about it. The only time that I did feel decidedly woozy was when I cut my finger deeply when removing a scalpel blade from the handle whilst cleaning the blood off the instruments post operation. Luckily I was alone in the sluice or it would have entailed going to occupational health and filling up all sorts of forms in case I had picked up some infection or other. As it was I hung on to the sink and just put my finger under the running tap in the approved manner.

At the end of each operation we accompanied our patient and the anaesthetist to Recovery and handed over the patient. The recovery staff were a particularly spirited bunch. I enjoyed my time on their ward because of this but found the work very routine. The only excitement concerned dental patients of whom there were quite a few, Guy's having the foremost dental school in the country. The dental surgeons still used an anaesthetic called ketamine. This caused the poor patients to become violent as they came to. It sometimes needed three or four of us to hold them down.

Life in the theatres tended to be a bit claustrophobic, as we could not leave the area in our break without changing out of our blues. I could not face this battle an extra time. I did once borrow a doctor's long white coat to cover my dress but was greeted everywhere with remarks like 'How's that?' and 'Give him out LBW, Miranda.' I suppose that I should have borrowed his stethoscope as well and with that round my neck I might have resembled a cricket umpire less.

My next placement was on Victoria, a maternity ward. I had been looking forward to this as I imagined it might be as satisfying as my years calving my beloved cows had been. It was not. One was closeted for hours on end with mostly unlovable, moaning women. Even the delivery never gave me the buzz I had experienced on the successful birth of a little calf. Those first few moments of life had always been so precious to the mother and me. Now I had to cope with the silly modern arrangement of a fainting father or one offering gratuitous advice. I quickly came to the conclusion that my cows were a lot more sensible mothers than their human equivalent. They were always so helpful and I felt we made a great team. The mechanics of the delivery were almost identical, so I suppose my vast experience was useful, but that was about as far as it went. We certainly could have done with a foetal monitor in our calving boxes.

The exact opposite applied on my next ward. This was the paediatric cardiac ward. I found this work immensely rewarding and all my skill acquired rearing calves came into play. It was even pure luck that I went to Rothschild ward. I had been given the handicapped children's ward, but the girl due to go to Rothschild thought it would be too heartbreaking and asked me if I would swap. Our main job was to nurse the babies to sufficient strength so that they could undergo lifesaving surgery. These were very sick babies indeed. They mostly started on naso-gastric tube feeding. We gradually weaned them off this on to bottle-feeding of milk. This took infinite patience and there were many setbacks along the way. One built up a close bond with the baby and this helped them to respond to our coaxing. It was such a joy when coming on duty and going up to the cot to receive that little smile of recognition.

I cared for one baby during my entire time on Rothschild. His name was Lenny. His mother was very young. She was a sweet girl and we got on really well.

Week after week he gradually gained strength. He always reserved a particularly lovely little smile for me and quietened in my arms. Sister told me that Lenny responded best of all to me. This made me very proud. Lenny and I even appeared on the six o'clock news one evening. An MP named Emma Nicholson had rescued a badly burnt Kurdish boy who was on the ward. She had brought along a BBC camera crew to publicise the plight of the Kurdish people who were being bombed by Sadam Hussein at the close of the Gulf War. They wandered round the ward with the camera and had a word or two with me, holding Lenny in my arms. I learnt later that Lenny had finally made the theatre but was close to death on leaving it. His mother picked him up and said 'Don't leave me, Lenny, don't leave me' whereupon he rallied miraculously and spent two days with her before dying peacefully in her arms. He will always have a very special place in my old nurse's heart.

We had a brilliant young paediatric cardiac surgeon called Anderson. He gave so many of our babies a future. The Rothschild nursing staff backed him up magnificently. They were a really fine team and it was an honour to have worked with them. The months I spent on their ward were amongst the most memorable of my time at Guy's.

Time raced by and our second year came to an end with yet another exam. It was a great relief to get through this and win my senior nurse's purple belt, but I was sad again to lose more of our set. It certainly was a very demanding course. We began our final year with the biggest learning curve of all, Accident and Emergency. The Guy's casualty department was a very busy one indeed. During my time at Guy's they even had a major IRA bomb incident at London Bridge station to cope with. In the event, although there were many flying glass injuries, fatalities were mercifully few.

A retired RAMC Major General who had served in the Falklands campaign ran the department. He introduced some innovative practices gleaned from his experience there. The one I particularly remember was the use of polythene bags to cover burns. This kept the wound clean whilst allowing the hands or feet to keep moving preventing them from becoming atrophied. The benefits of this had apparently been discovered by chance, as in battle they were the only things available to dress the high proportion of burns from the Argentine Exocet missile strikes.

Guy's being in the East End, a rough area, we dealt with many gunshot wounds. These were a fast growing phenomenon. In the past these would apparently have mainly been knife wounds. It was surprising how many of the poor beleaguered Metropolitan Police were on the receiving end of these. It was about this time that I became aware of the close bond that exists between policemen and nurses. I was the beneficiary of this special relationship later on. One winter evening on the way to go on night duty, as I set off round Regent's Park in my trusty old Ford cabriolet I was aware of a blue flashing light behind me. I stopped wondering what they wanted with me. A policeman alighted from his car and paced menacingly to my car door. I was informed that I was doing sixty miles per hour past St John's Wood barracks in a thirty mile an hour area. He produced a book from his pocket and requested me to get out of the car. When he recognised my uniform his whole attitude altered. 'I see you are a Guy's nurse, madam. Be careful in future,' he said, pocketing his book again and I continued on my merry way. Of course, I had no idea what speed I was travelling at. I did the long journey so constantly that I motored along in 'Auto-Pilot' and often on reaching my destination I had no recollection of the journey at all.

On our first day on casualty, Maggie suffered one of those incidents that happen to all nurses sooner or later. She was told to ring up the son of a lady that had died in one of the cubicles. He duly arrived and she showed him into the cubicle saying how sorry she was. To their amazement his mother was sitting up reading *The Daily Mail*. To his credit he saw the funny side and it was their laughter that I heard in the adjoining cubicle. Apparently the dead lady had the same rather unusual surname and was lying in the cubicle on the other side. This incident appealed to the sense of humour of the A&E staff. A kind of black humour helps keep nurses sane.

Daily we saw some terrible things. None more tragic than the little golden-haired toddler who was admitted one day just as we were about to go off night duty. He had been staying with his grandparents who had pushed twin beds together up against the wall to try and avoid him falling out of bed. He had somehow got his little head jammed between the bed and the wall and was all but suffocated. On his arrival we waged a desperate battle to revive him, but it was just too late.

The mortuary staff have this same black humour honed to almost an art form. We spent a day there early in our course watching post mortems. I found it the finest way to learn anatomy. Guy's has the most famous forensic medicine department in the world. In the medical school galleries are the most infamous murder exhibits in our recent history. It is a quite fascinating place. Bearing in mind the nature of their daily work I suppose one should excuse the staff their little fun, but even we found it a bit over the top.

The casualty department was a very restless place to work. Even in the staff room when one was having a break there was a constant stream of policemen, ambulance drivers, and paramedics coming and going day and night. They all seemed to smoke like chimneys too. I also found the homosexual members of the permanent staff a bit hostile to me as usual. Dealing with the patients one was confronted with violent drunks and deranged individuals. It was a common occurrence to get 'clocked', knowing that it was not considered cricket to retaliate in kind. Also, patients who had endured a long wait for treatment could get abusive.

There was a surprising amount of girls with abdominal pains. We gave them all a pregnancy test on admission and almost invariably the one's who said that they could not be pregnant were and vice versa. I saw so many girl's private parts I became quite dizzy! On examination there never seemed much wrong with any of them and they were quickly discharged. They also provided most of the overdoses and stomach pumpings. The latter was not a pleasant task, but I became quite adept at it.

On the plus side, we learnt a colossal amount about dressing serious wounds of all sort, removing stitches and dealing with broken limbs. Also it was good to work with so many of our own set as opposed to being all split up on different wards. They were a really nice bunch and I became fond of them all and enjoyed their company.

The Casualty Sisters and the majority of the staff nurses were very friendly, as were the Casualty doctors. The latter were young and lively like most of the junior Guy's medics. On night duty one heard their wild parties round the hospital. This carousing would go on into the night. One night they even chucked a piano out of the window, which went through the conservatory roof below with an almighty crash. Fortunately it was uninhabited at the time. Some of the more daring girls in our set attended a few of these, but said they were lucky to escape intact. They preferred taking advantage of the free tickets that most of the West End theatres generously sent round and were posted on the notice board in Henrietta Raphael (the nurse's home). Most of our set lived in Henrietta Raphael and had their own social life there. It was quite a matey place but none too comfortable, and rather a throwback to a more Spartan age.

I found my time on A&E the most exciting placement during my training. It is the shop window of a hospital and at the same time its engine room. Most of the acute cases come through it. Even the DOAs (Dead on Arrival) pull up to at its doors and are first seen by the Casualty Sisters. By the end of my stint there I began to feel a competent nurse for the first time.

I was given a choice of wards next. I chose Stephen, which was part of a cardiac unit with its own cardiac catheter theatre. My experience on Rothschild had fuelled my interest in this speciality. I was not disappointed and it was the start of a career-long learning curve in this type of nursing. We were indeed fortunate to have one of the leading cardiologists as our consultant. Dr Sowton had pioneered many of the techniques now so widely used. He was also an extremely nice man, never too busy to explain some procedure one was carrying out. This applied to his patients also. I was on duty on Christmas day every year that I was at Guy's and he made that last one as a student the best. He bought all our patients a present and accompanied his team round the ward handing them out. The younger doctors were dressed as fairies, shepherds and even a Father Christmas. I brought in some bottles of Buck's Fizz and we all sat down for lunch in one of the side rooms. Dr Sowton had brought a magnificent turkey and carved it himself. With the snow falling gently outside, the paper hats and the crackers in the old Hunt's House ward, it was quite a Dickensian scene

Hunt's House was the last of the old hospital buildings and ran along the side of the Guy's park. The only new part were the stairs, which had been burnt down at the height of the wartime blitz. The great benefit for me was being able to nip out at breaks and sit in the park to enjoy a cream bun from the Guy's tuck shop. All my working life had been spent in the open air and I began to feel like a caged bird when shut up indoors all day.

I made two long lasting friendships on Stephen. Junet Rogerson, one of the staff nurses, had her roots in the Lancashire cotton mills. She was great fun with a heart of gold. I have found these qualities in others with that same background. They are straight talking and extrovert characters. Nothing seems to get them down. Perhaps that is what it took to survive in the old mill towns. Junet was ever the Gracie Fields character and, as such, a wonderful nurse.

Sarah June Mead was a student in a set senior to mine. She was from a totally different background to Junet, but equally good company. She was more the archetypal Guy's nurse mentioned before. She was well educated and intelligent, with all the most important qualities of a fine nurse in compassion and an impish sense of humour. She has gone far in the profession and is now a Great Ormond Street cardio-thoracic Sister.

The three of us were on duty that New Year's Eve and we saw the New Year in together with every patient we could get out of bed. As the hour tolled, we all linked arms around the nurse's station and Stephen echoed to the strains of 'Auld Lang Sine'. I seem to remember Sarah June's future husband, Paul, was one of our company. After more celebrations we escorted the patients that had survived back to bed! In my long life I don't remember entering the gates of a brave new year in better style.

For me this comradeship in shared times of happiness and sadness too has been one of the great blessings of my nursing. The hard lonely years on the farm just dropped away and I regained that joy in life that I had in abundance as a young Guard's officer in my salad days. Nurses are a lovely group of girls just as I had found my fellow officers such splendid chaps. I count myself so fortunate to have lived amongst them both for at least part of my life.

A friend and I used to play a betting game on the underground journey from St Pancras to London Bridge. We called it 'spot the Guy's nurse'. Even in a crowded carriage I seldom made a mistake and it became 'a nice little earner'. There was a certain quality in them that stood out from the crowd. Just as I suppose there might be in me when we heard a little cockney tell his pall 'It's a geezer.' Much to my chagrin. in certain quarters I was thereafter known as Nurse Geezer.

We had a young patient called Bill in end-stage heart failure on Stephen. He could be abusive and difficult. but I gradually struck up a close relationship with him and he eventually softened towards me. His one great pleasure in life was smoking a Woodbine. I found a little tobacconist near Guy's that stocked them and used to bring him in packets of them. In spite of being very ill. he always insisted on reimbursing me for these. He was meticulous in calculating what he owed me. It was most touching. One evening I was in the drug cupboard over the far side of the ward from his bed when he finally died. At that moment I knew that he had gone. It was almost as if I felt him leave his body. It was a wonderful feeling of release that he was at last winging away from all his anguish on his way to paradise. His death affected the ward in a way that I have not experienced again. Yet he had incessantly cursed and shouted at us all in his pain and grief, poor Bill.

There was a quite extensive Turkish community living near Guy's and I first became aware of a phenomenon peculiar to their women whilst on Stephen. I found them very pleasant people and this finding has been reinforced when I visited their beautiful country recently. As a child I also remember hearing from an ancient warrior relative of mine that they were brave and chivalrous foes at Gallipoli. All that being so, their women do get monumentally constipated – and when I say monumentally, I mean it. I have since developed a technique to deal with this that involves the use of a hoist. In the interests of delicacy I will not go into the details. Suffice it to say that it is Miranda's contribution to the onward march of medical science. Perhaps even one day it will be known as 'Miranda's condition' if it could be translated into Turkish.

Before I left Stephen something happened that was almost like stepping back in time for me. Since my earliest days I had heard from Nanny that she was going to visit her brother Fred and his wife Irene in Rotherhithe on her days off. It was like background music to my life. My brother, John, and I had heard of their struggles during the depression before the war, of the dangers that they had suffered during the blitz and on to the dock strike when the army had been called in and the post-war years. I had never met either of them or had the faintest notion of where Rotherhithe was. I suppose that I had pictured them in my mind. Nanny had told us that he was a foreman engineer at the docks and that he wore a bowler hat. At the start of my last week on Stephen I was admitting a patient called Irene Sales when, suddenly, the penny dropped as to who she might be. She had obviously heard about us throughout all those years too. Now I could not say who I was, which was a bit tragic for me.

Irene looked exactly as I had always imagined her, and of course Rotherhithe and the docks were in the Guy's 'patch'. I looked after her for that week and heard so much about myself and family and, of course, dear Nanny herself. It was a very precious week for me. I hoped that perhaps I had been able to repay a tiny fraction of the great debt that we owed our beloved Nanny. Someone told me that Irene died a few days later.

Dr Sowton had a rule that before he would undertake long-term treatment of cardiac patients they had to sign an Affidavit undertaking never to smoke again. I suppose that he felt that that treatment would be nullified if they continued to smoke. He apparently told them that the scarce resources of the NHS would be better employed treating those who gave themselves a good chance of survival by giving up smoking. This proved remarkably effective in helping our patients to kick the habit. We had the unenviable task of reporting them if we caught them nipping out for a crafty Woodbine. In the Mad Hatter's Tea Party world of the NHS this seemed an eminently sensible policy. Of course it was far too sensible to survive beyond Sowton's time.

Life on Stephen was punctuated by cardiac arrest emergencies. The alarm bell would shrill and we would hurry to the bedside and carry out our allotted role in the resuscitation process. This procedure more often than not included the use of the defibrillator paddles to shock the heart out of VT or VF rhythms. During my time there the success rate was pretty high. One of these happy outcomes included the senior staff nurse who dramatically arrested whilst on the ward one morning. The poor girl had commented to me earlier when I had said that one of my patients was not feeling too well, 'He can't be feeling worse than I do.'

One of the main investigative procedures was the angiogram. This was carried out with the use of a catheter inserted via the femoral artery along the coronary artery to the heart. Its route was monitored on a television screen to pinpoint blockages. These often could be cleared by the inflation of a tiny balloon situated on the catheter tip. This was termed an angioplasty. The small theatre where these were carried out was in also in Hunt's House and so on catheter days we would spend the time taking patients to and from it. The procedure itself did not require a general anaesthetic or take very long. Following angioplasties, however, the patients found it a great trial on their return to the ward to lie flat on their backs for hours on end to prevent bleeding. Some of the doctors were much more skilled at introducing these catheters than others and one rather ham-fisted one use to cause haematomas to swell up, which entailed an even longer period spent flat on their back.

One of the things that I particularly remember about Stephen was the rest hour after lunch every day. The curtains were drawn across the great old windows, only staff were allowed on the ward and silence had to be observed. I found this latter rule particularly difficult to adhere to and was always being told, ' Shut UP, Miranda.' It was almost as bad as the therapy group sessions on George Savage when we all had to sit in total silence until a patient volunteered an observation. This silence would sometimes last as long as ten minutes. It would seem to build up in intensity almost to breaking point. David Shaw would be eyeing me sternly as if to say, 'Be quiet. We don't want any of your silly remarks, Miranda.'

My next placement was very different. It was at a nursing home down the end of Jamaica Road by the docks. We had a jolly little party on Stephen before I left. The male staff nurse, James, kissed me on the lips as he had done on several occasions before. I don't quite know quite whether this was meant for my pleasure or his. At any rate it was decent of him and good for my morale in the circumstances. I arranged to return to Stephen for my final placement, as by now I had determined that cardiac nursing was what I wanted to specialise in.

To reach St Olave's it was necessary to take a bus from London Bridge. The black drivers piloted their buses in the most erratic manner. One minute they would be driving like bats out of hell and then suddenly brake sharply. One had to cling on for dear life. It was rather like riding on the trams going to the Oval cricket ground in the old days. I don't quite know whether they drove in this manner out of malice or plain ignorance. I suspect it was a bit of both. I was constantly catching poor old dears catapulted across the bus. It was an achievement to arrive at St Olave's in one piece.

St Olave's had been founded by King Olave for Norwegian sailors and had been a hospital. This was in the process of being dismantled and the nursing home nestled alongside the old site. It was a lovely place with beautiful gardens, but not one Viking in residence. My fellow student, Caroline, and I thoroughly enjoyed our time there. The patients were not all that old and mainly suffering from smoking-related illness like emphysema. They had to be pushed around in wheelchairs as they were chronically short of breath and could not walk more than a step or two unaided.

The staff were first class and really tried to make a happy home for their charges, encouraging as much freedom for them as possible. Rules were kept to the minimum. Their daily outing was to one of several pubs in the area. Caroline and I would push them there and I at least would enjoy their hospitality in the form of a gin and tonic or two. Caroline, being a high-principled vegetarian, had to be careful not to be seen enjoying herself too much. In our own lunch break we went to a pub called the Fox & Firkin or something like that. They dispensed jolly good reasonably priced grub. By the end of our time at St Olave's even Caroline had got a bit of colour in her cheeks and was becoming really good company.

The nursing home owned its own ambulance but the regular driver was off sick, so I was allowed to drive it. It was the most beautiful autumn weather and we took the residents off on outings. I discovered that an ambulance could park anywhere, even on double white lines. It felt like ferrying the royal family about. My passengers loved it all. I particularly remember one rather sad journey. One of my patients named Bob who we were all very fond of died and I drove a party up to his funeral at a local cemetery. It was a beautiful place on the top of a hill overlooking London across to the Thames. Bob had apparently been an ace mechanic at the same local garage all his working life, since starting there as a boy apprentice in the 1930s. There was a great gathering there to see him off. Many of his old customers as well as his friends had come, quite apart from our lot. I cannot ever remember a more perfect autumn afternoon. It was a most memorable occasion and one could picture old Bob being there to greet them all in his kind friendly way.

We slowed down to the comfortable leisurely pace of St Olave's. Caroline and I would take coffee on the terrace on our arrival in the morning as the mist began to lift from the river, knowing that another perfect day lay ahead. We would then spend most of the day with the residents around the garden. One or two of the ladies were keen on horseracing and I would lay bets for them. So when it came to my project turn I brought a childhood game of ours called 'Good Going' to entertain them all. It certainly achieved that. It was a replica course of the Grand National with model horses, and jockeys in different racing colours. Everybody bet on a horse, which was moved by playing cards. My favourite old lady backed the winning horse and collected her winnings with great jubilation. I asked her to say a few words to the rest of us race goers. She did this with a great flourish starting, 'Unaccustomed as I am to public speaking...' We all ended up toasting her with some of the St Olave's sherry and a good time was had by all. Years later when I noticed one of the staff on a course she sought me out to tell me how fondly she remembered that afternoon. I remembered the wartime Christmases that we had played 'Good Going' in our doctor's house in Montpelier Square, round the corner from where we lived then. They were indeed happy days too. Dr Lorraine was a really kindly soul full of laughter and good cheer in those difficult times.

When I returned to Stephen at the end of the pleasant St Olave sojourn I had already been at Guy's for three years. We had still two months of our course to complete. After the final exam was passed the time began to drag for the first time. I rather wished that I had gone to Samaritan, the cancer ward, as originally planned. On Stephen it was very much the same as before. I had found caring for cancer sufferers most rewarding work. I felt also that I had a great aptitude for this form of nursing. If I had of gone there it might have changed the whole direction of my future nursing. On a strictly practical basis, however, I planned to try and return to Kettering Hospital on qualifying, to avoid the crippling daily journeys up to London and back. Kettering had no such ward.

At this time, jobs were very scarce and everything depended on just getting a post. As newly qualified nurses we had an even harder task than those who had already been staff nurses. Fate then took a hand in the guise of Sister Gale. She had just been promoted to manage the surgical directorate of which her old ward Luke was a part. A new Sister named Karen Smith had just come from Bristol to take over. There was one staff nurse vacancy on Luke. An existing staff nurse had just been interviewed for this and accepted it, but the following day had let them down and gone elsewhere. Sister Gale recommended me to Karen and I was called for an interview. As I sat in the familiar Luke Staff room waiting I enquired after any other candidates for the post. There was none. Sister Gale had spoken and 'it shall be done'. I hit it off well with Karen and of course knew most of the others. Lo and behold, I had a job before I practically had time to blink, ahead of the rest of my set. I was a bit dazed by the speed of it all. I had been so buffeted by rejections and apparently insurmountable obstacles put in my path getting my nursing career on the road at all that success was a new and heady experience. Against all the odds I had made it through to ' the promised land of milk and honey'.

In my army days of youthful confidence I expected nothing but than to carry all before me. I felt that I could walk on water then as 'the golden boy'. In a strange way, life was repeating itself. As on that triumphant day when I was commissioned forty years before, I set off to be fitted for my new uniforms. It was now the Guy's Sewing Room rather than Rogers of Jermyn Street, but equally exciting and equally magnificent uniforms, to my eyes, on that day.

There was still one important thing to do and that was to celebrate with my set. We survivors from the band that had come together more than three years before had been through so much together. They felt like my own family, rather like our Squad in G Squadron at Mons Officer Cadet School. We were a fine body of men then and we were a fine body of girls now.

So it was time to wriggle into the old halter neck for one last 'hurrah' and off to the Grosvenor Hotel for our third Guy's Ball. As I drove through Admiralty Arch and set off up the Mall I might have been in my faithful old Sunbeam the Talbot on that long lost day with Lydia on our way to Glyndebourne. The same haunting melody ran through my mind: 'If you don't get pissed tonight you'll never get pissed at all.'

Joys like this should have been long buried and gone forever at my age. Miranda had given me a second chance to ride once more like Tarquin The Great 'In triumph through Persepolis'. I was indeed a Guy's 'doll' now.

Chapter 13

The Promised Land

When I returned to Guy's the following week, I was somewhat brought down to earth by the news that I would have to pass a medical before starting on Luke. Also there was a cheery little letter from the UKCC congratulating me on being the oldest person 'in the history of nursing' to have qualified. At that moment I could have quite gladly foregone that piece of immortality. It was hardly the sort of news to warm the cockles of the heart of a lady of a certain age.

Instead of the venerable Tabard House, the medical was to take place in a brand new Occupational Health building situated outside Guy's rear gates. I couldn't believe my old boy would still be in charge of this. He seemed too much more be a relic of Guy's glorious past. Tabard House was more his setting. I was ruminating on this as a rather snappy and un-Guy's like young woman took my details. I was doubly glad that I had the old silk underwear on. A nurse whom I didn't recognise eventually came down to escort me up to a door, which said 'Consulting Room' on it. This wasn't Guy's form at all. One usually had to knock on several doors before finding the correct one. I felt much more comfortable with the old arrangement. They apparently were preparing for the wretched new century already. I muttered 'silly Asses' under my breath. Nurse gave me a sharp glance but said nothing and entered the consulting room behind me.

To my immense relief Gaspard's 'old mucker' was sitting behind the desk and rose to greet me with, 'How good to see you again, Mrs Ponsonby', adding, 'You can leave us now nurse'. We enjoyed an interesting chat on the merits of Ponsonby Place and a few hitherto unheard reminiscences about dear old Gaspard. He concluded by congratulating me on not having had one day's sickness during my time at Guy's and passed me fit. I wasn't even weighed this time. With a rather wry smile he shook my hand and passed the observation that I was the only nurse he had ever examined who had shed ten years during the course of their training! My faith in Guy's somewhat restored I set off up the Tower Block to arrange my first duties on Luke.

I must say I was rather proud of the fact that I had not missed one day or even one shift in my three years at Guy's. The nearest member of my set had apparently lost fifteen days. Perhaps the old boy was right when he said, 'They don't make them like you anymore, Mrs Ponsonby.' I felt this was even more so bearing in mind the fact that I had to travel two hundred miles every day and the girls only had to saunter a few hundred yards across the park to get to work.

My first shift as a qualified nurse was in charge of the ward, on night duty, with the assistance of a student nurse, Melanie, and an Agency nurse. It was rather a tall order as Luke was a very busy ward with a lot of acute patients. With my staff nurse's new uniform on for the very first time, complete with a white belt and ornate silver buckle, I was in no way daunted. I hung my own green stethoscope round my neck, to add a touch of professionalism as I saw it.

On the way up to the ward the porters and a lot of my other old chums around the hospital congratulated me on my new status. One of the best things about Guy's was how good the ancillary staff were and I got on really well with them all.

The drug round seemed to take forever and I could not administer the intravenous drugs, as I had not got an IV certificate yet. I had to call upon a Sister from another ward who was a bit bolshie at having this extra chore to cope with. At any rate when we finally settled down to the usual night routine, well after midnight, all seemed to be in order. I was fortunate in my assistants. Melanie worked away like a little beaver. The Agency nurse, Jim, turned out to be a very experienced Nursing Officer. He was very helpful and pleasant. I informed him that I was only just qualified, to which he replied soothingly, 'Don't worry, we have all been there.'

Then about two o'clock in the morning Melanie reported a dead old lady in her section. She had been very ill and white as a sheet, but we couldn't be quite sure when she had died. At any rate, all I could do was to bleep the House Officer to certify the death and ring the son who said he would be over in the morning. This sort of situation is one of the worst things that can befall a nurse. I thought: 'It would have to happen to me on my first duty.' I was absolutely 'on my chinstrap' by morning and I do not know how I made it home in the car.

The three of us continued for the rest of the week and things gradually improved as I began to get a hang of the ward routine. We were still frantically busy but more in control of our destiny. I was so lucky that we were such a good team. Mrs Morley, the Guy's Nursing Officer, had come to help with the IVs. She said she thought I had done very well in the circumstances but that, no matter how good a nurse was, to expect them to cope with a ward like Luke on their first few days qualified was asking too much of them.

Jim, Melanie and I went for a celebratory breakfast after our last shift, in a local café. We had eggs, bacon, sausages and beans. Never has a breakfast tasted better. I never saw Jim again, but Melanie became a great friend and still is to this day.

On commencing Luke it was no longer practical to travel by train as the early shift started at 7 o'clock. All the other wards had begun at 7.30, which the first train from Kettering enabled me to just make. Also British Rail, in their infinite wisdom, had cancelled all trains after 9 o'clock on Saturday evening. The shift ended too late for me to reach the station by this time. This would have made a season ticket even more expensive than before. The price of these had rocketed also. Even after night duty, when it was such an ordeal to drive, the life saving train breakfast had been cancelled. At first the main problem was parking. I was forced to use the multi-storey car park outside the hospital gates. This was expensive at about £15 per day and added an extra fifteen minutes to the journey. I arranged only to do long days, which helped greatly, and after a few months a pal in the car parking department gave me a pass to park in the consultant's reserved areas. This enabled me to park directly outside the Tower Block in which Luke was situated and proved an absolute blessing.

Even so, the journey was extremely tiring. It entailed rising at 4.15 in the morning and not getting home until 11 o'clock at night. In the winter one had to cope with fog and snow in those early morning journeys the weather was usually at its worst. The roads almost invariably had some delightful little tricks up their sleeves, aided and abetted by the IRA, which meant making detours. Fortunately, knowing London so well, I usually avoided getting hopelessly lost.

One evening going up for night duty I became stuck in a snowstorm on the M1 for hours. A kindly lorry driver invited me into his spacious cab and with a couple of other lorry drivers we played poker. Guy's nurses must have gone up in their esteem as I won £15 off them. I suppose it was all part of life's rich tapestry. At least those years spent in Life Guard officer's Desert Messes had not been spent in vain.

The agonising part of those journeys was trying to keep awake on the journey home. I used to keep opening and shutting the windows for some reviving air and even recited poetry. As a schoolboy I had to write out 'Ode to a Nightingale' a hundred times for some misdemeanour or other. After close on fifty years I was still word perfect. Keats would have been impressed. The other thing I found safest was to drive really fast up the motorway to negate the soporific effect of steady progress. Luke was at that time the busiest ward at Guy's and the long working days were exhausting enough in themselves. The only time that I used to hit really bad traffic was after night duty. I once fell fast asleep whilst waiting in a jam by the Hemel Hempstead exit on the M.1. Unable to wake me with his hooter, the driver behind me dismounted to see if I was all right. I awoke to hear him tell another motorist, 'She is definitely dead.' They were more than a little startled when I said, 'Not yet,' and continued, much refreshed, on my way.

In spite of this I was very happy on Luke. Karen, the Sister, and I got on really well and the senior staff nurse, Vanessa, was quite one of the nicest girls that I have ever met. She was everything a nurse should be. Also, some of my old chums like Donna, Sophie and Emma were still on the ward. Partly because of the stressful situation, we drew close together. I thought that we were a great team, certainly as good as any that I have been a part of. It was also good to be working for The Prof again. I renewed my acquaintance with Lady McColl on Christmas Day when the Prof was visiting us and she was sitting in the car outside. We had a smashing Christmas with a large breakfast on tables set up down the centre of the ward and the McColl turkey for lunch. I felt amongst friends. We were one large happy family. As the Social Officer, I organised an outing on the Thames for our Christmas party in the middle of December. We shared a river cruiser with some city types. The river at night was quite spectacular with all the old bridges light up. There was music and free wine. I wore a blue velvet dress and thought that I looked very demure. When I joined the dancing, however, the city boys jumped up to photograph me. Such is the penance of being Miranda. Plentiful wine lessened my embarrassment a bit. My main problem had been to get all our party on board before sailing time. I ended up refusing to let the crew raise the gangplank until I had counted us all on board.

A much greater penance for me was not being invited to my younger son's wedding. We had always been very close. After duty on Luke one evening I travelled down to Fulham to meet Toby's's fiancée, Carolyn. I was rather pushed in getting away from Guy's and must have omitted 'spending a penny'. I tried to rectify this when I alighted at Earl's Court station, but the loo was out of order in usual railway 'best practice'. So by the time I arrived outside Toby's front door I was pretty desperate. I was contemplating a quick dash up the stairs, but there was no answer to my increasingly urgent bell ringing. They obviously had not returned from work yet. A girl has got to do what a girl has got to do and I did. There was a little lake forming under me. Toby arrived at this moment. He noticed the puddle and said rather breezily, looking up at the bluest of skies, 'I didn't know it had rained'. I was soaking but as Carolyn also 'tipped up' before the front door was open I did not want to let the side down by admitting my accident. So I soldiered on, trying to make a good impression, in order to get invited to the wedding. The snag was that everywhere I sat a damp spot appeared, even though I had discarded my knickers in the bin at the first opportunity. As the evening wore on my skirt began to dry out a bit but the smell persisted. I noted surreptitious opening of windows. We dined in a little restaurant. I liked her a lot and thoroughly approved of the match. They broke the news to me then that they thought I would be too much of an embarrassment to them. I heard later that I had been called a 'Disgrace to my Regiment'. I was very proud of being a Guy's nurse and thought this was a bit unfair to me. I was sure that my dear Bermondsey people would never have treated me in this way.

It was about this time that we had our Passing Out Parade in Southwark Cathedral. It was an annual ceremony so we had to wait until the final Set of that year had passed their exams. It was a splendid affair. There was a short service conducted by the Bishop of Southwark himself. Then we went up one by one to be presented with our

Guy's badges. These are a nurse's proudest possession or were until the university ninnies abolished them. This disgrace was still sometime in the future then. We would wear these badges proudly on our uniforms from that day on. Wherever our nursing took us in future we could recognise a Guy's nurse and be recognised ourselves. There was a party in Henrietta Raphael after the ceremony with all the parents attending. It was the last gathering of our set and in that way a sad day also. A few of us dined at the Caprice restaurant in Mayfair to round off the day.

The following year I nearly killed myself driving back from night duty one morning. I had waged a desperate battle to keep awake all the way. I was only a few miles from home when I went out like a light. I suppose that I must have relaxed thinking I had made it. The car swerved across the road in front of an oncoming lorry and hit the kerb. The bang woke me up and I missed the lorry by a whisker. The good Lord must have been watching over me that morning. Perhaps he thought that I had some nursing left in me yet.

I had been beavering away on Luke for nearly a year then and with great regret decided that a live Kettering nurse was more use than a dead Guy's one. I handed in my notice and savoured my last few weeks at Guy's. The four years during which I had embraced the place body and soul had been amongst the happiest of my life. In true Guy's tradition they had been wonderfully kind to me. They had recognised in me that inner something that makes a nurse. They had guided and protected me, as perhaps no one else would have done, through to the Promised Land.

On my final day on Luke I heard my old Household Cavalry Trumpeters' notes floating up from Westminster, on the still balmy morning air, from the State Opening of Parliament. I looked one last time out of the open window across the hospital. I then said goodbye to all my friends and went into the little chapel to say a last prayer of thanks for all the gifts bestowed upon me by Guy's. I saluted old Thomas Guy as I passed his statue on my way out of the gates with tears in my eyes and their last words to me gladdening my heart. They had said I had made a true Guy's nurse and they were proud of me. I could not have asked for a finer tribute.

Chapter 14

A Country Life

I had been on 'the bank' at Kettering Hospital since the start of my student days, doing the odd shift when they were short and I was on leave. The bank was an emergency pool of nurses who could be called in when staff shortages occurred. I thus had now only to give Beverley, who ran it, my registration certificate to start work. I then set about finding a permanent post. This involved filling in application forms and attending interviews. I invariably got short-listed. I suppose they did this to live up to their 'Equal Opportunities Trust' billing. To actually give me a permanent post was, it seemed, a bit too equal for them. I was even told by one Sister that I was too high powered for their post. I had some cracking good interviews, by their own admission, but there was always eventually some rather lame excuse. The excuses became even lamer as time wore on. Even my old orthopaedic ward turned me down. Some of my old chums there were furious about it. I heard on the grapevine that the hospital was nervous about employing a Miranda. So much for my reference saying that they would be glad to employ me on my return as a qualified nurse. At any rate I paid a visit to the Sewing Room to be fitted with my staff nurse's blue uniforms. It was a great moment. When later I went to collect them a new student gazed at me in awe just as I had done five years before. As I changed into one, in the same cubbyhole, old memories came flooding back. It was indeed a dream come true.

I was not unhappy, as I had all the work that I could cope with on the Casualty Department. I was almost working permanently there. They were a great bunch to work with and it was interesting work. Also it was wonderful to be back in the countryside the whole time again. By now I had two Chows, Ming and a red male called Rowley. We now were able to spend time together and used to roam the countryside when it was cool in the winter. I began to realise how important emotionally they were to me when later poor little Ming died. Poppy came to be a companion for Rowley and they were devoted to each other.

It was about this time that I bought an old wooden-hulled Norfolk Broads cruiser called *Sir Bedivere*. She was 25 feet long with a Perkins diesel engine and two cabins. I was determined to enjoy my newly acquired freedom to the full. That was the great advantage of banking. I could come and go as I pleased within reason. The idea was that the family, particularly the grandchildren, would join me to make a happy family party. This never materialised, so the two Chows and I explored the Broads on our own. They loved it and even little Poppy became adept at jumping up on to the deck from the riverbank. We had many adventures and used to try and navigate isolated difficult reaches of the Broads to find a sheltered mooring.

I gradually began to get the hang of managing the boat on my own but never found berthing very easy. Sometimes I would make 'a right Horlicks of it'. I was always terrified of seeing the chows setting off on their own with me stranded on the riverbank. One day we braved Great Yarmouth and Braydon Water, going on down to beyond Beccles. Sometimes puttering along with the mist still on the river on a summer morning, setting out on some new adventure, nothing could seem more perfect. Guy's and St Olave's were in another world. The smoke of London did not exist for me anymore. I was more in my own element as I had been in Africa and the desert. I was in tune with nature again and my batteries, which the past four exhausting years had so depleted, were recharged. I became ready to assault that nursing citadel anew. Only this time I knew that it would fall inevitably before this Guy's nurse. It was just a matter of time. It took six months before a victory could be celebrated, but Miranda was on her way again and nothing would stop her caring for the Northamptonshire people as she had the Bermondsey clan.

In the meantime I was finding the variety of life entertaining on A&E. One minute I was treating cricketers with broken fingers. I was even able to speed back to the crease a Leicestershire county batsman. When the soccer season came round I was plastering up arms and legs. Strangely the majority of injuries came in casual kick-abouts during lunch hours. There were the usual tragedies of course. One I remember involved a pony and cart. This young couple were trotting along a country lane out by Melton Mowbray on a peaceful Sunday morning. Suddenly round a bend came a speeding car on the wrong side of the road. Their beloved pony was killed, the cart smashed and the couple severely injured. On a Saturday afternoon a farmer was collecting some kindling with his son. He had parked his tractor at the top of a small slope. Somehow the brake had released sufficiently for the tractor to roll down the hill and run over his son, whom we were not able to revive.

One disaster that affected me the most was the arrival of a dead 19-year-old cyclist. He looked so perfect in his racing colours and helmet with no apparent injury. The riders had been racing down the slipway on to the A14. The boy had his head down pedalling like mad and did not see a lorry unexpectedly halted at the bottom. He had run slap into it. There were also the girls with asthma or overdoses, the latter renewing my acquaintance with the old stomach pump again.

At night the demon drink was the main problem. It was odd how perfectly sensible men in their thirties with responsible jobs would go on regular benders every few weeks. They were brought in so paralytic that they were in danger of expiring. We put them on mattresses on the floor for their own safety. The following morning they would smarten themselves up and return to normal. One knew they would be back the following month or the one after. Sometimes in the long reaches of the night we would be empty with no patients at all. I even remember playing poker with another sporting nurse and a couple of policemen during one of these lulls. The secret was not to rub the ex-patient's names off the board. In casualty folklore this invited an influx of new patients.

On one particularly busy Saturday evening, the triage nurse needed a break and asked me to take over. This nurse classifies the patients according to the urgency of their treatment. That is: 'Immediate', 'Can wait' or 'Bugger off'. I approached the long queue in a brisk authoritative manner. 'Right,' I said in my best military mode. As I sat down at the desk, however, my chair, which was on castors spun away, and I went crashing down flat on my back on the floor. The patient that I was about to see had his arm in a makeshift sling covered in blood, but he helped me up. By this time a bevy of nurses, who had heard the crash, were doubled up with laughter in the doorway. At that moment I did not exactly see the funny side of my fall from power, but joined in, bearing in mind that a sense of humour is a nurse's most priceless possession.

I experienced one slightly tricky moment. Ever since setting out on my nursing career I had feared publicity. So far I had avoided this. One day, about this time, I apparently had treated a local journalist. He reported his findings to his paper. They had telephoned the hospital to enquire if there was indeed a Miranda in the department. I was hauled yet again before the ubiquitous Lynne Gale and advised, sensibly enough, to say nothing if approached. The nurses closed ranks round me and we heard no more on the subject. I suppose it was always there ticking like a time bomb ready to explode.

That autumn, on my usual job seeking round I applied for two six-month posts. One on the Intensive Care Unit and, at long last, one on the Coronary Care Unit, which was where I really wanted to work. Unfortunately the ITU interview arrived first. I had to come back from Norfolk for the interview and returned straight back there with instructions to telephone them later in the day when the interviews were completed. I was offered the post. On the principle that a bird in the hand is worth two in the bush I accepted. ITU was the one place that I had not worked as a student and knew very little about. Later I heard that I would have been offered the CCU post, as I was the only applicant. Such is life.

The Sister was new to Kettering and, I gathered, rather got cold feet after appointing me. The offer had been made, however, and it was too late to go back on it again. A&E was not really all that suitable for me in the long-term, bearing in mind the journalist incident. On a ward people had time to get used to me and become friends. I had never had any trouble there. On ITU the patients were not even fully conscious and I could have been the man in the moon as far as they were concerned.

On the other hand, my main strength as a nurse is what in the trade is called communication skill. Give me an old lady who is lost and in despair and I will bring her to life again, make her laugh and feel amongst friends and wanted, thus ensuring her recovery. I can lift the spirits in a ward and motivate people. This is what makes me tick as a nurse. Good technical nurses are ten a penny, but my gift is unique. Without it I would have retired long ago or perhaps never started at all.

At any rate, I knuckled down to learn the ropes but my heart was not really in it. The time that I really got job satisfaction was the odd hour after my patient was off the ventilator before going to a ward. On the plus side the staff were friendly and helpful. We were each allocated one of the four patients on the unit and were solely responsible for him. The busy time was 'on the hour' when the observations had to be recorded, unless there was some emergency or the pumps needed changing. Sometimes the sedation would lighten and the patient would go 'bananas' and pull out his tube. Quick action was needed then. At least there was only one patient to cope with rather than fourteen or fifteen as on Luke.

One of my first patients was a boy in a coma. He seemed to have a good many young friends. One evening a policeman came in and told me that he had stolen a microwave oven, amongst other things, from an old lady. In his haste to drive his van away he had hit a lamppost and the microwave had hurtled forward hitting him on the head. A case of poetic justice. I had always thought these vastly overrated things before this.

Rather strangely, I nursed two ex-members of the Hitler Youth movement one after another. They had both married English girls whilst prisoners of war and stayed on. They seemed nice enough chaps and had some fascinating tales to tell. One was a survivor from the Battle of Stalingrad. There cannot have been many of them. He was one of the last wounded soldiers to be successfully evacuated by air. They talked about the summer camps in the Bavarian mountains they had enjoyed as boys. How they had nightly singsongs round the campfire and the great feeling of optimism and sense of destiny at the time, after the terrible years of the Depression. It sounded a bit like our Boy Scouts if it had not been for the sinister future.

We had frequent dashes to the Neuro ITU in Oxford with patients. The ambulance drivers used to drive at break-neck speed, even in thick fog, but with great skill. We always arrived in one piece. The Sister at the Radcliffe Infirmary wore a white uniform that was short enough to be a miniskirt — very bizarre. I suppose that I might have been working there if things had worked out differently. Things so often hang by such slender threads. The canteen certainly served some smashing eggs and bacon.

The Christmas Day that I spent on ITU was so unlike Guy's. Nobody seemed to acknowledge that it was Christmas at all. I did not even have time for lunch, which, being as I was the only person doing a long day, was a bit rough. I was so tired by the time I got home I just flopped into bed. The chows were a bit choked off, but at least I was at home thirty minutes after knocking off. That was the wonderful thing about working at Kettering. I no longer had to face that terrible journey.

A new trend was emerging about this time. The anaesthetists on ITU were mainly from behind what had been the Iron Curtain. They were unspoilt and jolly good company. Being on a small unit we got to know them well. They had all served in the army and this gave me a certain affinity with them. I had some convivial meals at local restaurants with them. The first of these was on Boxing Day after yet another long day's duty. They had felt sorry for me not having a family Christmas of my own. We drank some fiery liquid of theirs similar to vodka and sang 'Silent Night, Holy Night' round the candlelight table. It made up for what had gone before and was so kind and thoughtful of them.

We came to know the relatives of our patients well and acted as a support in troubled times. Keeping them in constant touch with how things were going was important to them. I had one patient who was in such a poor way that a joint decision was made to switch off the ventilator. The Doctor had to carry out a set routine of checks before this could be done and then it was duly switched off. I thought myself that it was a merciful measure for the patient and the poor relatives.

The oldest Sister was a throwback to a different age and had been on the unit since its early days. Janice was a splendid character and the mainstay of the place. She was Officer Commanding Gold Fish. I was her '2i/c'. They lived in a glass tank in the reception area. We had to clean the tank out and feed them. They looked as if butter would not melt in their mouths but were little savages. One day I went out and bought a few companions to keep up their numbers. They promptly snacked the lot.

When I first arrived Janice was a bit bossy over my tank cleaning operations. I eventually grew a bit fed up with this. I accidentally on purpose tipped the contents over her and we came to a better working arrangement thereafter. In fact she amused me no end and I missed her a lot when my six months ended and I left. I was now back where I started, working on the old bank and restarting the discouraging round of interviews.

At first I used my freedom to choose when I worked, to enjoy a really good summer on *Sir Bedivere*, which had just come out of hibernation. I liked Barton Turf, where my mooring was. It was a pretty little unspoilt haven with no hire-boats. It took me only two hours and forty minutes to get down there. By now I had got my own special favourite spots to visit. I found travelling long distances in a day tiring, as I had to be at the wheel the entire time. Rowley and Poppy had become old hands by now and less of a worry, so we often moored up for a rest and to stretch our legs. Thus we travelled to far destinations in stages. I remember stopping one evening at Belaugh on the Bure. The chows and I climbed up a rather overgrown stairway, which emerged unexpectedly in the vicar's garden. It was a glorious evening and he was tranquilly enjoying a 'chote peg' with his lady wife. They greeted us like long lost friends and invited me to join them in a dry martini. Afterwards he offered to show us round his beautiful little church. I queried, 'What about the chows?' 'Bring them in. We are all God's creatures.' That summer we had many pleasant little interludes like that. I could almost write a slim bedside volume of our 'Tales from The Riverbank'.

In stark contrast to that charming old vicar's truly Christian attitude was my brother's towards me. He was a Roman Catholic convert. Apparently they regarded 'my change' as a sin against God's ordained scheme of things. Following this dictate he did not feel that he could have anything more to do with me. This was most unlike John who is a high-principled, kindly soul. We had always been very close and I am sure that if he had still been a member of the dear old tolerant Church of England things would have been different. This tolerance I see as a Christian virtue in itself. Thus when admitting patients if they say RC I write, 'No religion'!

All this did engender a feeling of loneliness at times. When I became Miranda I knew that I would be ostracised in certain quarters, but I did not envisage that it would be quite so complete. I had nobody left in my own world. I had a host of young friends through my nursing, but so missed, say, a day in the pavilion at Lord's, amongst old friends, catching up with all the gossip. I could not, of course, use my MCC membership now, being female. All this was borne home to me that summer in *Sir Bedivere* when I was down the River Waveney. I was so near to Benacre, the home my fellow 'strange bird' and best man at our wedding, John Gooch. How lovely it would have been to ask him to join me for a day on the river or just pop in to see him, as I would have done in the old days. I seemed to be like *The Flying Dutchman*, forever destined to sail the seas alone. It was this sort of thing that I missed so much. Being alone on Christmas Day and times like that did not bother me. The chows were lovely companions and, at any rate, I invariably worked, to give the youngsters some time at home with their own families and children.

Apart from that, it was a gorgeous summer. I even had to rig up a large umbrella over the helm to keep cool. We sailed up to the top of the River Yare into Norwich and out again pretty swiftly! We did battle with the bolshie anglers at the beautiful Bramerton Woods End. It was quite like *Swallows and Amazons*. I suppose that I could have qualified as the latter if I had been prepared to sacrifice one of my beautiful new breasts. These had grown quite splendidly and were my pride and joy. I certainly would never have had an implant so, if they had not developed, the whole project would have been a bit of a damp squib. I took them off to an invited breast screening that summer. I had to climb up into a sort of caravan in Oakham, not far from our old house at Barleythorpe. I was told to strip to the waist which I gladly did. I was not prepared for the next item on the agenda. This involved them being squeezed in a sort of glass vice. Not as bad as it would have been if they had been testicles but not far short of it. On completion the radiographer wrote something in a book and left me to dress. I looked at the book. She had written: 'This lady has remarkably firm young breasts for someone of her age with several children!!' Perhaps she had not been impressed when I cautioned her to 'play the game' when she first tightened the vice.

I was beginning to think that being female was a hazardous business when my new doctor at Gretton insisted on a cervical smear test. 'We carry these out on all new women patients,' he assured me soothingly. I duly turned up at his main surgery in Uppingham at the appointed hour. This time I was told to take everything off below the waist. It was reminiscent of my trysts with Bernard! I was then instructed to lie on my back with my legs apart. The nurse then inserted something like a mole trap up me. Now I had done this to patients on many occasions but did not feel it was quite cricket having it done to me. On examination Doctor did not seem to find what he was looking for and after a prolonged whisper to Nurse I was free to regain my dignity.

Eventually the first frosts arrived and it was time for *Sir Bedivere* to be taken out of the water and put in an old barn for the winter. During this winter I was in great demand on the bank! I seemed to fill in somewhere and stay on for a month or so until they were up to numbers again. I spent a few months round Christmas on a medical ward called Harrowden A. I found staff on the medical wards particularly nice. Then I had a long spell on the Coronary Care Unit as well as covering for another medical ward, Harrowden C. By the spring I was working one hundred hours a week at times. Every time I got home they seemed to ring me up for another shift. Looking back I really should have been firmer. When you are dependent on banking for work it is difficult to say no and there is always the fear that the work might dry up. It was now almost a year since I had left ITU I had had a short 'banking' spell on ITU at Peterborough Hospital straight after I left the Kettering Unit. It was not a friendly place like Kettering and Guy's, and there was so much work at Kettering that I soon gave it up.

In March I applied for yet another permanent post. By this time I should think that I had applied for more posts than anybody else in the 'History of Nursing'. Lo and behold I was offered a PERMANENT post on Harrowden C. As usual I was being told what a good interview I had had and was just waiting to hear the usual but... When the offer was made, I queried it, but they laughed and said they wanted me. I was a bit stunned at first. The news got around like wildfire. All sorts of people came up and congratulated me. I was quite touched; they all seemed so genuinely pleased. It had taken me two years since that memorable day that I had left Guy's to get my nursing career under way again. Rather appropriately in the circumstances I was to begin on April Fool's Day.

Chapter 15

A Member of the Team

My new ward, Harrowden C, was under great pressure of work at the time that I joined it. A first class young nurse had just given up the unequal struggle to provide what she considered a proper standard of nursing care. She had even left the profession altogether. The problem for well-educated, able girls was the abysmal pay: £12,000 to £15,000 per year with no prospect of significant advancement. It meant a life of comparative poverty unless she married a successful young man. There would be no respectable mortgages or decent provisions for a young growing family. Even a postman could better this rate of pay. Yet more and more was expected of nurses. Skills like cannulation (siting of venflons), which had been previously been carried out by doctors, were passing to nurses. She was also expected to give up her spare time undertaking courses and studying for university degrees. On qualification she was already a highly competent professional with over three years' training behind her. No other professional in the country would dream of putting up with these conditions. The Government's solution to the acute shortage of nurses that this partly caused was to try to recruit less qualified nurses from abroad at rock-bottom pay rates.

To this end the Last of the Pharaohs, still Director of Nursing, had set off to Sweden on a recruiting drive. No Scandinavian blondes had resulted from this jaunt. They obviously had more sense. So she next went to South Africa in pursuit of some Zulus. Surely they would come. The pay would be like a King's ransom to them. We cleared a storeroom on the ward for them to drop off their spears before coming on duty. There was a frantic and unavailing search for Zulu dictionaries. What had been overlooked in this bright initiative was the fact that they could not read or write and Zulu speaking patients were a bit thin on the ground. At any rate I am sure that it must have been an enjoyable trip and the poor old Zulus were relieved to be left in peace in their delightful little rondavel huts. Hunting for big game in the woods round Kettering would have been a discouraging pastime.

All this being a fact of life, nursing would have to depend on those with a real vocation for it to the exclusion of all else. They, and I dare to count myself amongst their number, would struggle on in their ever-dwindling numbers to carry the National Health Service on their backs. It would not be a dead end job to them but a fulfilment of their innermost selves. To augment their numbers they would have to recruit the less able girl who would not have been able to get a decent job elsewhere. This is already happening with the consequent dilution in the standard of nursing care.

Thus I was entering a ward where morale was low. On the plus side we had, in my opinion, the best Sister in the hospital to try and hold things together. Her name was Ann Guida and she set a fine example of good leadership. Her nurses respected and liked her, as I did myself. I saw my first job was to try and cheer them all up, poor dears. Ann had been able to keep a really fine bunch of nurses who I already liked very much from my time 'banking' there. We were particularly lucky in our, what were now known as, Health Care Assistants. In my time we had been called Auxiliaries. At least they were easier to spell now. We also had, without doubt, the best ward clerk in the hospital. Val was an absolute boon to us on our roughest days and her expertise in line dancing was invaluable. I did my best to put a smile on their faces again and lighten the atmosphere. One of the main things that my years in the army had taught me was the ability to smile in the face of adversity.

I had suffered a series of burglaries in my new house whilst away on my long working days. The day before I started on Harrowden C I had finally replaced my stolen grandfather clock after a long search. I was really pleased with my new clock. Without thinking I tried to report my pleasure to the staff by saying that I had had an orgasm every time it chimed. Ann commented, rather dryly, that I had obviously been kept busy. The others, rather to my surprise, fell about laughing. An old gentleman, holding his catheter bag in one hand, even looked into the staff room to see what all the commotion was about. From then on whatever I said tended to be greeted with laughter. Several people told me in my first few weeks how much morale had improved since my arrival. This did please me. I had so hoped that I would be able to achieve this first objective.

What were not so funny, depending on which way you look at it, were two incidents that occurred one morning around this time. The chows and I had gone for a walk and were returning down a farm track when a jogger suddenly came round the corner. I reined in the dogs on their leads but instead of going round us the silly little man ran straight at us. He had a sandy moustache and looked like a Scotsman. Rowley, rather naturally, thought that we were being attacked. He jumped at Sandy Moustache, who took evasive action. With relief, I thought no damage had been done but Sandy stopped and only retreated when Rowley growled at him. He said from a safer distance: 'Look at the hole in my new jeans.' He did have a dreadful Scottish accent. 'Rubbish,' I replied, 'the hole must have already been there.' 'LOOK,' he said pointing at Rowley who was proudly holding a piece of blue jeans in his mouth. The silly ass requested £40. I gave him £20 as I couldn't bear his nasty accent a minute longer. Thus I was not in the best of humour when I got home to discover a man peering in at my new grandfather clock. The loss of all my stolen family treasures boiled up in me. I grabbed him by the hair and with the chows growling at him dragged him into the telephone to ring the police. Every time he struggled I thumped him with appropriate endearments like: 'You turd.' He kept trying to say something, rather plaintively, which I finally listened to. 'But Madam, I have only come to read the electricity meter.' 'Tell it to the Marines', I replied, but on ringing the Electricity Board I discovered that he was indeed who he said he was. We both laughed and I apologised. I explained about my recent burglaries and gave him a glass of whisky. We parted the best of friends but the Electricity Board decided that it was safer for their employees if I read my own meter in future.

The nursing skills that I had acquired whilst acting as a 'Hired Gun' around the wards came in very useful now. At the time I was the only nurse able to site venflons and fine-bore naso-gastric tubes. Also to take blood, carry out ECGs and assist them with many other little tasks. This was fulfilling for me and I felt really needed and part of the team. No longer was I rung up at every hour of the day and night to fill in for some emergency. I could plan my life again. Also I would get six weeks paid leave. As a 'bank' nurse I was not entitled to even one day. This last rule has since changed and not before time too. Above all, however, was the feeling of security that I now had. I had been disgracefully discriminated against, but it served no purpose to complain about it. It was the way things were. My perseverance had again won through and I could now care for Northamptonshire people, as they deserved to be looked after. On a medical ward one came into contact with a very wide section of the local community. I soon found that I could not walk down the street in Kettering or visit Sainsbury's without grateful patients or their relatives coming up. I was a respected local figure again as I had been in my farming years. I was indeed doing a Profumo although I had not lied to the House of Commons or played 'the giddy ox' down at Clivedon.

The majority of our patients were elderly, as geriatric wards had been misguidedly abolished. This typical piece of lunacy is shortly to be rectified, but it has taken them ten years to rectify the error. Like the Project 2000 nurse training, it has done damage. It beggars belief that it has taken them ten years to realise that project 2000 has been a failure. Any nurse could have told them that after ten months or even ten minutes. Senior nurses who cannot 'hack it' anymore should be turned out to grass or fill in as domestics where they could do a useful job: certainly not given clipboards, or millboards, as we called them in the army, to run around with, desperately trying to justify their existence by inventing nonsensical changes.

With elderly patients their home circumstances very often had to be sorted out before they could be safely discharged. Thus we worked closely with the families and our brilliant social worker, Mary Markham. By the time you included the geriatric specialist, Dr Walters, occupational therapists and physiotherapists, it was quite a team effort. The whole team met weekly to plan matters. I always tried to put myself in the patient's place and imagine what I would have wanted had I been in their bed. Usually the patient's main concern was to get home. The saddest situation was for them to lose their independence and go into a 'Home'. I waged many a battle to try and avoid this fate for them. When I entered nursing, ten years before, all the talk was about the increased resources to enable the older patients to remain in their own houses, helped by community carers. These had not materialised so it was a tricky business. We just had to throw our weight about as best we could and exert pressure. The weak link was the District Nurses who appeared loath to play their part in this.

Our elderly patients were an endearing generation. One morning Ann escorted an old lady into the shower to assist with her ablutions. When the shower was turned on the lady exclaimed, 'Blimey, it's wet in here.' We became fond of them and it was a pleasure to care for them. As my own family had mostly died young I had not had to cope with this problem in my personal life. Some of the men still had nightmares from their experiences in the war. One night I heard screams coming from one of the bays. An old soldier was reliving a Jap attack in Burma. I was advised to, 'Take cover, take cover, I can see them moving out there.' On admitting a patient I always found out his old regiment first of all. This gave me a better picture of him than any thing else.

One day I was urgently called to the bay at the far end of the ward. One of the men had launched himself head first out of the window, which was three stories up. The heroine was a Health Care Assistant named Annette. She had grabbed his leg and was holding on for dear life. John, a student nurse and myself each took an ankle and held on but we could not lift him as he was clinging to a ledge below him. His ankles were greasy and our hands kept slipping. By this time a large crowd had gathered on the concrete below. The Fire Brigade were called to provide a ladder to assist. They did not materialise, but two window cleaners had seen what was going on. With great presence of mind they broke into a doctor's locked office on the floor below and pulled him to safety. They and Annette had saved his life and did really deserve a medal each. We were then subjected to some half-witted counselling. Annette had commendably taken everything in her stride. My arms were shaking uncontrollably from the strain and a tot of brandy would have been more appropriate.

I played a more solo role in another incident on a Saturday afternoon. Nan Currie, the bleep holder, who was the Sister temporally in charge of the hospital, sent an urgent request for me to go to the Assessment Unit as there was a violent patient who required treatment and the nurse in charge was in tears and beyond coping. I was very busy, as usual, with my own patients and not prepared to be messed about. The police were standing outside the patient's cubicle. They looked at me with open mouths as I strode in. He was a small Scotsman. We summed each other up and I think he came to the conclusion that if he tackled me he would come off worse, which at that moment was most certainly right. I briskly sited a venflon and set up a drip. Scotsman said that he was feeling sick and wanted to go to the toilet. I hauled him down the ward to the loo ignoring the police advice not to go in with him. He was not feeling like putting up any resistance by then. Such is a nurse's life.

Life on Harrowden C was hard and I always seemed to have to make use of every flying minute to get through the work. The ward consisted of six bays with six patients in each bay, plus three side rooms. This arrangement was cosier for the patients than the old open Nightingale wards at Guy's but it was harder to keep a constant eye on all the patients. Each of the staff nurses was allocated two bays with the assistance of a Health care assistant. Your day very much depended on which assistant you had and of course the condition of the patients. I tended to allocate a few suitable patients to my assistant and work on my own with the rest. This was only possible with an aid of a hydraulic hoist on some patients. I found these cranes brilliant once I had got the knack of using them. The only problem with them was the acute lack of space in the bays.

We specialised in diabetes and I enjoyed working with Dr O'Malley the diabetic consultant. A lot depended on these relationships. The patients got the best treatment when consultant and staff nurse worked closely together, as our information was vital to diagnosis and effectiveness of ongoing treatment. It was alarming how many patients were only in hospital because of the drugs their GP had prescribed them. Once I even requested Dr O'Malley to stop all drugs on a patient who was deteriorating. This having been done the patient improved dramatically and when I saw her in Sainsbury's a few months later she informed me that she had never looked back since that time. This type of treatment was often all they needed. All drugs have side effects that then require others to nullify these and so on. It is a merry-go-round. My years as a nurse have led me to believe that it is best to put up with minor ailments, untreated by drugs, if you want to stay healthy.

Another factor is taking commonsense measures to look after your own health. I was amazed at the damage smoking cigarettes did. I had no idea of the extent of it. Our hospital would have been half empty if Sir Walter Raleigh had left the Americans to smoke themselves to death and not introduced the pernicious weed into this country! Before they died, I saw the hail and hearty Queen Mum and Princess Margaret on the BBC News on the occasion of the former's one-hundredth birthday. The poor Princess was apparently paralysed in a wheelchair. They ought to have had placards stating. 'Age 101 – Non-smoker' and 'Age 71 – Smoker'.

I worked long days to give myself a few outings on *Sir Bedivere*. I started work at seven o'clock in the morning and did not finish until nine at night. After a couple of years of this I was exhausted, so when a couple of young friends invited me to accompany them to Spain in the early spring I accepted, provided that I could get someone to look after the chows. This satisfactorily accomplished, we set off to Andalucia. I had never been to Spain but to me, in recent years, it meant those ghastly package holidays. I had looked back a bit further in my mind to Ernest Hemingway. His tales of Grenada and bull fighting had entranced me when I was young. The call of the south had always been irresistible to me. The sun had renewed and refreshed me all my life. I had never used any sort of sun lotion to keep its rays off me even in the tropics. The English March weather that year was cold and wet. The Andalucian weather was like a perfect English summer day. It was like stepping into a brighter happier world. Frigliana was a Moorish little town with whitewashed houses sitting high above the sea. Our house was in the countryside below it. Sitting on the terrace in the morning sun taking breakfast I seemed to get a different perspective on my life. During the past few years I had adopted such a tunnel vision to achieve my objectives. I was now nearing the allotted span of life. Were there other things to be enjoyed before time ran out? Since setting off to Africa at seventeen I had thrown myself so utterly into every new enterprise I had undertaken. I had never really sat back and taken stock. Was this all there was to be?

My first holiday objective was to retrace Hemingway's steps to Ronda for the bull fighting. Ronda was the most beautiful place looking over the surrounding vineyards in the valley below. The 18th- century bullring was steeped in the history of the great matadors. Juan Belmonte's bloodstained tunic, from a goring, was in the museum beside to the ring. A statue of Joselito stood by the main gates. Bullfighting might seem a barbarous sport but it has a certain nobility. It is not like shooting an elephant. This is akin to murder. It had always upset me in Africa. I had shot big game but only when necessary. I shot buck to survive in the bush and, on one occasion, a rogue lion.

Our own Welsh Blacks, not sold as pedigree breeding animals or kept as replacements, were slaughtered at two years old. Fighting bulls did not enter the ring until three years old. Up to that time they led they led a free and natural existence on the great ranches in the south of Spain. They only fought once and had a chance against the skill and courage of their adversary. Thick mattresses now protected the horses of the picadors with their lances. It was 'Death in the Afternoon' but in a form acceptable to me. In Spain it is as popular as ever and getting into a 'corrida' is as difficult as obtaining Cup Final tickets. Caroline, my old St Olave's companion, would not have agreed with me but I am a product of the first half of the last century. We would disagree about many things.

We also visited the magnificent Palace of the Moors, the Alhambra. What were equally memorable were the little mountainside towns. Wandering round them was like stepping back in time to my own childhood. The builders still used mules to cart their rubble up and down. The farms were mostly family affairs with horses and donkeys in place of tractors. Peasant agriculture appeared to be alive and flourishing. The Spanish country people were pleasant and friendly. The restaurants were cheap and provided excellent food and wine. It was a lovely holiday.

I returned much refreshed to the demanding life on Harrowden C. We all went to a local nightclub for our Christmas outing. Nightclubs were alien places to me now. Their noise was so mind-numbing that conversation was impossible. The dancing was weird and wonderful. They were no longer the sweet, soothing places I had so loved in my youth. I felt out of place but joined in to the best of my ability. My third year on the ward raced by. I was like those Spanish donkeys working until I was ready to drop, without complaint or hope of an easier life. On New Year's Day I entered one of my bays and wished them all a Happy New Year. None of my patients was even up to returning my greetings. The Sisters told me that the atmosphere in my bays was totally different to the others. They were much more cheerful and imbued with my own 'joie de vivre'. If that was really the case, as I worked hard to make them, goodness knows what the others were like.

At long last a permanent post became vacant on the Coronary Care Unit. I went through the familiar admission routine with a lighter heart. I would now be selected on merit for the first time. I had one of my usual good interviews, 'Buts' were a thing of the past and I was duly selected. It was a thrilling moment for me. It had been a long tiring journey to the type of nursing I knew that I could do better than any other and was most suited for. I have not been disappointed. It has lived up to all my expectations.

I gave a leaving party for all my friends on Harrowden C at my house. I was going to miss them all. They had put up with my somewhat ebullient self with great good humour. We had been through so many hard times together and they had never failed me. I was going to miss the knockabout humour of the two domestics, Jenny and Maureen. It was impossible not to feel cheerful with them about. There would be no more reminiscences from 'My early life' by Allebone, tales of rounding Cape Horn from Jayne, the adventures of the Jellical cats from Jacquie, Jobs I might take by Caroline, My favourite roundabouts by Elaine or tales from the Vienna woods from Barbara. My line dancing would go to pot without Val.

I had gone through so many heartbreaking partings like this in my life and carried treasured memories of so many of the people I had so intimately shared a fleeting moment in time with. They had all bestowed such happiness on me. Of course one often saw them again, but once you were no longer a member of their little group it was never the same. You really walked out of their life as you moved on.

Chapter 16

Affairs of the Heart

Starting on CCU was rather like joining the Mounted Squadron at Knightsbridge Barracks had been nearly fifty years before. It was the same small elite unit. It had an atmosphere all of its own like Knightsbridge and the work was totally different from serving in the regiment or, in this case, on the general wards. CCU had changed greatly since I had 'banked' there three years before. A new consultant, Penny Astridge, who had just been starting then, was now the power in the land. She was almost an exact replica of Dr Somerville, the visiting cardiac consultant at Guy's, who worked at the National Heart Hospital. They were both able women who had made their way in a man's world. As such, they perhaps over compensated by throwing their weight about unduly. Neither of them suffered fools gladly, to put it mildly. The main thing was that they were both excellent cardiologists, but you could not imagine either of them putting up with a man in their life.

Penny had introduced a pacing suite on to CCU This enabled us to fit new pacemakers and change faulty ones. This extended the range of treatment we had to offer and added to the interest of the job. Almost immediately I was detailed to assist Penny with the fitting of a pacemaker. This was like my days in the Guy's theatres, being shouted at and having to wriggle into theatre 'blues'. This first day I had hurriedly grabbed too small a top and too large trousers. The former made me look like Raquel Welsh and the latter had a disconcerting habit of falling down without warning. Rhona, the cardiac technician, who also present, said it was one of the best comedy shows she had ever seen. On returning the patient to the ward I was greeted with great merriment and cries like 'Where did you get that hat?' whereupon my trousers promptly fell down. It was quite a day.

Our patients were mainly middle-aged men who had suffered a frightening experience. They had visualised the ' grim reaper' arriving for them during their heart attacks. Once we had stabilised them with the aid of the clot busting drugs, an important part of their rehabilitation was lessening their anxiety and cheering them up. This was where my natural ebullience was such help, as I had found it was on Stephen ward at Guy's.

Penny had the opposite effect on us nurses. She induced anxiety and could reduce nurses to tears and the team of doctors under her to gibbering wrecks. The only defence was to know your stuff and not appear cowed, even if you were. If she scented fear she would move in for the kill. She certainly kept us on our toes and ensured high standards on the unit. As you can imagine she had a poor bedside manner, but the patients appreciated the good care she gave them. She provided me with quite a bit of amusement and when she left to go to New Zealand I really missed her and still do, if only for the fact that you knew your patients were getting the best possible treatment. It was lucky I started when I did as she taught me an awful lot.

I settled down quickly on the unit and found my wide range of nursing skills could be of benefit to the staff, which was satisfying. The staff themselves could not have been nicer, as I already knew. I particularly liked the senior Sister, Maxine White, who ran the ward but, sadly, has now left to pursue one of those 'mill board' jobs. I quickly became proficient on the computers, which had become an essential tool in our work. None of the staff had mastered the addressograph machine. This produced sexy little labels with all the patient's details on them. These could be stuck on the many forms that we had to fill in. I learnt to work it and deal with its many vagaries. This job gave me great delight and I always knew that once a new admission had got his labels printed the worse was over for him. If inotropes, thrombolytics and various other treatments were not working, I found that printing some more labels for him usually did the trick. So in emergencies the shout would go up: 'Miranda, do you want to go and have an orgasm and print some more labels?' I thus felt I was playing a vital role in the patient's rehabilitation. This was job satisfaction.

The other procedure I was good at was cardioversion. This was giving a synchronised shock to revert the heart rhythm from atrial fibrillation to sinus rhythm. I think my height assisted this in that I could exert sufficient downward pressure on the paddles to effect the reversion. I had witnessed many unsuccessful cardioversions on Stephen ward and was somewhat sceptical of their effectiveness. Yet I was now achieving an almost 100% success rate and many satisfied customers. The other pressure that one had to exert was on the anaesthetist and ODA technician to get their synchronised attendance to assist. This took considerable force of personality to achieve. I got used to combating their various excuses. My main ally in this battle was a Russian anaesthetist from St Petersburg, known as Prince Igor. One day when we couldn't bring a Polish patient round after the anaesthetic I shouted in the patient's ear, 'Look out, there is a Russian by your bed.' He immediately sat bolt upright. Dear old Prince Igor commented that he must add this measure to his protocol in future.

I was also what was known as the DFM (Deputy Fire Marshal). This was attaining dizzy heights. To qualify for this much-sought-after position I attended a two-day Fire Course. I had gone on a week's jolly down to Maidstone to become Knightsbridge Fire Officer whilst with the Life Guard Mounted Squadron. We had been billeted at the luxurious Angel Hotel and had a whale of a time. Thus I was looking forward to renewing my fire fighting skills. We reported to Kettering Fire Station. After watching a video of burnt bodies, to get us in the right frame of mind, we had to find our way round a dense smoke filled room. The secret seemed to be to avoid swearing when barking one's shins on obstacles placed in one's way. I don't think that I came top of the class in this discipline.

I was good with the old hose and, by turning it on a lecturer who was blathering on, I got us to lunch on time. I then blotted my copybook by absentmindedly going into the Gents loo out of lifelong habit. We also had to play strange games round the hospital, similar to 'Hunt the Slipper'. We were despatched in pairs to various wards to find hidden messages. Just before this I had become covered in mud from head to foot while lying down to connect a hose to a hydrant point down a deep chamber. Thus my arrival in the Day Case Unit caused some consternation. In their defence I must have had an even more strange appearance than normal, but even so we were both a bit miffed when the hospital security guards were called to eject us.

We rounded up the course by practising taking a patient down the main hospital stairway on a sort of sledge. This got away from us and went sailing on down the stairs on its own, narrowly missing a consultant on the way. It stopped safely at the bottom and the patient was none the worse for wear. He merely said; 'Blimey! Like going down the Cresta Run.' The consultant tried to complain to us, but we were laughing so much that he gave it up and wandered off.

Every spring Penny had taken her dogs and a couple of nurses away for a long weekend in some country Inn. By my second spring on the unit she had already departed to New Zealand. I decided to carry on the tradition. The other two unattached nurses besides myself, Jan and Donna, were also keen on the idea, so were Rowley and Poppy, my chows. I located what seemed like a cosy little inn near Southwold, by the sea, which welcomed 'well-behaved dogs.' It advertised a 'delightful snuggery with log fire burning'. We set off in convoy with the chows in my car and Donna in Jan's. I was the pathfinder and tootled along below 100 miles per hour so that they could keep up. We arrived at Southwold for lunch in pouring rain. Most of the restaurants had not yet opened for the season. After quite a search we eventually located a rather seedy looking place. They gave us a quite splendid meal with plenty to drink. The only thing was that every time Donna went to the loo her boyfriend rang her on her mobile. He showed interesting timing. The only explanation Donna could give was that he was 'a bit of a shit'.

That conundrum solved, we donned our Macintoshes and took the chows for a walk on the beech along past the Martello towers. These had apparently been constructed to repel an anticipated invasion by Napoleon. Our 'cosy inn' was a really ramshackle, rundown looking place. We were cold and wet by now but there was no snuggery or fire to be found to greet us. So we repaired to our rooms. The beams in these were so low that the cupboard doors could not open. On top of this inconvenience it was difficult to move around without cracking one's head on them. At least there was a bath in my room, which could be negotiated by moving along bent double. The girls came in for a bath after I had warmed myself up in it.

We fled the place to dine elsewhere in a proper cosy inn with a real crackling log fire. When we returned the door was locked. With the judicious use of gravel thrown at the windows we eventually gained access. The following morning we came down for breakfast in better spirits. There was a couple also staying there with their dog. I had heard a programme about the use of chemotherapy to combat cancer on the wireless that morning. I was regaling the girls on this and how chemotherapy only depressed the system and made things worse. The man butted in and asked me to be quiet as he was undergoing chemotherapy. Nothing daunted I changed the subject and asked him what he and his wife were going to do on that wet and windy day. They did not know what to do. I told them that we were going to visit the Maltings at Snape. They replied that they didn't like snakes and wouldn't go there. Even I gave up after that.

What we did do was to go down to Southwold beech with the chows. There was such a storm blowing that Donna stayed in the car. Jan and I braved the elements. Right along that part of the beach there were pretty brightly painted beach huts all with names such as 'Dun roaming' and 'Devana', whatever that means. More appropriately there was one called 'Stormy Weather'. The only other people on the beach were a few middle-aged men in dirty raincoats sporting little grey beards. They did not return our cheerful greetings. We came to the conclusion that they must be paedophiles. They certainly looked like that. Rowley must have agreed with our verdict as he growled at them. A thing he did not normally do. Bearing this in mind and that Donna was still very young, we hurried back to the car to make sure that she had not been molested, but all was well.

That evening having taken the dogs for a walk I kept bumping into the snake charmer. We would then alter our routes to avoid each other and lo and behold come face to face with each other again round the next bend. Fed up with this I returned to the inn to find the door locked again. I knew Jan and Donna were in their room so I called 'Donna.' There was no reply in spite of repeated calls. I eventually resorted to gravel again and the landlord opened the door. The stairs were so steep he and landlady used a stair lift to get up and down them and that took time he said. I said to Donna, 'Didn't you hear me calling, you silly ass?' She replied that she had but could not think why I was standing outside in the rain. There was no answer to this.

The following day we went to Snape. Years before I had heard Ted Heath, when he was Prime Minister, describing a visit to the Maltings Concert Hall. Alfred Brendel had been playing Mozart piano sonatas and 'the music had gone on and on, magically, through that lovely summer afternoon'. This description had somehow fired my imagination and I had vowed to go there one day. Now the hall was deserted and locked. The outbuildings were full of junk for sale with many people wandering rather dejectedly to keep out of the rain. I said to the girls, 'I have never seen such a load of old rubbish in my life.' The owner heard this remark and indignantly said, 'I took a lot of trouble putting this collection together.' I picked up a battered tin oil jug with 'Shell' on it like the ones on the farm. 'I bet you had a job finding this treasure,' I said as a parting shot. He kept a close eye on us until we left to try out the tearoom. That was disappointing. We laughed so much over that weekend. The girls were very good company and on our return CCU were entertained by them with the tales of our adventures for days. I have only recounted a few of these.

A certain amount of quick thinking and reaction is needed on an emergency unit like ours. Recently I was discharging a rather dignified black gentleman whose potassium had been slightly low. In these sorts of situations we normally recommend eating bananas. Quick as a flash I substituted 'oranges' and felt sublimely 'PC' in averting a possible crisis. At other times it is the shrilling of the alarm bell that causes the patter of tiny feet, or not so tiny in my case, to be heard in the land once more. When one of the patients had an alarm clock with a similar sounding bell, its ringing sent us all running in different directions. This was doubtless good exercise, but not so good for the patient, who was laughing so much he nearly had a second heart attack.

One sunny summer Saturday morning, I was just getting ready to set off to London, when the long shadow of my African past fell across my path. I had obtained tickets for Mozart's *The Magic Flute* at the Royal Opera House in Covent Garden. A couple of CCU nurses were coming with me and due to arrive shortly. I had just completed a spell on night duty, which upsets one's bowel pattern. In trying to clear the decks I got a great concrete-like lump stuck. The pain was so severe that I could barely stagger to the door to let them in. I beseeched them to help me but they thought the situation was too serious for that and suggested taking me into our A&E department. I did not want them to miss the opera, which was due to start at two o'clock, and hoped that I would be able to follow them later if I could manage to drive myself to Kettering. They thought that this was silly, but I pretended I was feeling a bit better and prevailed on them to set off on their own. By the time I got my car out I was feeling faint but somehow managed to get to 'casualty' and explain the problem before passing out. I came to in an examination room, being undressed by a nurse I knew as 'Puffing Billy'. Having worked with them all in A&E the whole thing was becoming increasingly embarrassing. Fortunately I had not met the doctor who came to examine me. I later gave him the nickname of 'Moonraker' when he joined us on CCU and he became a great favourite of mine. I was lucky as he was highly skilled. Puffing Billy stood beside him, puffing, as he began to remove the offending object. He advised a general anaesthetic but I refused, still dreaming of Mozart later in the day. The whole thing was aggravated by the scar tissue from my unfortunate Rhodesian experience and fistulas were mentioned. I was split again and required stitches. Other nurses I knew assisted in this, but were very good and never teased me about it later.

I never, however, quite lived the incident down with Moonraker. He would often look at me with a knowing smile and seemed proud that I had been his patient. I had an uncomfortable feeling that Miranda's unfortunate bare bottom would never completely fade from his memory and might be used in some future CV to gain him a distinguished medical post! At any rate, I never did make Covent Garden and my £160 ticket remains in one of my drawers to this day.

On our long frantic days, which start a seven o'clock in the morning and don't end until after nine at night, laughter is often the only thing that keeps us sane, as it did in my army days. Only now instead of sharing it with The Hon E S Biddulph and The Hon Nicky Beaumont my comrades are 'Been around a long time' Linda and 'Desert Island' Donna, but they still make my world go round as of old.

Chapter 17

Jamie

As the years passed, I am now in my tenth year on CCU and twentieth since my operation, I felt increasingly isolated because of my new sex. Of course my colleagues on the unit were friends, but at home the telephone never rang anymore. I so longed to ring one of my old friends. After all, so many of them had even started school with me at the outbreak of war. We had grown up together and even our families had been friends. A few of us had been in the cricket eleven and shared exciting stands at the wicket on long summer afternoons. Then there was the family atmosphere of the Life Guard officer's mess during our years in the Household Cavalry. If ever there was a band of brothers it was we.

Of course it was my own fault for surrendering to my female self. My own family cannot be blamed for shunning me. I have not even been allowed to see my younger son Toby's children. I am going to miss dreadfully not being able to take them out when they go to Eton. The elder boy is a promising cricketer too, I hear. I have spent the last fifteen Christmases on my own, apart from being on duty for part of the day. The worst of these was when I was at Guy's. Being on duty on Boxing Day also, I had arranged to stay in London at the home of an aged relative who had gone up to Scotland over Christmas. She had turned off the heating by mistake and there was not much to eat. It was freezing and Ming, my little chow, and I clung to each other for warmth. By the time the house warmed up a bit it was bedtime. I thought of all the lovely family occasions round the tree in the past. On the farm, the children used to decorate an old stone barn where the calves slept at night. In fact, Christmas has always been very special to me.

I suppose it might be thought that I should have kept Harold, my old pal I used to go up to Oxford to see. He obviously found me attractive and had proposed to me. In bed it had worked well, even if he was a bit frantic, as mentioned before. Penetration was achieved with the aid of the old wheat germ oil and I experienced what I took to be an orgasm. Quite how I achieved this I hadn't a clue! I was totally ignorant as to how my private parts had been refashioned. Harold was a vital part of becoming Miranda. He was there at the very beginning. Having suffered such a grievous emotional and physical trauma I needed to know that I was indeed a fully fledged member of the female sex. He was a well-educated and interesting companion. How the devil he did not twig about me I shall never know. I am sure he would have been horrified if he had found out.

I think what he saw was an equally well-educated widow, living in a 17th century manor house. She was obviously part of the landed gentry. He found her tall, slim and younger than himself. In short, he was smitten. On the other hand I had just escaped from a long and stifling marriage. I had just won my freedom after thirty years. Nothing was going to make me throw that away. Legally I could not have married him anyway, as stated above. We could have remained as friends and shared our Christmas, but my Guy's commitments made this difficult. Perhaps, if I had done my training at the Radcliffe in Oxford things might have worked out differently. It must be remembered that I had to put my new career first in order to live. I was very short of money at the time. In the event, in due course he married an ex-St Thomas' matron. She was nice and they were happy in the few years left to him, dear old Harold.

In these early female years, I attracted attention often. Being six foot tall did not help. People would stare or, more generally, giggle and make humorous asides to one another. Only once did I react to this taunting. I was sitting on a bench at Ladywell station on a late winter afternoon waiting for a train home after a dispiriting day traipsing round on my mid-wife training. A black man stood himself in front of me and asked me, 'Are you a man?' Quick as a flash I retorted, 'Are you a monkey?' I said it without thinking. but at least it had the desired effect of shutting him up.

The great difficulty with my momentous change was having to go it on my own. Jan Morris, whom I met with Harold in Oxford, wrote a most moving account of her sex change in the 1970s. Her great blessing was a loving wife and understanding and supportive children. Her friends, being perhaps a trifle more enlightened and trendy than mine, appeared to have adapted to her new state. Also, she had a ready-made career as a writer and journalist to continue. In my case I really was starting from scratch. To try and break into nursing, at that time, was about the most difficult thing I could have 'set my cap at'.

If I appear to have taken things in my stride, like the testicle being left inside me, it was because I had no one to turn to. I just had to get on with it. As I mentioned before, my family doctor and old friend David Brentnall, who signed my first Miranda passport, thought I was on some sort of undercover mission. I could not go back to him again. Therefore I did not know what the pain was and assumed that it would clear up in time. I am sure a close friend would have made me go straight back to Mr Harrod, who had carried out the operation.

Five years ago a new nurse, Jamie, started on CCU. On her first day I was helping her with a somewhat unstable post-heart attack man. We were 'going to town' on him setting up various intravenous infusions. She informed me that he had four venflons sited to attach these to. I couldn't find the fourth and in my best clinical parlance asked her to put the pump line I had in my hand 'on the end of his tiddlypush', whereupon our patient whipped his pyjama trousers down and held up what Jamie called his 'Winky Woo'. We were both reduced to tears of laughter and became firm friends thereafter. I am glad to report that the patient survived and said 'Winky Woo' was returned to base in good order.

Over the ensuing months and indeed years, as the song goes, 'I became accustomed to her face, her ups, her downs....'. However hard the going on the unit was at times, we seemed to remain cheerful and full of fun when working together. We had a young blonde Senior House Officer called Vicky for about five weeks. She noticed this and said how much better CCU was with us there. This atmosphere definitely cheers up our patients and is beneficial in their recovery. Vicky wore a fine variety of pink blouses for the entire five weeks and we always remember and refer it as our pink period. On leaving, Vicky stated that she was going to try and 'poach' Jamie and me to be her practice nurses, when she became a GP. She was even tolerant of my frequent indiscretions. Such as when I knocked a huge bottle of Lucozade off a prim old lady's bedside table on to my toe, exclaiming ' F*** A Duck!' the lady, rather quaintly, on hearing this, remarked, 'We used to keep ducks.' When I ran into Vicky, some time after she left us, She rather wistfully said that nobody called her a 'silly ass' on her new ward.

On a freezing winter day earlier this year, I took Donna and Jan, who had been on our Southwold outing, together with Jamie, to see *Journey's End* in London. This is a play about a group of British officers in a trench before the last great German offensive of the First World War. R C Sherriff, an ex-officer, who had experienced it, wrote it after that war. I had a part in it at school, but the play was cancelled. I knew that it was going to be moving for me. So many members of my family had perished there and I was brought up hearing the harrowing tales of the survivors. What I didn't know was how it would affect the girls. As the final barrage came to a thunderous ending and the curtain came down, I looked across at Jamie who sat speechless in her seat with tears in her eyes. As ever, she was on the same 'wavelength' as me. This is rather remarkable, bearing in mind the vast difference in our respective ages and backgrounds. I am really a product of a different Imperial past. Jamie is still in her thirties, very much into texting and the wonders of the modern age.

Jamie was born in Barking and still retained the slight cockney twang of a Londoner. She is fair, blue eyed, with a slim, athletic build and ballet dancer's calves. The latter inherited from her mother, as I now know. There is a fine fair down on her arms which suits her and is very much part of her. She has the impish cockney humour with a ready smile. One evening I stayed late when she was taking over from me for night duty. She was in tears and I tried to comfort her. My ex-wife June was ugly when she cried. Jamie was beautiful.

Fundamentally, I have a certain feeling of relief at just being alive. I have escaped almost certain death on a number of occasions. None more so than in Aden, in a wadi ambush. Standing in the turret of my Ferret armoured car I dropped my map. As I leant down to pick it up, a 'dum-dum' bullet whistled over my head. These bullets, fired by the Shamshi tribesmen, do not have a sharp point and cause terrible wounds. I was very lucky on another occasion. My Ferret hit a mine on the Dhala road. The sandbags placed on the floor plating must have taken some of the blast. My driver was killed but I was thrown clear. Apart from superficial cuts and bruises and temporary deafness I was unhurt. My fellow officers even joked that I seemed more sensible following it than before! My shredded uniform was kept as an example of the durability of a Life Guard.

Also, in the London blitz, death stalked us nightly. Thus I had not tended to agonise over my sexual predicament. I did now, however, need to understand more of what had happened to me. What form had the operation taken? How was it that I could still have a form of orgasm? Was I really a woman now? I could not find Mr Harrod, who had carried out the surgery. The Rotherham clinic appeared to have gone. My present GP was none the wiser. He even inquired what form the operation had taken.

Jamie came down, with a group of my nursing friends, to Llanstefan on the west Wales coast for a week's holiday. Amongst that group were my old Guy's companions, Sarah June and Melanie. It was the former and her husband, Paul, who had greeted the New Year in such memorable style all those years ago at Guy's. Melanie had shared my first hours as a qualified nurse. It was one of those lovely early parts of the summer, with warm sun day after day. Jamie and I would wander along the near deserted beach, with the surf swirling round our ankles. Her willowy frame was above medium height. I noticed how the skin on her legs was of a different texture to that of her fair arms. She discussed her present life. I somehow, for the very first time since becoming female, felt able to share my innermost thoughts and worries with someone. It was like suddenly having a beautiful loving daughter.

We shared those magical June days with our jolly group of friends. We swam, played croquet, went on boat trips and took tea in Dylan Thomas' boathouse. His Renault Clio was still parked outside it! We even arrived just too late to have to deal with a cardiac arrest beside the sea! Of an evening we, or rather they, prepared great feasts, followed by rivers of wine and a card game called appropriately 'O Hell'. We would finally stagger up to bed in that most pleasant of tipsy states. It doubtless led to my rolling out of bed in the early hours one morning. The glass top of the bedside table and a massive lamp followed me on to the floor, causing cuts and bruises. These wounds were further aggravated by the top of the loo seat busting up beneath me and a stumble dismounting from my Saab. Jamie tended my wounds with the aid of steri-strips.

On our return home, all this led to Jamie initiating me into some the wonders of the fair sex. It was almost as if I had been in 'No-Man's Land' for the past seventeen years. I was introduced into the rigours of make-up and 'eye shadow' as opposed to 'five o'clock shadow'. We boldly set off to Stamford on a 'Buy Miranda a Bra' expedition. I had never owned or worn one before. I learned that what I had worn, to cover my blushes, on my nursing medical examinations, was really a camisole top.

We bogeyed up in a cubicle at the top of a Lady's Lingerie shop. There the mysteries of '42C' and '38DD' were unveiled. We laughed so much that I was quite incapable of putting the wretched things on. Jamie had to do it for me. This entailed putting them round the waist back to front. Then twisting them round and somehow pulling them up. Then the straps had to be put up over the shoulders with contortionist wriggles. The exciting bit came when one had to push one's 'boobs' home into them from the top, with a triumphal flourish. It seemed a funny way to go on. By the time we repaired to the George Inn for lunch. I was 'knackered'. I must have struggled into more than a dozen different sizes. What the ladies in the adjoining cubicles made of our merriment I dread to think! They went very quiet. The shop assistant looked as if she had completed a long and tiring journey by the time it came for us to leave. It was a case of 'Come back, Nada, all is forgiven', when I think of my impatience with my sister when she took so long to get ready. Indeed this applied to every girl who had kept me waiting over the years. Little had I known!

The reward for all this effort came that evening, at a dinner party given by a doctor, married to one of our nurses, to which I had taken Jamie and Donna. A splendid toast was drunk to my new bra. It made it all worthwhile. To cap it all, the following afternoon I played my first croquet game wearing it 'Chez-Jamie'. Playing for Guy's and later for the army I triumphed.

Another great female occupation, even preoccupation, seemed to centre upon leg hair removal. I remember my old love Annabel telling me, with a giggle, that girls only shaved below the knee. This was borne out on the beaches of my youth. Most girls sporting down on their thighs of varying colour and density. This never appeared unattractive to me. The girls I had worked with at Guy's said they used an ordinary razor whilst sitting in the bath. Things had obviously moved on since then. Jamie and her pals used an electric appliance, called an epilator, on the entire leg. This apparently pulled out the hairs, which then proceeded to grow back under the skin. This in turn necessitated the use of a loofer to remove that skin. It sounded a full-time job to me. Certainly it made their legs look beautifully smooth and smart. It made my occasional forays with an electric razor seem a bit basic. Doubtless I shall be dragged, kicking and screaming, into 21st century methods before long!

I had not bought any clothes for a number of years. I suppose I must have looked a bit 'down at heel' to Jamie. I had found it difficult to find clothes that looked right on me. We set off, in the open top Saab, to a large Marks and Sparks, one scorching July day, to rectify this. It was an education in itself to see Jamie go to work. She was totally focused on every piece of clothing she thought might do for me. It did not seem to matter if unsuitable garments were left strewn about a bit. Only when she was fully satisfied and we had been to a cubicle for a trying on session, did she relax. I had always thought how smart and well dressed she was herself. Now I began to look much more feminine when dressed by her. She had unearthed some really lovely things for me. It brought home to me what I had missed since embracing the female sex. I had really been a bit lost in this new world before. Yet as a young officer I had always known what was the right thing to wear. I had been a sort of male Jamie with an equally slim build. I am sure I had looked just as smart.

The other great thing I was taught was the art of texting. I had not even realised this existed. This exchange of confidential loving little messages seemed to me to be a lovely innovation. I had always been a great letter writer. So often, however, in my life, these had got into the wrong hands or, unbeknown to me, failed to reach their destination or been misunderstood. In fact at the time of my divorce I had written what I considered to be 'letters from the heart' to a member of the family. These had, by chance, ended up with quite the wrong person. Now, when Jamie was on holiday in some distant land, with her family, and I was feeling a bit lost and lonely, the tiny 'peep peep' would bring her back to me for a precious moment.

Paradoxically, the closer we two became the more feminine I felt. I began to get pleasure again in just being a woman, as I had at the very start of my great adventure. Recently, I had begun to grieve at the loss of my family and old friends. Even the attentions of the hospital chaplain, known as 'The Boogie Woogie Bishop from Baluchistan', which had begun to irk me, now seemed appropriate and flattering. Nursing in a bra began to take on a whole new meaning. The grateful kisses from my patient's male relatives, erstwhile treated as a bit of a joke by me, became right for Miranda, even if they were a bit bristly. The touch of their hands on my bare arms was what a girl would expect!

Laura, Vicky's best friend, was our Senior House Officer on my first bra week. She was a sweet girl and most encouraging about my new clothes when I had to visit the unit out of uniform. During the week I was able to discuss bras, amongst other things, with her and it felt just like two girls together! She was relaxed and friendly. I would catch her eyeing me with amused tolerance when I came out with one of my more bizarre offerings. I think I was becoming more my real self. I was so used to having screw up my courage to come on duty in the public gaze. For so long it had almost been like going on stage. I suppose having Jamie had given me an inner confidence. Her absolute insistence on complete frankness had perhaps cleared away some of the dark recesses of the mind; a realisation that those little secrets that I had guarded since childhood and nobody had been able to prize from me were not so terrible after all. Unconsciously I think I had hidden from her the fact that the first time I had consummated a sexual act had been on my wedding night. The skirmishes with Jennifer, the nice Ma Feather's girl, had been just that. It no longer seemed anything to be ashamed of. The young perhaps do not realise what innocents we were. We put women on a pedestal and treated them with great care and deference. They were the most wondrous creatures to us. It was almost as if they had come from another planet. The modern girl is so much more sexually aware than we ever were.

Yet again, however, I was brought down to earth when one of my best friends from my Knightsbridge days, Everard de Lisle, was recently tragically killed in a car accident. He lived nearby and I had spent the night before my wedding at his house with him and his parents. His wife and I had also been pals when we were young. We used to ride across the Yorkshire moors together when staying at her home. I remembered the time that I had leant across and kissed her, unaware that her entire family were behind us in their car! I had introduced them to one another and we were mutual godparents to each other's children. I was not informed of his death nor invited to the funeral. I only heard about it later from a chance remark by one of my patients. At least, as my godson later told me, my letter of condolence was quite the best of the many that they had received. It was almost as if I was a pariah who had carried out some terrible crime and must wander in the wilderness for the rest of his or her days. Even poor Profumo was finally 'brought in from the cold' after his peccadillo with Christine Keeler and lying to the House of Commons. He had richly earned it by toiling for years at Toynbee Hall, in the East End of London, on behalf of the poor and needy. I feel that I have given myself body and soul to nursing the sick and dying for the past sixteen years. I am a respected and well-known local figure, but not, it would seem, to my own sort.

I did attend Everard's rather grand memorial service in Leicester Cathedral, some time after his death. It was an extraordinary experience for me. For a start, I heard myself being discussed by some erstwhile friends sitting behind me. Neither they nor the many old Household Cavalry comrades recognised me. I barely recognised them. I had last seen them many of them as young men. It was if a malign fairy had touched them with her wand and turned them in an instant into grey old men hobbling along with the aid of sticks. After the service, which was beautifully carried out, I drifted with everyone else towards a gathering in the vestibule. Now was my last chance to greet some of them but I could not cross that divide. It was just too wide. I drove sadly away out of their lives forever. It had upset me terribly. I wondered if I should have come, but I wanted to pay a farewell tribute to my old friend.

The difference in age between my present companions and myself was brought home to me at The Royal Opera house one night. I had taken a box with three of the girls who worked with me on the Coronary Care Unit. At the interval they went out to 'spend a penny'. I remained sitting, with Mozart's music still echoing round my mind. A lady in the adjoining box leant over and said kindly, 'How nice to see a mother taking her three daughters to the opera.' I could have corrected her by pointing out that they were more like my granddaughters, but let the opportunity slip!

As I think I saw Jamie as a daughter, the age gap was not an issue with her. She firmly believed that we should seek an examination by a specialist to try and find out how my private parts had been refashioned and whether in fact I did possibly have ovaries or something. She thought the knowledge thus gained would settle my mind.

I very much agreed that it might well be of great benefit to me. Jamie had great difficulty in finding a suitable expert until Laura, our SHO, came to the rescue and found a Mr Standing whom Vicky, of the pink period, had worked for.

Jamie telephoned his secretary, who was keener on getting my credit card details than arranging a private consultation without a GP referral. I duly set off to Uppingham, on a sweltering July morning, to seek this. My GP was sitting in a remarkably luxurious and airy room, looking very pleased with himself, as well he might, following the recent mad pay award to his kind. I found it difficult to explain why I wanted to see Standing, so blurted out that I was having difficulty with 'sexual relations'. Whereupon he gave me a very funny look. I dread to think what was going through his mind! At any rate, he pulled himself together and gave me a little talk on the virtues of oestrogen cream. He then enquired after my waterworks. 'Oh, terrible,' I replied. This did the trick, as Standing was an urologist, as well as carrying out sex change operations. I got my referral but emerged feeling rather shaken, to be greeted by a grateful ex-patient of mine. She restored my self-confidence somewhat.

That same warm summer night I was transported back in time to my former life as the mainstay of my beloved cows. My son Rollo telephoned to ask my assistance with a difficult calving. I arose from my bed willingly, as I was very unhappy with Jamie across the seas and far away. In this state I had found sleep so hard to come by. I was unused to this level of suffering. I was out of practice! As I drove the six miles down into the valley and across the River Welland, it occurred to me that the last time I had experienced this longing was over Annabel. That was over fifty years ago now, but still so vivid to me in that soft and gentle darkness. A few tears went plopping down on to the steering wheel. I hadn't felt that sweet yet sad taste in my mouth for many a moon. Were they shed for Jamie or Annabel or perhaps myself and the loss of all that I had once lived for?

Arriving at the farm, I walked up the familiar path, to the calving boxes. I had trod this under the stars for more than thirty years, on so many similar nights. Rollo greeted me in his calm unhurried manner. I started to strip off my shirt as of old. Calving is a messy business and you need to insert the arm up to the shoulder on occasions. I noticed Rollo staring at me. It suddenly dawned on me that it was not perhaps altogether usual for ladies to stand naked above the waist without the old 38DD on board. Even if it had occurred to me, I would have been loath to mess my bra up, as I needed it to wear under my nursing uniform in the morning. I felt Jamie would have approved of these sentiments but was not quite sure on this point!

At any rate, the welsh black heifer was number one priority at that juncture. She did also give me a rather funny look as I entered her box. I consoled myself that this could have been because I was now a stranger to her, rather than the sight of, what were by now, my fairly lively bare breasts! After half an hour's hard work Miranda emerged glistening like a 'Rhine Maiden' with a smashing bull calf in her arms. By the time I had hosed myself off, baby was up and drinking from her proud mum. My old joy at the birth was still there. I would have liked to be a fly on the wall to have heard how Rollo described this pantomime to his wife, but perhaps he was too weary by then, like me.

Since entering the female ranks I have worn a wig, although I have a fairly good head of hair. In fact 'the change' had made the hair grow thicker. Nevertheless the female's crowning glory could not be achieved without it. It also certainly saved a lot of messing about. I suppose this practice was not all that unusual. I remember my mother wearing a wig for many grand occasions. In the 18th century they had been generally used. The only time that I find them uncomfortable is in very hot weather, particularly on a hospital ward. The hair has to be cut fairly short under them and there is a problem, how to go to the barber dressed like Marie Antoinette. Once, in fact, when I was at Guy's and without a change of clothing, I had simply gone in, sat down, pulled off my wig and requested a short back and sides. This had, however, caused rather a stir. So now on my trips to Uppingham I wear trousers and as loose a shirt as possible hoping to pass myself off as a man! A sort of exercise in role reversals. The tricky bit is removing the wig in the street just before entering the barber's shop. I dare not be seen without it for fear of running into one of my old patients. As can be imagined, this manoeuvre does not always go quite as planned. Either one drops the damn thing or bumps into a departing customer with it half on and half off. Such is the life of a Miranda.

Outdoor activities can also present their own interesting situations. Once when I was surfing I caught a great wave beautifully, only to see my wig racing along beside me on the very same wave. Also, gale force winds have to be catered for. At the start of my time on CCU I decided to buy the unit some proper mirrors. I set off to the local Wilkinson's and as I walked down the street the high wind sent my wig scurrying down the road ahead of me. I ran after it and eventually managed to stamp on it only, on looking up, to notice a bus queue watching spellbound.

When assisting in the siting of pacemakers in our little pacing suite, we have to dress in theatre blues, which include a tight hat. This tended to squash down my wig and spoil it. I now keep an old knackered model in the car and keep the hat on this and whip the entire contraption on my head when no one is looking.

Tension-filled ambulance journeys have been part of life on CCU since I started there. The reason for this is the fact that we have no cardiac catheter theatre at Kettering. At Guy's we simply took the patient across the corridor to our own little theatre to carry out advanced cardiac procedures on patients whose life was threatened. Even that little journey could be nerve-racking with someone unstable. We now have to escort them by ambulance to Glenfield Hospital in Leicester. This takes at least forty minutes on a 'blue light' with a following wind! One particular trip I shall never forget saw us caught up in a traffic jam on the M1. I did 'what a nurse has to do' and leapt out of the vehicle to cajole a van driver to move out of the way and allow us to get on to the hard shoulder. I was not on board for more than five minutes when a broken down van blocked our path again. I jumped out and rounded-up a gang of waiting lorry drivers. Between us we managed to push the offending vehicle out of the light. It ended up in some bushes down an embankment! By this time I was occasioning some ribald comments. 'Crikey, look at Action Nurse' and ' Don't ladder your stockings, Sister' being a couple of them. This story had a happy ending as we delivered our lady 'shaken but not stirred' to her destination in 'double-quick time'. At least those excitements were preferable to some of my other joys such as breakdowns and cardiac arrests en route. It is always nice to deliver a live patient at journey's end!

All the nurses on CCU now work double shifts. Previously I was the only one who did. This entails coming on duty at seven o'clock in the morning and working until eight at night. It is around four that one begins to feel the pace. It is at that time that our little evening 'Domestic' arrives. She is a schoolgirl known as Gubbins by me, or more generally, 'Gubbins Darling'. She is a ray of sunshine and lifts our flagging spirits. The fact that she can handle Miranda shows her maturity and even virtuosity! She is so much part of the dear old tottering National Health Service. As was the aged gentleman, who when asked by Jamie, if he wanted to see the Chaplain, replied, 'I haven't been to the cinema for years.' We looked at each other in puzzlement for a minute, visions of the 'Boogie Woogie' Bishop in Hollywood springing to mind, before the 'penny dropped.' That wistful smile on his old face was in memory of Charlie Chaplin. To paraphrase The Eton Boating Song:

> The private sector may be more clever,
> The Government may make more row,

But we'll row, row, row for ever,
Steady from stroke to bow.
Others may fill our places,
Dressed in the old light blue.
As we recollect our races,
We to the flag will be true,
We will still swing, swing, together
And swear by the best they allow,
And nothing in life shall ever sever
The chain that surrounds us now.

At long last, the great day arrived to see Mr Standing and find out what had happened to me in 1989. I picked up Jamie at Kettering Hospital, as she had arranged to come on duty late that day and I would return her there on our way back. The BUPA hospital seemed an oasis of calm after our working atmosphere of frantic battle for survival. It was a different world from the NHS. We parked the car and strolled through well-tended gardens. The only person to be seen was a gardener standing on one leg, for a reason not too obvious to fathom 'en passant'.

Inside the hospital the same calm prevailed. It was somewhat shattered by my forgetting to lock the door when 'spending a penny'. A gentleman burst in on me and retired in confusion. I only hoped it was not Mr Standing, as this would have started us off on the wrong foot. When finally ushered into his august presence he turned out to be a thoroughly approachable chap and not at all the sort of person to burst in on ladies with their pants down. The pants off syndrome would occur all too soon.

Jamie, wisely, had told me to keep quiet and she would prepare the ground. She first of all had to cancel all the symptoms expounded to Fish Paste (my GP). This was done with admirable finesse. We could now start on a 'level playing field' as it were. The first conclusion he came to was that my early operations requiring pink liquid were probably normal realignment of the male genitalia such as dropping a testicle down or something like that. This did not, however, explain the remarks I had overheard the doctor in the white coat make about me being female.

He classified me as a true transsexual who had imagined himself to be female since birth. The reason for this was, apparently, still undiscovered. The cause could be either nurture or genetic. As I had fathered children he ruled out my being a hermaphrodite. Also, he felt that further investigations, such as a chromosome saliva test or ultrasound scan, would be superfluous, as my fertility showed that I could not possess ovaries or anything like that. Jamie pointed out my breast size. He replied that 30% of transsexuals had that good development, without implants, following surgery With reference to my previous life as army officer and farmer, he said that many of his clients had led macho lives deliberately trying to mask their femininity. I told him my difficulty in getting hold of the old medical notes relating to my operation. He informed us that these would have been destroyed by now. This applied to anything in the private sector in the 1980s.

The climax of the consultation was now reached. The examination to judge Harrod's handiwork. I was told to remove my pants and shoes and lie on the couch with my skirt up round my waist. Jamie was at first unsure of her role in this. She had a little local difficulty with the cubicle curtain. At one stage she appeared to be wrapped up in it but with a few muttered 'Oh Hells' extricated herself and was welcomed to join Mr Standing at his side. As he carried out an internal examination he explained it all to her as a fellow member of the medical profession. My vaginal passage was short and the labia majora needed to be restructured from the excess skin left after the removal of the testicles from the scrotum. Also, he pointed out how this excess scrotal skin could be used to make a longer vaginal passage. In fact, Mr Harrod had formed two passages in me, one within a space in the pelvic cavity and the main one outside the body in the empty scrotal sack. The examination caused me quite a bit of pain. I shut my eyes and did not suffer too much embarrassment as a consequence. As a nurse, the thing that came into my mind at that moment was whether I could be catheterised. Jamie told me afterwards that exactly the same question occurred to her. She supposed that this was not surprising, as almost the only time we delved up this part of the female anatomy was to carry out this procedure. The difficulty was always to find the correct hole to insert the damn thing. She had identified this orifice in me and therefore did not feel that it was necessary to ask Mr Standing about catheterising, as it appeared obvious it could be done.

After I had dressed and sat down beside Jamie again, he advised us that by doing the above-mentioned surgery he could tidy up the loose folds of skin and make a larger deeper vagina if I so desired. It was too late to fashion a clitoris, as the nerve endings would have been taken away already. This latter practice was not yet developed in 1989. He then drew a diagram showing my operation and how he could improve it. Jamie asked him how much this would cost. He was a bit reticent about this. He did not give an answer. He was adamant that my present queries were due to the fact that I had never undergone counselling. He advised me to see their own psychiatrist who specialised in these matters. Jamie thought that this was a good idea. I was a bit doubtful. However, he said that he would not carry out any surgery until I had done this. So I agreed and we made an appointment on our way out. He had a rather outlandish foreign name which did not sound too promising.

It seemed to us to boil down to the fact of whether I would ever have sex again. I feel that I have always been very highly sexed. I have never been the slightest bit neuter before or after my operation. Standing had explained that I still had the gland from the tip of the penis inside me. My orgasm with Harold was thus accompanied by a slight ejaculation from this. He said that the female usually 'peed' in the same situation at any rate. Jamie having helped me to awaken my female self again, I really feel the need to make love once more before I 'shuffle off this mortal coil'. In fact, I have come to the rather startling conclusion that my sexual drive could have been so fulfilled if I had married the girl that I loved above everything else in my life, that there would have been no urge to change sex to find ultimate satisfaction and happiness. Thus, it was Annabel who held the key to my life. I do not even know if she is still alive, but I sense she is still somewhere out there. I remember dear old 'Batkins' (The late lamented Andrew Burnaby Atkins) telling me that Annabel's husband, Richard, was very like me in looks and personality, which is bad luck for him if it was indeed so!

As we returned to the car, the gardener was on two feet again and so obviously all was well with the world on his side of the potting shed. We stopped off at a little Italian restaurant for lunch, to fortify Jamie prior to her stint on duty. Over a Dover sole I thought how lucky I was to have such friend. I would never have gone through that ordeal on my own. My mind was so much more settled now. Perhaps I could enjoy a little Indian summer of happiness before it was too late in my much-cherished new sex. Would I even attract another Harold to make love to me again? If I kept my courage up all might be well with the world on my side of the potting shed as well.

We had to wait a month for the psychiatrist's appointment. The only one he had was at eight in the evening. This was difficult for me as I was on duty that day and could not swap my shift. With great difficulty I got the night nurse to come in early so that I could hopefully hand over my patients by seven thirty. Oadby was a good thirty minutes drive away. Jamie was waiting at the main hospital entrance with her engine ticking over. We just made it to be told that the doctor had tried to cancel the appointment that afternoon. I could have castrated him on the spot, but he soon turned up looking rather flustered and in a rush.

He refused to let Jamie come in at the start of the consultation, which further irritated me. The first thing he said to me when I sat down was, 'I suppose you want gender reassignment.' I replied 'Haven't you received Mr Standing's notes?' He had not, even though their respective offices were only two doors apart. He knew nothing about me at all. I was beginning to think I should have stuck to the NHS!

He treated me like some juvenile delinquent who had just come in off the street making impossible demands. As a battle-hardened cardiac nurse who had made her way as a female in the most demanding of professions for the past sixteen years, it was downright insulting. Instead of exploding, I fetched Jamie. She calmed things down and began a masterly review of my life. He started to get fidgety and looked at his watch. He then cut her short, said he would recommend me for surgery and to pay at the desk on the way out. This farce cost me £150. I cannot understand why Mr Standing, in my case, felt it necessary to have his approval. Unless on the principle of 'If you scratch my back, I'll scratch yours.'

As a transsexual you are always up against it. Recently I was offered a 'Gender Recognition Certificate' which I was informed would lead to a birth certificate as a female. What a difference this would have made to me in all my early titanic battles in the nursing profession. Although I did not really need it now I decided to apply. It seemed like the end of the search for the Holy Grail was within my grasp. It was like being awarded my Guy's badge. At long last, Miranda was Miranda. No sooner had I received it, however, than I received a stunning letter from the pension people stating that my state pension would now be reduced by £1000 per annum. The rationale for this is apparently that a female retires at 60 and therefore her additional earnings are less than a male. It did no good to point out that I was officially a male then and earned the money as such. They replied that I was classed as a female now. Right, I said, therefore I should have received my pension at 60 not 65. This would be worth about £20,000. No they said you only became a female on receipt of your 'Gender Recognition Certificate'. It is a case of 'Heads you win. Tails I lose'. It is the logic of 'Alice in Wonderland'. As my Equitable Life pension went 'belly up' I shall now have to work until my dying day. At least the new law makes this possible, but perhaps it will not apply to transsexuals!

To forget all these irritations and disappointments, Jamie and I set off to Wimbledon to spend the weekend with Paul and Sarah June Regan. Rain belted down all day. We stopped for lunch in Kew Green on the way there. It was an excellent meal. The rain lashed against the windowpane as we talked and talked. I was happier than I had been for years. Those years had fallen away and I felt like the joyful Rhodri of my salad days again.

The Sunday was a beautiful autumn day. We all went off to see the Mill House in the middle of Wimbledon Common. I had not been back since we left it on the outbreak of war in 1939 when I was six. The happiest years of my childhood had been spent there. It was the only time all the family had been united. My brother John had once been back, but on looking through the garden gate had been confronted by the then owner. He told her that he had once lived there. She replied 'Well you don't live here anymore, so bugger off'. This had upset him a lot.

There it was now, basking in the hot sun and looking as beautiful as ever, to my eyes, with its large luxuriant garden full of flowers. Woolgar, our old gardener, would have been proud of it. We rang the bell but no one answered. Agile Jamie climbed the gate and took some photographs. To cap it all I spotted a 'Black-un'. The Common Rangers were ex-Life Guards. I chatted with them and discovered that the Mill House had just been sold for £6 million. No wonder we children had loved it so and spent the war years longing to return to 'our home'. I think if I had been on my own I would shed some tears for that lost world of happiness. I kept 'a stiff upper lip' and I don't think even Jamie realised my choking emotions.

The following day, after that little trip to paradise, we were back on duty again on the Coronary Care Unit. Jamie, for the umpteenth time, bade me speak more softly. She challenged me to answer the telephone when our consultant responded to his 'bleep' and pretend to be her. I duly adopted what I fondly imagined to be a convincing falsetto tone. The Consultant listened wearily to this for a while and replied, 'You sound as if you have been castrated,' before putting the telephone down. It was further proof that someone in my position simply cannot win!

Where I do win is the fact that I am very young for my age. Most of my old friends are either dead or in their dotage. As mentioned before, this was brought home to me at Everard de Lisle's memorial service. I am certain that none of them would be capable of enduring my long working days, so full of physical and mental stress, which I still do full time. Jamie classifies me as stronger than any other nurse, male or female, on CCU. I still jealously guard my 100% attendance record. One of my patients, the other day, said to me 'You are beautiful, you are such a tall stately lady,' yet I am very much a 'hands-on' nurse.

How much this is due to the hormones, with which I have flooded my body ever since changing sex, I am not sure. I have certainly enjoyed perfect health. I once stopped taking them for six months. I felt I was not quite so mentally alert during this period. Of course, the elixir of my youth may just be due to motivation. As the RAMC Colonel, who had to pass me 'Fit for service everywhere', following my bad back injury at The Guard's Depot at Pirbright, noted in my medical records: 'The motivation of this Officer Cadet is so excellent...' So perhaps it is just me.

The upshot of this feeling of comparative youth and well-being is a need for sexual fulfilment. I have had no sex-life since Harold nearly fifteen years ago. Even then the pain during penetration was pretty challenging. I accepted it then rather as a virgin must. This is what I was as a female. My hopes of overcoming this lie in Mr Standing's skill in refashioning my vagina. These feelings of feminine desire are so different from those Rhodri felt. I wonder if the opposite sex quite realise this. I certainly had not before experiencing them. I often lie naked in bed riven by them. Even my breasts seem to harden and rise.

I qualified as a nurse at 60 years of age, by which time the vast majority of nurses have retired. I am now in my mid-seventies. I suppose one day I shall just go up in a puff of smoke and be no more. Helen, our stalwart Health Care Assistant, has promised to 'lay me out' in proper style, without a neck brace to spoil my trip to paradise. She is such a kind, motherly sort of girl that it almost makes me impatient for that day to arrive! Then, as long as Jamie is there to hold my hand, with her warm smile, lighting up the dimples in her cheeks, I shall die happy. I will then carry the memory of my beloved and faithful friend on my 'long journey into night' without her.

Chapter 18

Miranda

Since returning from Guy's, I have been at Kettering for fifteen years. Most of the people in the hospital who stood in my way have gone now. I have outlasted them all. My nursing career is approaching its twentieth year. It is longer than I was in the army. I have not missed one shift in all those years. I have given the NHS excellent service, but it took quite exceptional fortitude on my part for them to allow me to serve them at all. I am the first person to have achieved this. I can only hope that I am not the last and that my success will light a beacon for others to follow some day. That is the reason that I have told my story.

The reason why I took this dramatic step I have tried to fathom and explain. A factor in this, that finally pushed me over the precipice as it were, could be the male menopause. Like many others before me, it hit me very hard. It very unsettling and gives one a feeling of impending doom. There is a desperate urge to recapture some of the joys of one's youth before it is too late. In spineless men this manifests itself as depression. In the more dashing types it is running off with a younger woman. In my case, being of the latter persuasion, it was running off with myself!

As far as my long marriage to June was concerned, it started in the hunting fields of Leicestershire, like her parents before her. Like them, it had a Guard's background. June and I were totally different people caught for a brief moment in the same world and perhaps imagining that it would be there forever. She bore me children to be proud of and was a loyal wife. We built up a successful farm together and worked very hard. We virtually never argued and there was no strife in a happy home. Eventually, however, our colossal disparity as people began to pull us apart. As I saw the sands of time running out I began to reach for the stars. Sensible June stayed rooted on mother earth. No trip through the heavens for her. They say the break-up of a marriage is never only one partner's fault. In our case I feel it was entirely mine. I just wish that we could have remained good friends. We had, after all, given each other the best years of our life.

Guy's died when the casualty department was moved to St Thomas' Hospital recently, as the Bermondsey clan, it served so faithfully, go there now when in trouble. The spirit that inspired generations of doctors and nurses going back to Thomas Guy himself in the 18th century is dead. I was amongst the last people to be imbued by it. I do hope that I have been able to pay tribute to it in this book and provide a little last memorial to it for those of us who loved and served it in our different ways.

I see no reason to be ashamed of making Miranda. I served The Life Guards and my Queen loyally, when called to arms, like my Ponsonby ancestors before me. I may be eccentric, like so many of them, but perhaps it is that individualism that has enabled us to achieve great things. Major General Sir John Ponsonby, in his book *The Ponsonby Family*, wrote: 'In every walk of life . . . the family seem to have taken their own line and to have acted according to their convictions without regard to the consequences.'

Sometimes when I sit in front of my fire on a winter night, with my chows lying round me, I feel like that legendary schoolmaster Mr Chips did with his boys. The hundreds of people that I have looked after seem to walk in an endless line past me. I remember their faces and a few of their names, but most of all the battles that we have fought together to save their lives. They never forget me and that is perhaps what I am proudest of.

I have had to undertake this last great adventure of my life, with one notable exception, without the support of my family. The loss of them at a time of life when one normally draws closer than ever to them, as they extend with the addition of grandchildren, has been a blow. I have also, as mentioned before, lost all my old friends. I have perhaps condemned myself to an isolated old age. In losing Rhodri I have lost a part of myself. I shall never again experience the intoxicating pleasure of holding a girl in my arms and feeling her velvet cheek against mine. In 'dancing to the music of time' I shall never be entirely one thing or the other. As a crotchety old man said to me on Harrowden C, 'You are no use as man or woman.'

On the other hand, I have long since stopped bothering if I am laughed at. I have entered a new profession, which has brought me great fulfilment. This I would never have done without Miranda. I have many new young friends who are happy to judge me as I am. In my heart of hearts I feel I am still me. In fact, I am probably more true to my real self than ever before. Miranda has also given me a new lease of life. I have not aged, as I would have done. I have gained the respect of local people. I have become a valued member of the local community with power to do good and help them.

Above everything, I have been happy as Miranda and therefore should not regret the dramatic step that I took. I am at peace and as I play my beloved Mozart into the night my cup is full and I fear no evil. The journey has been long and tiring but, with apologies to G K Chesterton, I still look forward to the future rather than back to the halcyon days of my youth.

> 'For there is good news yet to hear and fine things to be seen
> Before I go to paradise by way of Bringhurst Green.'